Geopolitics and the Diplomacy of the European Energy Security

Yusif Huseynov

Geopolitics and the Diplomacy of the European Energy Security

Role of Azerbaijan

LAP LAMBERT Academic Publishing

Imprint

Any brand names and product names mentioned in this book are subject to trademark, brand or patent protection and are trademarks or registered trademarks of their respective holders. The use of brand names, product names, common names, trade names, product descriptions etc. even without a particular marking in this work is in no way to be construed to mean that such names may be regarded as unrestricted in respect of trademark and brand protection legislation and could thus be used by anyone.

Cover image: www.ingimage.com

Publisher:
LAP LAMBERT Academic Publishing
is a trademark of
International Book Market Service Ltd., member of OmniScriptum Publishing Group
17 Meldrum Street, Beau Bassin 71504, Mauritius

Printed at: see last page
ISBN: 978-613-9-82494-6

Zugl. / Approved by: Geneva, Geneva School of Diplomacy, Doctoral Thesis, 2017

TABLE OF CONTENTS

FOREWORD

I met Mr. Yusif Huseynov at Geneva School of Diplomacy where he attended my graduate course on *Geopolitical Analysis* and *Geoeconomics*. During the two semesters of this course he focused his research work on the topic of Geopolitics of Energy. His doctorate dissertation was a natural continuation of his graduate research to enhance his knowledge on this important topic. As a member of the jury of his doctorate dissertation *"Azerbaijan in Geopolitics and the Diplomacy of European Energy Security"*, I highly appreciated the quality of analysis developed in his well-documented doctoral thesis.

Energy security is a very important issue for contemporary Europe in the context of major geopolitical upheavals in the international system. As Dr. Huseynov highlights in his dissertation, Eastern Europe and in particular, Azerbaijan can play an important role in energy geopolitics from a European prospect. The links between energy trade and the role of Azerbaijan in the European strategy of energy supply diversification is not so much explored from a geopolitical and geo-economics perspective in the existing literature. Therefore, the doctorate dissertation of Dr. Huseynov brings important elements that can enhance the existing literature on the geopolitical aspects of European energy security. Moreover, Dr. Huseynov carried out interactive research and conducted interviews with various experts in the field of energy geopolitics. The effective integration of these interviews in the analysis enhanced the argumentation of the author on the potential role of Azerbaijan in the energy supply diversification of Europe.

Geopolitical analysis is not only an effective tool to make an assessment on a contemporary situation but it integrates as well strategic foresight in order to anticipate the possible evolutions of a given situation. The anticipation of possible futures can contribute significantly to informed decision-making processes. This is particularly relevant in energy geopolitics where strategic decisions can affect counties for a long term. Dr. Huseynov integrated well these anticipation aspects of geopolitics in the final parts of his thesis.

Geopolitics has a practical use as an interdisciplinary approach to establish an objective diagnostic of a given power rivalry by taking into consideration the enduring and variable factors of physical and human geography, the interests of state and non-state actors and their respective strategies. Once a given geopolitical configuration is explained and scenarios are developed on the potential future evolutions of a given situation in different time frames, then state authorities can develop and implement a strategy on how to defend national interests in relation to the given geopolitical situation. In this context, geopolitical knowledge is particularly important for diplomats who are in the forefront to promote the interests of their respective states in international arena. Dr. Yusif Huseynov is an example for a talented diplomat who applies geopolitical skills at his daily work at the Permanent Mission of Azerbaijan to the United Nations in Geneva.

I would like to recommend the reading of this dissertation not only to the experts in energy geopolitics but to an enlarged public ranging from university students to persons working in various economic sectors, public servants, diplomats, employees of International Organizations, and other interested individuals who would like to learn about energy geopolitics.

Mr. Gyula Csurgai Ph.D.

Director of the Geneva Institute of Geopolitical Studies
www.geopolitics-geneva.ch

CHAPTER ONE – INTRODUCTION

EUROPEAN ENERGY SECURITY

In the 21st century, hydrocarbon resources remain one of the most vital components of economic, political and social areas of most of the countries in the world (Global Data, 2014). Throughout modern history, these resources have consistently played an influential role in the economic and political developments of the major states and empires. Particularly in recent decades, the accelerating rate of economic development in many countries, the increase in the world's population, and the increasing scarcity of the world's total remaining energy resources have made it very challenging for all countries to ensure ongoing growth and development (Ojeaga, and Odejimi, 2014). At present, energy resources are the main sources for every state's modern industry and society. Currently, the main resources being employed are coal, crude oil, and natural gas. Therefore, the importance of these energy resources to the chief areas of the economy has automatically influenced the foreign policy and diplomacy of a significant number of countries. According to many researchers, the global demand for crude oil and natural gas is expected to grow continuously for the foreseeable future (Dumitru and Marin, 2014). The demand for energy is expected to experience significant growth not only in most industrialized countries of the western world but also in developing economies of the eastern world. In this framework, most of the countries' very sensitive position in the field of energy and in terms of its own security has become a major challenge in the implementation of both their geopolitical and geo-economic interests. It doesn't matter whether countries are located in the east or in the west, the aims remain the same: to maintain stable and secure access to the world's energy reserves (Ojeaga, and Odejimi, 2014).

Global energy markets have undergone many challenges since the 1970s and energy reserves, such as crude oil, natural gas, and renewables, have become the primary sources of energy that most countries are using as a means to meet their demands (Ostander, and William, 2012). Currently, in the global energy market, crude oil still remains one of the most significant fossil fuels for many countries to secure their energy demands. Therefore, in the foreseeable future, the continued progress and advancement within and natural gas and crude oil fields will continue to be critically important in the major world economies. It is expected that up until around 2040, the world's demand for oil will continue to increase (Dargey, and Dermot, 2010). The same situation is also expected in the gas market and the role of natural gas will likewise grow due to the high demands of the world economies. Due to the emergence of new major economies, and the continued stable demand from the western countries for the energy resources, the global energy market is being shaped and structured in an ever changing and dynamic way (Shieber, 2012). The role of fossil fuels will remain vitally necessary for global energy security. However, due to the negative impacts that fossil fuel consumption has on the environment, new advancements in the technological sector, and shifts in the geopolitical arena will have a significant impact on the position of fossil fuels in the distant future. Nonetheless, the current situation of global energy demands will remain the same, just as it has been for the last couple decades, namely, being dependent on hydrocarbon resources as a main source of energy.

Energy security is a crucial field for all the countries to focus their attention on, particularly in terms of being able to secure stable access to energy reserves together with energy partners in order to maintain ongoing economic development (Global Data, 2014). Under the energy security policy, stable energy supplies, mainly natural gas and crude oil resources from the world's energy-rich regions, have become the core targets of many energy dependent countries. It is for this reason that locating reliable sources of energy and energy security strategy has become the main topic on the agenda in international discussions (Gupta and Surbhi, 2015). Furthermore, the competition over the world's remaining limited energy resources has also become a major policy of many regional and global powers. This competition has not only affected the dynamics of global energy politics but it has also shaped the foreign policy of many countries. Currently, it is seen that the economic growth and development of many countries are highly dependent on the stable and secured flow of energy supplies. As it has been witnessed in the last couple of decades, any abrupt or unannounced interruption of the energy flow to their economies due to any reason has had a significantly negative and unpredictable impact on their economic growth (Gupta and Surbhi, 2015). Therefore, from a strategic point of view, the implementation of a successful energy policy is considered to be the primary objective of many countries. Given the difficult characteristics of energy politics, the 21st century has been the most difficult century for building and maintaining long lasting energy policies since its beginnings. This has mainly been due to conflicts, economic crises, and political instabilities around the globe. The rivalry between global and regional powers over the control of energy resources has created an even more challenging situation for many countries. There are varying levels of competition that exist between countries such as the Russian Federation, the United States, China, Iran, Turkey, as well as the European Union. This competition has affected the strategies of the energy-producing countries (Christoffersen, 2016). This outcome has become very influential to the national interests of each country in terms of building their energy cooperation strategies.

It is well known that starting from the 19th century, coal had been the most consumed and most important energy resource for the development of civilization. However, the 20th century was the era in which crude oil replaced the role of coal and became the foremost dominant energy source and it, therefore, formed the basis for global energy cooperation. However, it could also be argued that the beginning of the 21st century has demonstrated itself as the era of natural gas in global energy cooperation (Smil, 2015). The recent discoveries of huge natural gas fields in different parts of the world and increases in the production of natural gas reserves have accelerated its consumption in many countries. It should also be noted that natural gas resources differ significantly from the other popular energy resources. One reason for this is because its production and consumption produce relatively low levels of carbon emissions and it, therefore, has a significantly lower negative environmental impact. Also, the lower price of natural gas, compared to the unit prices of other fossil fuel resources, has made it very attractive to many countries in the world, especially in the western world (Gjelten, 2012). For many western countries, due to natural gas' above-mentioned features, it has been proposed as a potentially necessary bridge in the much-needed shift from the consumption of fossil fuels to more ecologically sustainable green energy renewables. Natural gas reserves are the main energy source used to power generators and its compatibility with the use of renewables is a strong incentive to use this resource in many modern energy-producing technologies. However, the natural gas market is very complicated due to many challenges in terms of ensuring the security of transportation, storage, and stability for its usage in the global energy market (Smil, 2015). Therefore, since the production and transportation of natural gas have become very challenging, most of the states have intervened and created policies aimed at securing the necessary natural gas supplies in order to create stable and diversified natural gas infrastructure over the last two decades. The countries of the European Union are the main example in terms of implementing these policies and in preventing such challenges to the continued security of its natural gas supply (Szurlej, 2013).

In recent years, countries of the European Union have faced a number of difficulties in regards to improving their energy security, especially in terms of their increasing natural gas consumption. Natural gas supplies are extremely vital for EU countries and as has been seen in the last two decades, the European Union has put a great deal of effort into investing in the securitization of its energy supplies (Shaffer, 2015). The green movement and environmental regulations in the European Union have pushed the European Commission to focus more of their concentration on natural gas reserves. As mentioned, this is mainly due to the fact that its consumption produces lower carbon emissions and has relatively low environmental impacts. However, this is not the only challenge that the European Union faces in terms of shifting its energy consumption from classical fossil fuels to more renewable and environmental friendly fossil energy resources (Leal-arcas, 2015). An increase in demand for energy resources, especially for natural gas, and a continuation of this tendency of the European Union countries has brought more security challenges to its energy consumption. Many statistics from 2015 clearly indicated that the rate of the natural gas dependency on Russian supplies was more than 30% and the same figure relates to crude oil dependency as well (Papatulica, 2016). Despite the fact that world economies have been facing economic difficulties since 2008, the European Union and Russia remain interdependent on each other and this has increased significantly to the point where both parties' ongoing economic prosperity is heavily reliant on the other. Currently, more than 50% of the energy that is being consumed by the EU countries is imported from outside of the European Union and expenditure on the imported energy resources totals more than 1 billion euros per day. From this, it is extrapolated that the European Union spends in excess of 400 billion euros per year to meet its demand for its energy needs (Sefcovic, 2016). Russia has traditionally been the main crude oil and natural gas supplier to the European continent. In 2015, over 158 bcm of natural gas was supplied by the Russian Federation to the majority of EU countries, fulfilling approximately 25% of the total gas needs of Europe (Eurostat, 2016). Russian natural gas exports have remained at around the same value and in the near future they are expected to continue to stay at the same level due to a slowdown in the economic growth of the countries within the European Union. As it has been indicated in many statistical reviews, the importation of Russia gas supplies and the percentage of total imports that are received from Russia have already made many countries of the European Union highly dependent on Russian gas supplies (Eurostat, 2016). It should also be noted that more than 75% of the Russian produced natural gas exports were delivered to the European energy market. Therefore, this interdependent situation in the framework of international energy relations indicates that both sides need each other in order to implement their energy policy (Rosenberg, Elizabeth, et al, 2016). However, in terms of the European Union, its heavy dependency on a single supplier has made it significantly more vulnerable to disruptions to supply. In order to meet their supplied energy needs, the countries of the European Union have traditionally received energy resources from European and non-European regions, such as Norway, Russia, the Middle East, and North Africa (Papatulica, 2016). This single and dominant supplier, namely the Russian Federation, has brought about a range of difficulties and obstacles to the EU countries. These difficulties mainly involve supply disruptions, primarily as a result of political disputes and interests, conflicts and wars in neighboring countries, and the implementation of strategies concerning the diversification of energy routes.

At the same time, the security of energy is unevenly distributed among the member countries of the European Union. The countries of the Eastern Europe, such as Poland, Hungary, Slovakia, the Czech Republic, the Baltic States and most of the countries in the Balkan region are highly dependent on Russian energy supplies, compared to western European Union countries (Dusciac, Popescu, and Parlicov, 2016). Therefore, the vulnerability of the eastern European Union countries is becoming more visible in terms of maintaining their energy security. Despite this fact, the Netherlands and Norway, with their indigenous gas reserves (although Norway is not an EU country but an important energy resource provider nonetheless) do not supply the eastern EU countries with the volumes necessary to decrease their dependency on Russian gas resources (Global Data, 2014).

In terms of their energy security, many countries of the European Union are now in a very weak situation due to their high dependency on Russian energy supplies. This weakness became abundantly visible when the gas dispute between Russia and Ukraine occurred in 2006 and 2009 (Rustamov & Stergiopoulos, 2011). This was the first time that the European Union countries could not resist the gas cut and it became obvious that Moscow remains the main player in the energy sector of the European countries, clearly demonstrating its overwhelming dominance in several European energy markets. It also became evident for European countries that Moscow's cut in the volume of gas, which was flowing into the European market via Ukrainian pipelines, is also a threat to its own energy security. These concerns subsequently became a reality when the war took place in the eastern part of Ukraine in 2014, which was followed by Moscow's annexation of the Crimean Peninsula (Comsa, 2015). This event and the aftermath highly increased the vulnerability of political concern of the countries of the European Union in terms of the energy security. The events in 2014 convinced the European Commission to finally adopt the policy of creating a more dynamic European Energy security strategy. In order to avoid any gas shortages in the short to long-term future, especially in light of the events that took place in Ukraine, the European Commission has created the Energy Union of the EU countries as way to prioritize the energy security field as the main focus of the European Union (Gümüscedil, and Yasin, 2015). An increase in the number of shortages of gas flowing into the European energy market and an unstable energy cooperation with Russia in terms of price and regulations of the energy sources have prompted countries of the European Union to prioritize energy supply diversification. As a result of this, the decision that was taken by the European Commission has assisted in the building of a strategy to diversify the energy imports from the other regions. Therefore, intensified negotiations of the countries in the European Union in the 2014-2016 period with other energy exporting countries has motivated EU countries to diversify their energy supplies. As mentioned, this is particularly the case for the eastern countries of the European Union. It is important to mention that eastern countries of the European Union have been highly dependent on Russian gas supplies for a significant amount of time and the creation of the common energy policy mostly serves the interests of these countries. In general, the need for natural gas supplies has always been in high demand in EU countries, especially from Russian supplies. As a result, European Union countries have been urged to diversify their energy supplies and to find alternatives for additional energy sources. The diversification policy of the European Union and the strategy to import gas from other regions of the world, especially from the Caspian basin (Central Asia and South Caucasus) and the Levant Basin (the Middle East and Mediterranean) has become the top priority of the agenda of the European Union. To be specific, huge natural gas and crude oil reserves in the Caspian basin, primarily in the Republic of Azerbaijan, Turkmenistan, and Kazakhstan did present themselves as the most appropriate and reachable energy supplies for the European energy market (Ruggiero, Francesco, et al, 2015).

In the aftermath of World War II, energy security and policy became a major part of the integration of European countries. This integration was formed under the energy security policy created by the European Coal and Steel Community in 1951 (Berger, 2013). As is known by many, this energy community laid the foundations for the eventual creation of the current European Union. Therefore, the subject of energy is not an unfamiliar field for the countries of the European Union. Currently, the EU energy market is highly diverse, with a mix of different energy resources. As is the case in many other countries around the world, crude oil makes up the highest share of the European energy market. This is followed by natural gas, coal, nuclear power plant energy, and finally renewables. However, despite the fact that the European energy market is highly mixed with a variety of different energy options, most of the European Union countries are nonetheless dependent on external energy resources. Reductions of domestic energy reserves, especially in crude oil reserves and due to the highly environmentally conscious demands of the European Commission, have pushed countries of the European Union to rely more on natural gas reserves. As a consequence of this, the European Union countries are constantly increasing their energy demands and, due to the decrease in its own fossil fuel energy resources, the

European Union has become highly reliant on outside supplies. This dependency has led to a number of weaknesses for the European Union in the form of political instability, supply disruptions, and price shocks. There is a great deal of evidence for these vulnerabilities, such as the Russian-Ukrainian gas crisis, instability in the Middle East, and unstable prices for energy resources. As mentioned, these issues have prompted EU countries to revise their security policies in the energy sector. Especially since the events surrounding the 2014 Crimean crisis, the European Union's policy towards its energy sector has become the main topic of discussion, the emphasis being to find alternatives to its reliance on a dominant supplier (Gümüscedil, and Yasin, 2015). Since the Crimean crisis, the European Union has taken important steps towards reaching this goal and has investigated a range of alternative energy resources in both the Caspian basin region and in the Middle East (Levant basin) and whether sources from these regions could assist in the realization of the European Union's energy security goals.

With the Soviet Union's fall and the subsequent independence of Central Asian and South Caucasus, the countries of the European Union have been presented with two important opportunities to optimize their energy security (Bajrektarevic and Posega, 2014). First of all, rich crude oil and natural gas reserves in Azerbaijan, Kazakhstan, and Turkmenistan have provided an important opportunity for EU countries to cover their increasing demand for energy. Secondly, rich energy reserves in these newly independent countries have given countries of the European Union the chance to greatly diversify their energy supplies and decrease their dependency on the Russian energy imports. Since 1991, the European Union has been following a policy that furthers the possibility of gaining access to the Caspian Sea through a secure energy corridor. The implementation of the Baku-Tbilisi-Ceyhan (BTC) crude oil pipeline and the Baku-Tbilisi-Erzurum (BTE) natural gas pipelines have laid the foundations of the Southern Gas Corridor, which will start in Azerbaijan and pass through the Georgian and Turkish soil to reach European energy market (Yesevi and Tiftikcigil, 2015). This energy corridor's importance has become significantly more visible as a result of the above-mentioned geopolitical events. Therefore, with the leadership of Azerbaijan in the Southern Gas Corridor and the implementation of further energy projects, such as the Trans-Anatolian (TANAP) natural gas pipeline and the Trans-Adriatic (TAP) natural gas pipeline, the role of South Caucasus and Central Asian countries in the European energy security policy has increased to a large extent (Ibrahimov, 2015). The construction of these projects under the Southern Gas Corridor and the expansion of the overall volume of natural gas being directed towards the European market would automatically lessen Russian control and dominance over the European energy market. Before the construction of the Southern Gas Corridor, Russia was traditionally the only country that Caspian energy resources were being transported through. However, since the development of the BTC and BTE pipelines, Azerbaijan has become the second country and the only alternative to the Russian Federation's transport of crude oil and natural gas from the Caspian basin (Yesevi and Tiftikcigil, 2015). These initial pipelines were the first steps towards building the west oriented energy infrastructure and the experience gained from these pipelines became the source of inspiration for the building of even larger and more secure energy pipelines.

The successful implementation of the Southern Gas Corridor has given an important advantage to the European Union countries to further expand their energy infrastructure towards the Central Asian countries. Kazakhstan and Turkmenistan, with their proven rich natural gas and crude oil fields, have strongly attracted the European consumers (Plenta, 2011). However, the undefined legal status of the Caspian Sea as well as ongoing geopolitical rivalries between the Russian Federation and the Islamic Republic of Iran within the Caspian basin have served as an obstacle to the implementation of an energy project that could potentially connect the eastern and western shores of the Caspian Sea (Bajrektarevic and Posega, 2016). Unlike Azerbaijan, Central Asian countries could not turn down Russian soil as a route to export their energy reserves. In addition to this, the implementation of the proposed Trans-Caspian natural gas pipeline has been postponed. Despite the fact that the Russian Federation and the Islamic Republic of Iran use the undefined legal status and other arguments to thwart energy cooperation with Central Asian and European countries, both sides are continuing in their negotiations to find a solution to the problem of connecting both sides of the Caspian Sea with an energy pipeline. The European Union's continued commitments and a new energy policy since the Crimean crisis with Russia indicate that Central Asian countries will become an important part of the Southern Gas Corridor. Therefore, Azerbaijan remains the key country and geographic corridor for both Central Asian and European countries to be able to promote such an energy policy (Bajrektarevic and Posega, 2016).

In 2012, when the European Union placed sanctions on Iran, it banned crude oil exports from the country and blockaded any international energy companies (especially western energy companies) from investing or participating in the development of the Iran's energy sector (Rafique and Shah, 2013). These sanctions resulted in the suspension of any energy cooperation between the two sides. However, after the lift of these sanctions in 2016 as a result of a nuclear deal, the energy a relation between Iran and the European community has been largely restored (Davenport, 2016). This is especially true regarding the transportation of Iranian natural gas reserves since this has become the main target of the European energy cooperation in their newly formed relations with Iran. Within this policy, Turkey and Azerbaijan, with their collaborative efforts towards the implementation of the Southern Gas Corridor, have become the main alternative for European Union countries to import the Iranian natural gas reserves. Iran's participation in the Southern gas corridor would likely ensure a more diversified and secure portfolio for the European Union's energy imports. Also, the substantial reconstruction and upgrading of the existing energy infrastructure between Turkey and Iran could serve as the framework for Iran to provide more natural gas reserves to the European energy market (Javed, 2016). Therefore, Iran's long awaited return to the global energy arena, as well as the normalization of relations with the European union countries significantly increase the likelihood that the European Union will be successful in the diversification of its energy supplies. Even though the sanctions have been lifted since 2016, the role of Iran will not yet be visible due to its currently outdated and undeveloped level of energy infrastructure. Western sanctions over the years have caused Iran to fall far behind the current trends in technological energy advantages. Hence, in order for the European Union to bring Iran closer to the European energy market with high volumes of natural gas imports, it needs to help by providing Iran with new technological advancements in the field of energy. Such investments would make one of the alternative supply routes possible for the European energy market within the next couple of decades (Javed, 2016).

A very similar energy policy of the European Union is followed as a set of guidelines to develop access to the newly discovered and abundant Levant basin natural gas reserves (Prisecaru and Ail, 2014). The contribution of the Levant basin energy reserves would further secure the diversification of the European gas supplies. The European Union's policy to meet its demand for energy and the creation of a network of diversified energy infrastructure around its borders is its main goal. Furthermore, new discoveries in Cyprus and Israel would significantly aid the European Union in its aspirations to achieve its target in energy strategy (Dagoumas and Flouros, 2017). Energy projects that are being constructed under the Southern Gas Corridor, such as the TANAP and TAP gas pipeline projects are also some of the most vital options for Levant basin countries to transport their own natural gas resources via these pipelines. Starting with a small volume and subsequently increasing the total capacity with the expansion of the Southern Gas Corridor, the volume of the natural gas transportation could be significantly increased within the foreseeable future. The amount of energy resources being transported could potentially accelerate with continued investment and growth of infrastructure would rise exponentially, leading to even greater volumes reaching Europe. The expansion of the energy infrastructure towards the Levant region and the Caspian basin also increases the role that Turkey will play in the framework of European energy security. Turkey's role as a key transit country for most of the alternative energy-producing regions increases the importance of the country substantially. Currently, Turkey is the main alternative route for Central Asian, South Caucasus, and European Union countries to build an energy infrastructure that bypasses Russia and Iran. At the same time, it is also the shortest route for Iran and countries within the Levant basin to export their natural gas reserves towards the European energy market (Arinç and Özgül, 2015).

ENERGY HISTORY OF AZERBAIJAN

Republic of Azerbaijan, which is the largest country in South Caucasus region, is home to approximately 9.7 million people. The country is geographically located at the crossroads of Europe and Asia, playing a particularly important role in the Eastern European region. Located on the western shores of the Caspian Sea, Azerbaijan borders the Russian Federation to the north, Georgia to the northwest, Armenia and Turkey (note: Turkey borders via an enclave of the Nakhchivan Autonomous Republic) to the west, and Iran to the south. The country is considered to be one of the most ancient populated regions in the world; an area in which crude oil has been used for many centuries (Namazova and Taghizada, 2015). In particular, the city of Baku, located on the Absheron peninsula, has been exporting oil to various neighboring regions for many centuries, long before crude oil had become commercially traded on the global market. According to many historians and travelers, the Absheron peninsula (especially in the vicinity of the Baku region) has been a major center for oil wells and since the ancient period of its history, crude oil has been extracted for the lighting of houses and also for medical purposes. Furthermore, there is some evidence, which strongly suggests that extracted crude oil was also used in the military sector. Due to the burning and glowing nature of crude oil, the land of Azerbaijan became the holy land for the Zoroastrianism religion, whose practitioners engaged in the worship of fire. For many historians, Azerbaijan is considered to be one the most important places for people following the Zoroastrianism faith (Namazova and Taghizada, 2015). Even until the present day, fire is one of the main symbols of the country. The Zoroastrian temple near Baku city, with its continuous, permanently burning fire, emphasizes the prominence of fire in the ancient history of Azerbaijan. The traditional belief in the fire also plays an influential role in contemporary Islam in the region and present day cultural celebrations. An example of such an event is the Novruz holiday, which is the celebration of the first day of spring and which is also considered to be the main holiday celebrated annually in Azerbaijan. Although oil has been an important aspect of Azerbaijani history, the main crude oil development in the country is considered to have occurred in the middle of

19th century, when the first oil well was drilled in 1847 (Gidadhubli, 2015). This event meant that Azerbaijan was to be the first country in the world in which an oil well was drilled. Very soon, Baku also became the place where the first oil refinery was constructed. Together with economic developments and western investments in the technological and engineering sector, the extent of crude oil exploration, production, and transportation increased substantially (Khan, 2016). This development resulted in Azerbaijan becoming the world's main oil center.

Starting from the late 19th century the Rothschild family started to invest in Baku's oil wells. It wasn't long before the Rothschilds became the main player, holding domination of more than 40% of the crude oil exports from Baku city. However, it was not only the Rothschilds but also other prominent western figures and companies, such as the Nobel brothers and Shell, who also played a significant role in the Baku crude oil fields (Gidadhubli, 2015). This brought the first ever oil boom in the history of the industry, in which Baku became the global center for industrial investments. During this period, Baku became the chief global provider, producing around half of the world's total crude oil demand. Moreover, Baku alone was providing 98% of the Tsarist Russian Empire's demand for crude oil (Johnson, 2010). In 1918 after the Bolshevik revolution in Tsarist Russia Azerbaijan declared its independence and this resulted in the creation of the Azerbaijan Democratic Republic, which became the first democratic republic in both the Eastern world and the Muslim world (1918 – 1920). Nonetheless, Bolshevik Moscow invaded Baku in 1920 and subsequently nationalized the entire oil industry. During the WWII period, Baku alone supplied 75% of the crude oil demands of the entire Soviet Union, and Baku oil played a pivotal role in winning the many battles against Nazi Germany (Johnson, 2010). Until this present day, however, Baku city has not received a "Hero City" award title, which is the title given to cities that played the most heroic roles during the World War II period. This is despite the fact that without Baku oil, the Soviet Army would not have survived any major battle against the German Nazi military forces. Starting from the 1950s, oil production in Azerbaijan started to decline until the eventual fall of the Soviet Union (Johnson, 2010).

With its independence from the Soviet Union in 1991, The Republic of Azerbaijan experienced deep economic difficulties, especially in the crude oil sector (Khan, 2016). Outdated and unmaintained soviet energy infrastructure, weak planning and management of the energy sector, and finally a lack of foreign investment into the energy sector of the country resulted in the sharp decline of oil production in the energy sector. Furthermore, the Armenia-Azerbaijan Nagorno-Karabakh conflict and the occupation of 20% of the internationally recognized sovereign territories of Azerbaijan by the Armenian forces brought about enormous damage both to the energy sector and to the economy of the country during the first years of its post-soviet independence (Kirvelyte, 2012). In spite of all the challenges that Azerbaijan has faced over the last hundred years, the government of Azerbaijan has once again successfully challenged its threats and has set into motion the foundations for its own modern crude oil and natural gas golden age by signing the "Contract of the Century" with the Western Oil Consortium (Khan, 2016). This contract laid out the framework for development of the Azeri, Ciraq, and Gunesli energy (crude oil) fields. The agreement was followed by a deal concerning gas fields that would give permission to western companies to work together with the State Oil Company of Azerbaijan (SOCAR) in the development of the Shah Deniz gas field and other gas fields in the Caspian region of Azerbaijan. These deals have attracted an enormous level of foreign investment into the energy sector. It is estimated that between 1992 and 2015 the Republic of Azerbaijan, under the conventions of international crude oil and natural gas contracts, has received more than 60 billion USD worth of investment into its energy sector (Namazova and Taghizada, 2015). These investments have become the most vital source of funding that Azerbaijan has needed in order to rebuild its energy infrastructure together with international oil companies. It can therefore be said that despite all the challenges that the country has faced in political, social, and economic fields during the post-soviet period, with the assistance of international companies it has successfully created strong foundations for the redevelopment of the traditional energy sector of the country and make its ancient oil legacy a reality once again.

The implementation of this strategy has become so successful that in a very short time Azerbaijan has created a strong sense of energy cooperation with global energy players, especially with the international western companies. They have been working together in the Caspian Sea in an effort to further the exploration, construction, production, and transportation of the country's energy resources. It is expected that Azerbaijan's revenues from the energy sector will reach more than 200 billion USD by 2024 as a direct result of the implementation of the abovementioned new infrastructure proposals (Damirchi, Ashir, and AliasgarAliyov, 2013). Since 1994, when the "Contract of the Century" was first signed, international energy companies have been participating in the redevelopment of the energy infrastructure and joined the projects on the crude oil fields (Khan, 2016). The following energy companies received an invitation from the Republic of Azerbaijan to gain the opportunity to be participate in the shared project: BP (17.2%), AMOCO (17%), SOCAR (10%), Lukoil (10%), Pennzoil (4.8%), Unocal (9.5%), Statoil (8.5%), TPAO (6.7%), EXXON (5%), ITOCHU 7.4%), Ramco (2.08%), and Delta (1.68%) (Damirchi, Ashir, and AliasgarAliyov, 2013). As the president of the Republic of Azerbaijan, Ilham Aliyev stated, "'Contract of the Century' is the main source of the landscaping work, sustainable economy, and large foreign exchange reserves. Azerbaijan came under certain pressure during that hard and difficult period. The decisiveness, courage farsightedness of Heydar Aliyev and his connection with the people ensured the signing of the 'Contract of the Century'" (Trend, 2016). As it is indicated in his statement, Azerbaijan has received a great deal of political pressure from several countries to reconsider the signing of the contract with the western consortium. When looking at the energy history of the Republic of Azerbaijan, it is clearly evident that the experience that Azerbaijan has gained over the past years makes the country a valuable and attractive development partner. In the future, Azerbaijan is expected to become the major destination for many countries to cooperate and develop energy-based relations because Azerbaijan has undoubtedly proven its role as a reliable partner for many countries and investors.

AZERBAIJAN AND THE EUROPEAN ENERGY SECURITY

The fall of the Soviet Union was the first time since 1920 that western international energy companies have had the opportunity to enter the Caspian basin. An invitation to the companies from the Republic of Azerbaijan has been an important geopolitical and geo-economic step in gaining back its energy legacy. Therefore, the participation of western energy companies has not only provided a lucrative opportunity to these companies themselves, but it has also served the goals of Azerbaijan to integrate itself into the western energy market (Damirchi, Ashir, and AliasgarAliyov, 2013). However, it has not been a substantially difficult task for Azerbaijan to attract international companies despite the fact that the country has been facing many challenges in its political, social, and economic fields. Due to its geo-strategic location, together with its rich crude oil and natural gas reserves, these companies have been eagerly attracted to the promising young nation. As a result of this, Azerbaijan has become the main geopolitical player in the Caspian basin in a very short time period. Due to its rich energy resources and strategic geographical position, the country has also become one of the key players in regional and international politics (Namazova and Taghizada, 2015). Both as an energy-producing country and as a transit country, Azerbaijan has established the "East-West" energy corridor (Sierra, 2010). The promotion of a Western-oriented energy corridor has allowed western countries to seriously consider the role of Azerbaijan in reaching the rich Caspian energy reserves. Opportunities to transport rich Caspian crude oil and natural gas reserves towards the European energy market while effectively bypassing the Russian Federation and the Islamic Republic of Iran's territory have created a strategic opportunity to build energy cooperation with the newly established South Caucasus and Central Asian countries that have gained independence since the fall of the Soviet Union (Dilbazi, 2010). This situation has resulted in the implementation of the Baku-Tbilisi-Ceyhan (BTC) crude oil and the Baku-Tbilisi-Erzurum (BTE) natural gas pipelines. The proposal of these two energy pipelines marks the first time in the history of oil pipeline infrastructure that the Caspian Sea has been connected to the Mediterranean Sea. This provides an opportunity for Caspian energy reserves to flow to the western energy market without any unforeseen difficulties. Currently, the majority of the crude oil produced is being exported via the BTC pipeline (80%), and a smaller of the amount is being transported via the Baku-Supsa and the Baku-Novorossiysk pipelines (Yesevi and Tiftikcigil, 2015). As it is clearly visible, Azerbaijan has largely succeeded in the planned diversification of its export routes, resulting in the avoidance of any dependency on a single route. Therefore, this diversified energy exporting infrastructure of Azerbaijan provides an important opportunity for

Kazakhstan and Turkmenistan to transport their own crude oil via the BTC pipeline. The Sangachal port, which is the largest energy terminal located in the south of the capital city of Baku, receives crude oil from tankers from both Kazakhstan and Turkmenistan. With the proposed energy projects, such as the Trans-Caspian natural gas, Trans-Anatolian natural gas (TANAP), and Trans-Adriatic (TAP) proposed natural gas pipelines, Azerbaijan is endeavoring to become an important natural gas supplier to the European gas market from the Caspian basin (Ibrahimov, 2015). Even though Azerbaijan has been known as a traditional oil producing country, the country's role as a natural gas producer and exporter has become more visible and hence Azerbaijan will be known as a gas producing country in the near future.

Proven crude oil and natural gas reserves in the Republic of Azerbaijan have highly attracted investors from the Global energy market. Currently, the country's proven crude oil reserves reach 7 billion barrels and natural gas reserves reach up to 2.6 trillion cubic meters (tcm) (Azerbaijan Oil & Gas Report, 2015). The largest energy reserves are mainly located on the national border of the Caspian basin and as a result of this, most of the energy infrastructure works are being constructed offshore in the Caspian Sea. The famous Azerbaijani energy fields, such as Azeri-Chirag-Guneshli (ACG) oil fields and Shah Deniz (King of Sea) gas fields, are located offshore of the Caspian Sea. Currently, the first phase of the Shah Deniz field is being operated by the British Petroleum company and with the start of the second phase of the gas field, the Shah Deniz gas field will become the main source of the TANAP and TAP projects and would carry resources from the Caspian Sea to the European gas market (Azerbaijan Oil & Gas Report, 2015). However, there are a number of other proven rich crude oil and natural gas fields that are located within the territory of the Republic of Azerbaijan. These crude oil and natural gas fields are 1) Bahar - offshore crude oil and natural gas field, 2) Gum Deniz - offshore crude oil and natural gas field, 3) Darwin Bank - offshore crude oil field, 4) Absheron - offshore natural gas field, 5) Ashrafi - crude oil and natural gas field, 6) Dan Ulduzu - crude oil and natural gas field, 7) - Karabakh - offshore crude oil and natural gas field, 8) Nakhchivan - offshore crude oil and natural gas field, 9) Shafaq-Asiman - offshore crude oil and natural gas field, 10) Umid - offshore natural gas field, and finally 11) Babek - offshore gas field. These proven rich energy fields are viewed as a guarantee for the long-lasting energy cooperation between the Republic of Azerbaijan and the European countries (Azerbaijan Oil & Gas Report, 2015).

The vital role of the newly emerged countries from the Caspian basin in the diversification of the natural gas supplies to the European Union energy market has become an important policy of the European Union Commission. The Caspian basin has attracted the attention of consumers in the European energy market because of its vast quantities of crude oil and natural gas reserves (Journal of European Studies, 2015). One of the main factors that led to this attraction was the removal of the Soviet Union blockade, which provided a significant opportunity for the Caspian basin countries to gain geopolitical and geo-economic importance in the eyes of European countries. Therefore, the South Caucasus countries, specifically Azerbaijan, serve as transportation routes for energy resources from Central Asia. This effectively places Azerbaijan in a position in which it can serve as an important passage between Asia and Europe. Since Azerbaijan gained independence, one of its major policies has been to develop cooperation with its regional and international partners and to integrate itself into the Euro-Atlantic community, particularly by offering its highly demanded energy resources (Pinar, 2009). Within this policy of Azerbaijan, energy cooperation with EU countries, political and economic relationships, as well as a strategic military partnership with NATO countries have become the vital targets of the foreign policy of the Republic of Azerbaijan. Azerbaijan, as well as other South Caucasus countries, has undergone difficult economic, social, and political circumstances during the communist regime and particularly during the transition period (Bishku, 2012). The Azerbaijan-Armenia Nagorno-Karabakh conflict resulted in economic and political instability and turmoil during the early post-soviet period. As a consequence of this, after the ceasefire agreement, Azerbaijan has found that the best way to realistically solve these tensions is to develop its economy and integrate itself into the European energy market (Johnson, 2010). The Republic of Azerbaijan has unique access to the proven natural gas and crude oil reserves of the Caspian basin and this position will continue to allow the country to help to secure, stabilize, and diversify the supply of energy into Europe (Pinar, 2009). Azerbaijan's ongoing development of direct relations with the Euro-Atlantic community was initially very novel to the Republic of Azerbaijan's leaders and representatives. It was only after the fall of the Soviet Union that everything changed for Azerbaijan. As an independent state, Azerbaijan did its best to choose a path to follow its own independent and sovereign foreign policy within the strategic long-term interests of the country (Grison, 2013). In terms of its economic and political advancements, Azerbaijan is considered to have a very balanced policy with both the Euro-Atlantic countries and with the Russian Federation (Bishku, 2012). The country is also assisting in the regional development of the larger South Caucasus by facilitating political stability and economic growth. By ensuring that its neighboring countries are also undergoing infrastructural development, Azerbaijan can expect long-term prosperity and stability in the region at large.

When looking at the primary commitments of Azerbaijan, it becomes very visible that the country is determined to be part of the European Energy Union policy and is committed to showing full support in playing one of the most important roles in European energy security. Azerbaijan's determination to cooperate with the European energy community was first declared when the country regained its independence and signed the necessary contracts with the international energy companies (Grison, 2013). Since then, Azerbaijan has been working tightly with these countries in the construction of an infrastructure network aimed at transporting energy resources directly from the Caspian basin to the EU energy market. It is clear that Azerbaijan has no hidden agenda and its primary goal is to allow the European Union to diversify is energy imports (Pinar, 2009). Azerbaijan has demonstrated itself as very committed to becoming a strategic natural gas and crude oil supplier not only as a producer but also as a transit country for the transportation of the Central Asian countries' energy resources. Furthermore, due to its significant geopolitical positioning, located at the crossroads of the European and Asian continents, Azerbaijan has been recognized as one of the main players in the Caspian basin region (Grewlich, 2011). The country's key role in providing an alternative energy transportation route, allows the countries of the European Union to decrease the threats to their energy security and to implement their plans of diversified energy routes. These actions will serve to promote the important advantages of having Azerbaijan as a partner in the European Union's desire to not rely solely on exports from a monopoly, such as the Russian Federation. Currently, the abovementioned energy policy of EU countries is being coordinated in line with the position of the Republic of Azerbaijan. This is because Azerbaijan's strategic location is the key route for this energy policy to be realized in terms of transporting Caspian basin energy reserves that bypass both Russia and Iran (Kolb, 2012). Particularly during the period when the Islamic Republic of Iran was under western sanctions due to disagreements over nuclear policy, there was a significant increase in the independent Republic of Azerbaijan's importance as an alternative corridor and hub for the crude oil and natural gas reserves of the Caspian Sea.

Not only does the Caspian Sea lack access to the ocean but also countries that surround its shores are all landlocked. (Bilgin, 2010). This situation has an effect on Azerbaijan's energy reserves in the Caspian Sea, which cannot be easily transported to the European energy market. This state of affairs has brought about many challenges for the secure transport of natural gas in the direction of Europe. These obstacles are being overcome by the development of a network of energy pipeline infrastructure, which plays a significant part in providing Europe with energy security. These regional developments that are backed by the European Union also give options to exporters in the Caspian region (Frances, 2011). However, from the countries of the Caspian region, Azerbaijan stands out as the most engaged with the European Union's energy policy and the country continues to cooperate with the western world in the implementation of pipeline infrastructure projects. Azerbaijan's important part in the development program was announced during multistate level agreements involving EU countries, whereby the primary objective was the "creation of an energy partnership" that would support the role of Azerbaijan in its securitization of energy flow into Europe. The foreign policy of the Republic of Azerbaijan and official statements made by the government officials have made it very clear as to what the country's role in the European energy policy will be. As has been clearly illustrated in Azerbaijan's foreign policy, in accordance with President Ilham Aliyev's leadership, has been helping EU countries, as well as Turkey and other Balkan states, to achieve the goal of diversifying their sources of both crude oil and natural gas (Khan, 2016). The Azerbaijani government has committed all of its resources as a gesture of demonstrating its interest in creating and developing energy infrastructure to access the European Union's gas market. Since its independence, Azerbaijan has been exhibiting both its natural resources and its political cooperation as a display of commitment to the plan (Bishku, 2012). In this sense of goodwill, the President of the Republic of Azerbaijan states the following:

"In near future, we will become important parties and close partners in the European energy market. This partnership will last for decades, as natural gas reserves will be enough for use and consumers at least for 100 years. Therefore, the cooperation in the field of energy security will be long-term and strategic" (Caspian Energy, 2016 URL).

As it can be clearly seen from the recent statement given by the president, Azerbaijan and countries of the European Union are working very closely to implement a plan concerning the diversified energy infrastructure of the European Union.

In the overall strategy of securing diversified energy routes, EU countries have acknowledged particular countries that could potentially play the roles of exporting natural gas and crude oil to Europe (Bilgin, 2010). It is clear that the diversification of energy security in Europe will require multiple routes from the Caspian and South Caucasus regions on top of the existing pipeline infrastructure. These existing routes could be used by Europe to engage with Turkey, Georgia, and Azerbaijan and cooperate on their development. (Yesevi and Tiftikcigil, 2015). Azerbaijan has been suggested as a key part of Europe's diversification plan. The previous President of the European Commission, Jose Manuel Barroso, stated that Azerbaijan is now in a situation in which it can play a dual role; both as an energy producer and transporter (Dimitrova, 2011). In this framework, the commitments of Azerbaijan, in terms of helping particular countries of the European Union to benefit from strategic access and a link to Central Asian energy reserves, create an important status for Azerbaijan in becoming one of the identified nations that has prime potential as an exporter and transit route of energy resources to the European energy market. Azerbaijan has been suggested to be a region that serves as the key corridor for Kazakhstan and Turkmenistan to export their energy reserves to the European energy market (Rustamov and Stergiopoulos, 2011). Currently, through the use of tankers, the above-mentioned Central Asian states are transporting some of their energy reserves to the western market in small volumes. However, due to the unresolved legal status of the Caspian Sea and due to geopolitical rivalry in the Caspian basin, there has been a postponement of the implementation of the larger energy infrastructure, which would connect Azerbaijan and Central Asia across the sea. Furthermore, energy resources from additional Central Asian countries, such as Turkmenistan, could also enhance the diversification of Europe's energy imports (Bilgin, 2010).

Azerbaijan is located in a highly sensitive region of the Eurasian continent. Therefore, Azerbaijan, while implementing its energy exporting policy, is a country that is dealing with various challenges while simultaneously implementing very important policies concerning regional balance. The fact that Azerbaijan is a neighbor to the Russian Federation on its northern borders and to Iran on its southern borders creates enormous challenges for the country to build energy-based relations with the European Union. The situation is further complicated by an extensive period of absence of the western community in the Caspian owing to the communist era, which creates further difficulties for Azerbaijan to invite western energy companies to the region (Bishku, 2012). However, Azerbaijan has increasingly made commitments to facilitating the long-term prospect of gas and oil supplies being imported from diversified sources. Furthermore, this commitment should be taken into consideration when looking at the contextual events portraying Azerbaijan as a staging platform for the implementation of Europe's diversification policy. Azerbaijan is following a policy of balanced geopolitical maneuvers to work with all of the Caspian basin countries, including Iran and Russia so as to ensure that European countries have access to its energy reserves (Kazantsev, 2010). This decision has been driven by the desire for Azerbaijan to gain political influence over the outcome of the regional dispute regarding the Caspian basin energy reserves and infrastructure.

Azerbaijan is still a relatively new country and because of its historical legacy, it must carefully balance its relationship with both Moscow and Europe. The country's foreign policy clearly demonstrates the approach that is required in order to achieve such a balance when implementing its own energy strategy (Pinar, 2009). Azerbaijan has been prompted to focus on the necessary tactics for gaining a share of the European energy market as well as negotiating European leaders and consumer representatives on issues regarding other factors, such as events concerning Russia and Iran (Grison, 2013). When considering the transportation of the energy supplies and the positions of all of the surrounding countries, Azerbaijan has a degree of leverage during the negotiation process with Europe. Even though Azerbaijan has aligned its political interests with those of Europe, it nonetheless has a responsibility to fulfil its national interests by obtaining securitization of the resources that it sells (Abilov and Isayev, 2015). In addition, Azerbaijan is actively exploring other European countries that could potentially be the recipients of its energy exports. In the same way that Turkey, Georgia, and

Azerbaijan were capable of building the Baku-Tbilisi-Ceyhan and Baku-Tbilisi-Erzurum projects, so too will there be a push for further collaboration and cooperation on other proposed energy projects that will undoubtedly lead to further achievements. In tackling the many challenges that Azerbaijan faces, there will be a greater sense of accomplishment and this will serve as motivation for the necessary actions for other projects to succeed, which will further contribute to reaching the objective of energy diversification and security in Europe (Emadi and Nezhad, 2011).

Azerbaijan is the country that founded the Southern Gas Corridor and, together with its western partners, implemented the energy pipelines that meet the interests of the countries of Europe (Indeo, 2013). But it should be taken into consideration that the diversification policy of the European Union does not only meet the western communities' interests, but it also meets Azerbaijan's interests towards the implementation of its own energy policy. As it is well known, diversification of the energy exports routes is the primary goal of the energy-producing countries. Since the Soviet Union period, energy infrastructure that existed in the Republic of Azerbaijan has been routed towards Russian soil, and there has not been a single pipeline or piece of energy infrastructure that has been directed towards the western route. Since the early stages of its independence in 1991, Azerbaijan has paid a great deal of attention to this matter in order for the country to build diversified energy export routes and avoid being dependent on a single export route (Khan, 2016).

RESEARCH STATEMENT

This study specifically examines the European Union's increasing natural gas demands over the past several decades. In this context, the role of Azerbaijan in the supply of natural gas and crude oil is evaluated. Lacking their own natural gas resources, the countries of the European Union face the need to satisfy increasing levels of consumption. Consequently, the external importation of energy sources, such as natural gas and crude oil, is going to continue to increase with time. The increasing demand for imported energy reserves has left Europe reliant on and vulnerable to dominant players, such as Russia, and this places the future security of Europe's energy supply into doubt (Finon, 2011). Many European Union countries are highly dependent on a single energy supplier. In particular, many eastern European Union countries are entirely reliant on natural gas supplies from the Russian Federation. This high dependency on a single Russian natural gas supply has created many challenges for these countries. Supply disruptions, political or commercial disputes, conflicts, and crises, as well as infrastructure failure are a serious threat to the European Union's energy security. Gas disputes in 2006 and in 2009 between the Russian Federation and Ukraine, which resulted in supply disruptions to the European countries during winter, annexation of the Crimean Peninsula, the subsequent war in Ukraine, and many other events have left the countries of the European Union with no choice but to diversify their energy supply routes in a foreseeable timeframe (Banciu, 2015).

This study specifically focuses on Azerbaijan's foreign policy and its relationship with the development of the gas and oil production and transportation industries. It also examines political and economic tensions within the region, which have served to strengthen the country's western orientation. It has been suggested that geopolitical factors and the 'energy game' will remain the key driving forces behind the formulation of Azerbaijan's strategic goals. These objectives have caused Azerbaijan to steer its actions towards playing an important part in the energy security of Europe. Since becoming independent, the nation has taken on a Western-oriented agenda with regards to its economic development path. This has been made clear by the fact that Azerbaijan has encouraged Western companies to invest in its energy transport and production infrastructure, even in spite of the Russian Federation and the Islamic Republic of Iran's opposition to this strategy.

The research paper looks at the geopolitical and geo-economic challenges that the European Union is currently facing and studies the role of Azerbaijan, Turkey, Russia, the Islamic Republic of Iran, as well as the Central Asian states, such as Turkmenistan and Kazakhstan. It analyses the existing energy infrastructure by examining regional gas supplies from Russia, Azerbaijan, Kazakhstan, Turkmenistan, Iran, and the Levant basin, including the role of transiting countries. In particular, this research paper also examines the other developments and events that highly affect the European energy security policy. Such events include the Georgia-Russia war in 2008, the Ukraine-Russia Crimean conflict in 2014, the Turkish-Russian crisis and subsequent coalition following the crisis in which a Russian jet was shot down in 2016, the global economic crisis, fall of energy prices, the lifting of economic sanctions on Iran, the unresolved legal status of the Caspian Sea, and many others. This study outlines the integration of Azerbaijan into the energy policy of the European Union and the relevant political and economic factors that play a role in energy projects with EU support. If Azerbaijan doesn't have the opportunity to exist in such an energy policy, there would be no way for the countries of the European Union to consider buying energy resources from the Central Asian countries. Therefore, this paper looks at the commitments of Azerbaijan from a geopolitical and geo-economic point of view.

Importantly, the research paper analyzes the pipelines that currently exist that connect Azerbaijan with the European continent as well as future proposed projects aim at diversifying Europe's energy supplies. In the context of the current and future infrastructure, Azerbaijan's relationships with its regional neighbors, such as Iran, Turkey, Russia, Turkmenistan, and Kazakhstan is examined. It is highly necessary to analyze the interests and the positions of the countries that are involved in the energy security of the European Union. Energy pipelines that are surrounded by significant levels of political involvement shape the geopolitics of the regions that they are passing through. Therefore, energy pipelines that start from Azerbaijan and pass through Georgia and Turkey and stretch further westward to the European energy market bring about many geopolitical challenges to the involved countries. It does, however, develop a sense of unity in political and economic spheres between the countries that share the pipeline corridor. Great evidence for this is the example of the energy pipeline cooperation between Azerbaijan and Georgia in the South Caucasus region. Due to the establishment of successful energy pipeline projects, both countries have removed any economic and political obstacles quickly, despite some disagreements, in order to maintain friendly relations between the two countries. Such an example can also be observed between Azerbaijan and Turkmenistan over the undefined legal status of the Caspian Sea. Therefore, this research paper pays detailed attention to this example in order to prove that energy cooperation promotes economic and political solidarity between involved countries. In the framework of the energy cooperation, economic ties do tend to decrease the different political views and encourage the involved countries to sit down and resolve any disagreements. It is because of this reason that this paper studies Azerbaijan's relations with the countries that are involved in the energy based economic relations.

RESEARCH QUESTION

In the framework described above, this study seeks to answer the following question:

In what ways could Azerbaijan assist in improving the European Union's energy security and how could the leadership of Azerbaijan within the Caspian basin and South Caucasus regions facilitate this goal?

How well prepared are European Union countries to achieve energy diversification policy from alternative routes?

To what extent could Azerbaijan contribute to the European Union's energy policy both as an energy producing and as a transit country within the Southern Gas Corridor?

What are the challenges both for the European Union and for Azerbaijan in terms of building further energy projects?

The research questions highlight the strategic importance of the Caspian basin region. This is due to its important geographic position and the fact that the region contains vast reserves of energy, particularly within Azerbaijan's territory. While keeping its attention focused on energy, the European Union has been playing an active role in the geopolitical events that are shaping the gas and oil industry in the region. There are also other regional actors who are heavily involved and desire to have control over the energy reserves. An increase in the demand for energy in the Republic of Turkey also brings Azerbaijan closer to the Turkish energy market. Azerbaijan has been contributing to the energy security of the Republic of Turkey and since Azerbaijan's independence, both countries have worked closely together not only to secure the European energy security, but also to meet the energy demands of the Turkish economy. Today, Turkey is the 16th largest economy in the world and is expected to grow extremely fast and many economists predict that it will become one of the top ten largest economies in the world (Poladian and Dragoi, 2013). However, in order to reach such a status, there needs to be strong and committed energy partners that supply the country with stable and sufficient crude oil and natural gas supplies so that it can secure its own energy policy. Therefore, this research paper examines the European Union's challenge in the Caspian basin from this point of view.

The regions adjacent to the Caspian Sea are surrounded by global and regional powers that seek to further their own interests within the region. This situation has led to significant problems for Azerbaijan. Because of the rising production of energy and the increasing demand for secure supplies of energy, Azerbaijan is now a regional hub for transportation between the surrounding powers. This situation has led to conflicts of interest between these various powers. In particular, Iran and Russia will not accept the entering of European countries into the Caspian basin region through Azerbaijan. In some ways, Azerbaijan is caught in the center of the geopolitical arena, in which it must juggle ongoing tensions between the European Union and Russia as well as Iran. Consequently, this study also seeks to identify the key events within the Caspian region and determine the consequences that they might have on the European Union's energy security. In response to this, this study analyzes and discusses the diplomacy and energy geopolitics of the whole region with an emphasis on Azerbaijan's important role.

CHAPTER TWO – LITERATURE REVIEW

INTRODUCTION

This study has analyzed a sizeable volume of books and articles focusing on the European Union's energy security. The majority of this literature directly investigates the potential for the diversification of EU energy supplies. Within the subsequent analyses, it is revealed that Azerbaijan's role in the energy sector has a significant link to the diversification of energy in Europe. Azerbaijan's rich energy reserves and strategic location has made it very apparent in the available literature. The European Union's energy security policy and the challenges that it faces have been thoroughly analyzed in the relevant literature and for the most part, this analysis covers the most pressing issues that countries of the European Union face in terms of their energy security. The available literature pays significant attention to the post-soviet period and further implementation of the diversification policy of energy routes. The role of the Caspian basin countries and the historical role of Russia as a supplier of energy to Europe is very visible in the reviewed literature. Furthermore, the role of these countries accounts for most of the available research in the energy security field.

Azerbaijan is seen as one of the most important countries in the world in terms of gas and oil production. Since becoming independent in 1991 after years of functioning under a communist regime, the country has actively sought to export its energy resources to the European continent for sale as a means of storage. It is for this reason that my research has selected articles depending on whether they cover the role of Azerbaijan facilitating energy security for Europe. It is very important to mention that the available literature highly covers the role of most of the countries involved in the field of regional and global energy security policy. The literature on the European Union, Russia, Turkey, Iran, the South Caucasus, and Central Asia covers most of the findings. The Literature that was discovered demonstrates that a great number of scholars and academics have been involved in studies focused on the European energy security policy building. Due to the constantly changing nature of the sphere of global politics and the occurrence of new geopolitical decisions between various countries, the literature is often affected in terms of its description and analysis. Especially since the Russian annexation of the Crimean Peninsula from Ukraine in 2014, there has been a significant increase in the number of researchers examining the role of Russia from an energy security point of view. The available literature since 2014 has mostly concentrated on building a strategy that seeks alternative sources of energy and reduces the reliance on Russia energy supplies. In recent years, there have also been significant increases in the volume of literature available concerning Turkey's role in European energy security. Even though Turkey is not a member of the European Union, the country's role as an energy consumer as well as a transit country for the supply of energy to countries of the European Union has been very well documented in the available literature. New proposed alternative energy infrastructure would mostly pass through the soil of the Turkish Republic. Turkey's strategic location and its fast-developing economy, as well as the changing dynamics of its relations with energy-producing countries, such as its relationship with Iran, Russia, and Caspian basin countries have been highly analyzed by many researchers and academics. As it was mentioned above, there are increasingly fast and unpredictable changes in the global politics and as such the role of countries such as Iran in European energy security has been highly considered and discussed in the recent literature since the lifting of sanctions. Therefore, when analyzing the role of the countries, especially in terms of energy diplomacy and geopolitics, it is important to examine the background history and refer to recently published pieces of literature, including the daily-published journals and newspapers. Therefore, the publication dates of the articles that have been reviewed have played a very important part in my research in terms of their accuracy and actuality. Due to this, up to date articles have been reviewed to determine the role played by Azerbaijan, Russia, Turkey, Iran and Central Asia in securing the European Union's energy policy. Moreover, most of the literature has been chosen according to its publication date. Only articles published between 1990 and 2016 have been reviewed.

Articles were also chosen according to their content. They had to pertain to this study's main aim, which was to ascertain whether or not Azerbaijan could be successful in securing the European Union's energy security and the best ways to achieve this. As an author, I did not face any major difficulties in finding relevant articles that could be connected with the research question of my thesis. For example, after the Russian Federation faced Western sanctions due to the Crimean conflict, the countries of the European Union have turned their attention to the South Caucasus and Central Asian countries in order to implement a new energy diversification strategy. When analyzing the literature that discusses seeking out alternative regions to partially replace Russia's dominant role in energy supplies, automatically the first regions to come up in the discussions are the countries of Azerbaijan, Kazakhstan, and Turkmenistan because of their rich energy reserves. Available literature also covers and discusses the role of the energy transit countries.

As stated, the evaluation of available literature was predominantly focused on the energy security Europe and the potential to diversify imports so as to include energy products from the Caspian basin and the South Caucasus regions. Within this analysis, the present research also investigates the role of Azerbaijan as an alternative supplier for European energy demands. Throughout this study, literature with relevant data has been examined and conclusions are organized into the form of a critical analysis. It was not difficult to obtain appropriate literature relating to the subject of the potential consumption of Azerbaijan's energy reserves in the European Union. This is mainly because of the topic's presence in the field of international politics. In the process of undertaking this research, I have had the opportunity reflect on the current geopolitical atmosphere. This has led me to divide the findings of this study into multiple sections when exploring Azerbaijan's potential role in the energy policy of the European Union. There is further subdivision based on particular pieces of infrastructure that could be developed in order to provide diversification to the European Union's energy security.

Available literature mostly illustrates the view that the Republic of Azerbaijan, with its rich natural gas and crude oil reserves, can contribute to the energy security of the countries of the European Union, which could decrease the European Union's reliance on supplies of natural gas from Russia. This has been demonstrated in research papers and reports on the huge natural gas and crude oil energy reserves of the country, especially in the national sector of the Caspian Sea. It is also important to point out that the literature mentions energy fields with proven crude oil and natural gas reserves that have only recently been discovered in the region. There are also many pieces of literature that suggest there are several existing pipelines that demonstrate Azerbaijan's potential as a stable and dependable trading partner. Due to this idea, I will pay specific attention to the role of the existing pipelines such as the Baku-Tbilisi-Ceyhan (BTC) crude oil and Baku-Tbilisi-Erzurum (BTE) natural gas pipelines. The volumes of product that the above-mentioned pipelines contribute to the energy security of Europe will be reviewed as well. Furthermore, there is a great deal of literature that has studied the political and economic pressures on the existing pipelines during both the construction and operational periods. Recent literature points out that the existing energy infrastructure has established the energy corridor for the European Union countries to reach the Caspian's energy fields. The stable and uninterrupted transportation of the energy resources via these energy pipelines to the European energy market has been indicated in most of the findings and a significant amount of literature backs up the reliability of the energy corridor that begins in Azerbaijan.

Literature that examines the role of Azerbaijan in the planned projects has also clarified the level of commitment that the country is willing to make and discusses the prospect of supplying larger volumes in the future. As a result, this research project has analyzed pieces of literature that cover the planned energy projects investigated their potential capacities, their contexts, and the surrounding political agendas that are playing a role in the continued progress of the Southern Gas Corridor. From the literature that has been reviewed, it appears that the Republic of Azerbaijan has appreciated the attention that it has received from the European Union with regard to the proposed pipelines. The construction of the Trans-Anatolian (TANAP) natural gas pipeline project has highly dominated the recent discussions and examinations of the European diversification policy. The literature points out the leadership role of Azerbaijan, together with Turkey, that has been taken since the decision was made to begin the construction of the TANAP natural gas pipeline. A similar situation applies regarding the Trans-Adriatic (TAP) natural gas project. Furthermore, both of the projects that are currently under construction are considered to be main parts of the Southern Gas Corridor according to most of the available literature. As such, the political and economic features of the pipeline have been analyzed by the literature relating to the diversification policy.

Finally, the research findings and literature both discuss the role of Azerbaijan in accessing the rich energy resources of Central Asia, particularly with respect to its access to Turkmenistan's natural gas reserves. Turkmenistan holds one of the world's richest gas reserves. The European Union's interest in the Central Asian region is very significant and therefore the literature also pays specific attention to the proposed pipeline, the Trans-Caspian natural gas pipeline, as well as potential access to Turkmenistan's rich energy reserves of natural gas. After reviewing most of the available literature and research findings it is plain to see that in the context of energy security in Europe, Azerbaijan is playing the strategic role of both a transporter of Central Asia gas towards Europe and also a producer. Current EU activities in the Caspian basin region have demonstrated Azerbaijan's twofold role and how it could potentially ensure the diversification of European energy routes.

EXISTING AND PROPOSED INFRASTRUCTURE

Energy security along the transit corridor and the relationship between the countries that share the area will be reviewed with reference to the existing literature. This will be accomplished through analysis of the planned projects. Although the studies that were examined focused specifically on the projects individually, in their entirety, they demonstrate the European Union's common policy on energy security with regards the Southern Gas Corridor (SGC). Studies relating to the subject have discussed the entire proposed infrastructure that could lead towards diversification of energy supplies within the European Union.

The literature concerning the already existing pipelines has also been crucial to the development of the investigation and argumentation herein. A number of researchers chosen to study already constructed pipelines due to the fact that their transport routes are laying the foundations for the creation of a transit passage, which is now of great importance to the energy security of the European Union. Richard (2009) states that since the collapse of the Soviet Union and the subsequent toppling of the communist regime in Azerbaijan, the country has joined together with Georgia and Tukey, with the support of the European Union and the United States, in order to foresee the construction and maintenance of the Baku-Tbilisi-Ceyhan (BTC) pipeline (Richard, 2009). According to Richard, the BTC was the first energy pipeline to be constructed without the approval of Moscow. The United States took measures to prevent the involvement of Russia in the implementation of the BTC pipeline (Youngs, 2009). The BTC pipeline received support from an international consortium including TPAO, Statoil, INPEX, Itochu, TotalFinalElf, ConocoPhilips, SOCAR (State Oil Company of Azerbaijan), and lastly British Petroleum, which has the largest share in the consortium (British Petroleum Report, 2009). According to many scholars, the implementation of the Baku-Tbilisi-Erzurum (BTE) project is also considered to have laid the gas infrastructure from the Caspian basin that bypassed Russian and Iranian territory. According to Alipour, the implementation of the projects has not only had a direct impact on the improvement of the European energy security policy, but it has actually had an enormous impact on the entire Caspian basin and Black Sea regions' economic and political developments (Alipour, 2015). Alipour also comments that after the collapse of the Soviet Union, like all of the ex-Soviet countries, Azerbaijan and Georgia faced extreme economic and political challenges in the South Caucasus. However, the successful construction and continued operation of the gas pipeline has meant that these countries have been able to significantly improve their economic and social sectors. Alipour states that the BTE pipeline, together with BTC pipeline, have strengthened the political cooperation between Azerbaijan, Georgia, and Turkey. This has resulted in the creation of a long-lasting energy corridor for the countries of the European Union (Alipour, 2015).

According to the American-Israeli scholar, Brenda Shaffer, a shift towards the use of natural gas as an alternative to crude oil has occurred in the European Union. As such, proposed natural gas pipelines originating in the Caspian basin region have become the focus of energy security policies (Shaffer, 2014). In her article, she states that unlike the 19th and 20th centuries "the twenty-first century is the era of natural gas" (Shaffer, pg 71, 2014). In particular, she concentrates on Azerbaijan and mentions that this country is especially vital to this shift in energy consumption, firstly in its role as a producer of natural gas and secondly because of the important role that it plays as a part of the transit corridor between Europe and Central Asian countries, such as Kazakhstan and Turkmenistan. Therefore, BTE, being an important piece of natural gas transportation infrastructure from the Caspian basin, meets the European demands for natural gas consumption. Arguing from the same perspective, Winrow also indicates that natural gas consumption is playing an increasingly important role relative to total energy consumption and this is having an effect on the supply diversification of energy being imported in Europe (Winrow, 2013). He brings the natural gas resources importance to the forefront and states that countries like Turkey, which serves as a transit hub as it did with respect to the BTE pipeline, contribute to the creation of a stable energy corridor and access point to the energy markets of the European Union.

Literature that exists on the proposed infrastructure dominates the research findings, and as such, most of the literature examines how the proposed energy projects would support the European Union's plan of diversifying the routes of energy exports. Literature that specifically touches on the role of Azerbaijan shows that a high number of scholars are involved in discussing the European Union and Azerbaijan's commitments in terms of implementing the proposed pipelines. However, an important detail to mention is that the literature that exists on this topic only concentrates on the proposed natural gas pipelines. This is because all of the pipeline projects are mainly concentrated on the transportation of the natural gas reserves. As mentioned in the literature, all the proposed pipeline projects such as TANAP, TAP, Trans-Caspian, AGRI, and Nabucco are the natural gas pipelines that were covered in most of the discussions. However, as it was mentioned in the introduction chapter, due to fast changes in global politics and the shift of various geo-political interests, the governments of the involved countries that subsequently implemented them into active construction phases selected some of these pipelines. According to the Volkan Ozdemir, H. Bugra Yavuz and Emine Tokgoz, TANAP and TAP projects are the only pipeline projects that have been committed to and that are currently being constructed that will expand the transportation of the natural gas towards the European energy market. In particular, TANAP is said to be a unique and very important project within the Eurasian natural gas network (Volkan, Yavuz and Tokgöz, 2015). On the other hand, projects like the Nabucco natural gas pipeline, AGRI LNG, and Azerbaijan's Georgia-Black Sea-Bulgaria Route, CNG, have been postponed and the realization of these projects in the close future is under question. Therefore, in the literature review chapter, I have chosen each of the postponed proposed projects because they have, until recent years, created competition with TANAP and TAP projects to take in the agenda of the European Union's energy policy. As mentioned, literature that exists on the postponed projects dominates the discussion. This is the case particularly for the Nabucco project, which was once paid important attention by the energy policy makers of the European Union. Therefore, in this chapter, there will be a literature review on the Nabucco, AGRI, and Azerbaijan's Georgia-Black Sea-Bulgaria Route - CNG projects. This review will be implemented in order to understand the geopolitics and geo-economic interests that are behind the implementation of the policy.

THE LNG – AZERBAIJAN-GEORGIA-ROMANIA

According to Global Insight, a proposal from multiple governments referred to as the Azerbaijan-Georgia-Romani Interconnection (AGRI) seeks to develop a new Liquefied Natural Gas (LNG) infrastructure network that would connect the involved countries (Global Insight, 2010). In addition to this, Socor mentions that AGRI was originally envisioned as a section of the proposed Southern Corridor that would take natural gas to Europe from the Caspian region (Socor, 2010). The AGRI could have been viewed as a new contestant with multiple competitors seeking to transport gas along the southeastern European route. According to Global Insight, a key advantage of natural gas liquefication is that it can be moved externally and does not rely on a pipeline. The AGRI project seeks to develop two terminals for LNG; the first would be located on the Georgian coast while the second would be situated on the coast of Romania. It is expected that the abovementioned terminals would permit the flow of Azerbaijani gas to Georgia through the Caucasus region. If development goes ahead as planned, this gas will be liquefied in the port city of Kulevi in Georgia. It will then be loaded onto tankers and shipped across the Black sea to the Constanta terminal on the coast of Romania (Global Insight, 2010). According to Codoban, the LNG will then be re-gasified and transported to the Romanian gas grid from where it will be distributed to European consumers (Codoban, 2012). The AGRI proposal to deliver LNG is considered to be the highest paced project that has been commenced to focus on the delivery of natural gas to EU countries. Adrien Videanu, the Romanian Minister of economy, stated "this is the fastest and one of the most efficient to bring Caspian gas to the EU" (Socor, 2010). As Socor mentions in this article, the development proposal is been receiving backing from multiple nations that have expressed their concern regarding the 2009 stalemate between Turkey and Azerbaijan over the gas sale and transportation agreement. Nonetheless, their collaboration on the BTC and BTE pipelines has hinted that there are no reasons for either country to deadlock any negotiations on future energy projects (Socor, 2010). Therefore, Socor indicates that the strategic maneuver of Azerbaijan regarding AGRI and putting pressure on Turkey will both serve to increase the position of Azerbaijan in terms of its ability to negotiate on the sale of gas as well as transportation price (Socor, 2010).

Furthermore, according to Codoban, several reasons are suggested to account for why the proposed infrastructure is to be implemented. One of the main reasons is that Azerbaijan and Turkey are involved in an ongoing disagreement concerning gas prices and transit tariffs. He follows by saying that once the dispute on different views is resolved with an agreement, AGRI will lose its importance. But he adds that such maneuvers would also create an obstacle for implementation of a pipeline project known as Nabucco (Codoban, 2012). According to Socor, during the period of discussions between Azerbaijan and European countries, including talks with Turkey, Azerbaijan was displeased because of the way it which it was seen by Nabucco supporters as merely a supplier instead of being treated like a proper consortium member. Due to this period of intense negotiations, the situation is causing Azerbaijan to consider striking up supply deals with Russia and Iran, or even Bulgaria and Romania (Socor, 2010).

Following the same view, Stefan has stated several players would prefer the AGRI project to complement the previously proposed pipeline project, Nabucco. He says that such a situation is unlikely and presupposes economic and political determination of governments as well as the capacity of Caspian reserves. However, there is also the possibility of a situation in which a significant volume of gas supplies will be diverted away from Nabucco as a result of the AGRI project. (Stefan, et al, 2012). Some scholars have the opinion that AGRI has a number of disadvantages. The viability of the project is often put into question, particularly when taking into consideration the fact that Azerbaijan and Romania are the only active players involved in the operation of the Black Sea closed loop transporting LNG (Global Insight, 2010). Georgia plays the part of intermediary in this arrangement (Global Insight, 2010). According to Maracz, the LNG export route has since been prioritized by AGRI team because it is anticipated that they can beat the extended delays that the Nabucco pipeline is expected to have before reaching the market. The Nabucco project has been escribed as "long in promises and short on financing" (Maracz, pg 19, 2011). There were once plans for AGRI to supply up to 8 bcm of LNG directly to the EU market by ferrying the product across the Black Sea using tankers. Stefan mentions that AGRI would lead to the avoidance of Russia and Turkey, which are the two main transit corridors that are capable of transporting gas. As such, AGRI would serve as a way of further diversifying the energy supply routes into Europe (Stefan, et al, 2012).

According to Maracz, because of the geopolitical influences surrounding the planned projects, European energy companies and countries within the region have put forward further projects in order to diversify Europe's supplies (Maracz, 2011). Azerbaijan has been working with Georgia towards the construction of a larger infrastructure network linking the Black Sea with the Caspian Sea. Maracz also states that European nations have begun to engage in individual negotiations with Azerbaijan on the proposed pipelines. Due to its access to the Black Sea, Romania wants to strengthen the Black Sea-Caspian Sea transit corridor. This demonstrates the country's ambition to take a part in European energy security. The AGRI project has concentrated mainly on LNG as a means of transporting energy products abroad. Maracz (2011) states that countries of the eastern European Union are particularly vulnerable to decreases in the supply of gas from Russia and this is motivating such countries to seek out energy supplies from alternative sources.

"Azerbaijan, Georgia and Romania have agreed upon, in April of this year [2010], to transport gas from the Caspian Sea via the Black Sea to Europe bypassing Russia. Later this year, Hungary also has joined this so-called AGRI consortium. As a result, EU-member states will be less dependent on the gas pipelines carrying Russian gas through states that are under Russian control" (Maracz, 2011).

Maracz optimistically supported the implementation of this project and suggests that the interconnection will reinforce the Southern Gas Corridor. But as a matter of fact, due to a delay of the project and a reduction in the interest of the countries involved, the implementation of the project is now being brought under serious question. In the same context as Maracz's statements, Codoban suggests that the European Union is in a situation in which it is left with no alternative option apart from offering its support for the realization of the project. Codoban makes the following statement.

"Through the AGRI project, Romania could become the second largest energy platform for the EU, after Turkey; and it could become, making use of its membership, the EU's main energy player in the region, thus becoming a nodal point for Caspian hydrocarbons transit to Central Europe" (Codoban, 2012).

It is argued that Romania will have the opportunity to play a significantly greater part in the European Union that this will help the broader region to become integrated into Western Europe (Codoban, 2012). It has also been suggested that LNG transportation practices and technology within the regional countries will be developed by AGRI and this will serve to reduce political disagreements regarding the transit pathway directed at the European Union (Socor, 2010).

THE CNG – AZERBAIJAN-GEORGIA-BLACK SEA-BULGARIA

In 2010, an agreement was signed between Azerbaijan and Bulgaria with the intention to transport Azerbaijani natural gas to Bulgaria. From there, it would carry on to various locations within the European Union. A key feature of this agreement relates to the transport of Compressed Natural Gas (CNG) from Azerbaijan, through Georgia and across the Black Sea to Bulgaria (Oxford Analytica, 2010). According to Global Insight, similarly to the LNG agreement with Romania, the CNG agreement with Bulgaria was also envisioned to serve as a means of circumventing the existing obstacles and hurdles related to the transport of energy resources through Turkey (Global Insight, 2010). During the ratification formalities, the former Bulgarian President, Giorgio Purvanov, emphasized this project in the wider context of Southern Gas Corridor as a means of carrying energy resources through Europe. He anticipates that Azerbaijan will double up as a transit country for natural gas from Turkmenistan to Europe and thus solve the perennial

Caspian-Central Asian gas problem (Global Insight, 2010). The president of Azerbaijan, Ilham Aliyev, noted that the CNG project would "make Azerbaijan a direct supplier to the European Union... advancing the European Union–Azerbaijan strategic partnership on energy" (Pasturia, URL, 2010). According to Oxford Analytica, one of the main benefits of CNG has been that it has allowed for the transportation of natural gas externally to a fixed pipeline. Nevertheless, AGRI's CNG extension remains an unprecedented and untested solution. So far, CNG has mainly been transported via road in relatively small quantities. According to Oxford Analytica, the transportation of compressed gas over the Black Sea requires specially designed tankers that are often more expensive than tankers designed for LNG, although there can be significant cost reductions due to the mode of delivery. This is because there is no re-gasification process required with CNG and this evades costly processes or installations (Oxford Analytica, 2010).

During the year 2010, the collaboration between Georgia and Azerbaijan drew attention towards Bulgaria in relation to the energy link between the Caspian Sea and the Black Sea. According to Issayeva and Parkhomchik, Compressed Natural Gas (CNG) was chosen as the method by which carry gas towards the European Union from the Caspian basin under this policy (Issayeva and Parkhomchik, 2015). The scholars of this article state that both LNG and CNG projects would have allowed for the transit of resources without a pipeline and the projects are still gaining attention from the European Union in terms of creating direct access to the Caspian basin via the South Caucasus region and thus bypassing Turkish soil as well. However, both scholars mention that LNG and CNG projects only promise transportation of just a small volume of natural gas and this would not be sufficient to satisfy the demands of the EU countries. Oxford Analytica states the following regarding the proposal:

"Concerns over the reliability of gas supplies from Russia have led Bulgaria to participate in alternative schemes involving the movement of gas across or around the Black Sea. One option involves the use of CNG: this technology is relatively untried, but it represents an interesting alternative for smaller volume flows." (Oxford Analytica, URL, 2010).

This article suggests that Bulgaria is showing desperation in the face of uncertain future energy supplies and is enthusiastic to secure the energy security of the European Union with the establishment of alternative supply routes. Pasturia also points out that Azerbaijan could gain access to the energy markets of Europe without the involvement of Turkey in the CNG project (Pasturia 2010). However, according to Volkan Özdemir, H. Buğra Yavuz and Emine Tokgöz, the TANAP and TAP projects have discharged the actuality of the implementation of the CNG and LNG projects that would connect South Caucasus to the Balkans (Volkan, Yavuz and Tokgöz, 2015). They state in their article that TANAP is a unique and very important project and Turkish soil is currently the most appropriate route for Caspian basin natural gas resources to reach the European gas market (Volkan, Yavuz, and Tokgöz, 2015). Therefore, as has been thoroughly analyzed in the literature review, CNG and LNG projects have currently been put aside and the realization of this project is no longer on the present agenda of the involved countries.

THE NABUCCO GAS PIPELINE

One of the most discussed postponed energy projects was the Nabucco natural gas pipeline. This was the one of the most widely talked about project of the European Union and was expected to diversify supplies of gas so as not to be so dependent on Russia. This project was being discussed before 2000 and it drew in significant levels of attention from the surrounding regions

(Barysch, 2010). Barysch also states that the project was predicted to decrease the European Union's reliance on energy supplies from Russia. The capacity of this pipeline would have been 31 bcm annually. This would have provided a source of healthy competition to the market as the monopolistic position of Russia could have decreased to some extent in the eastern part of Europe (Barysch, 2010). Barysch further mentions that the Nabucco Pipeline, which is also known as the Turkey-Austria gas pipeline, was expected to link up to the BTE pipeline and lengthen connection from the Caspian regions, through Erzurum, Turkey, and on To Baumgarten an der March, Austria (Barysch, 2010). The launch of this project has taken several years to gain approval from the representatives of Austria, Hungary, Romania, Bulgaria, and Turkey. However, six companies have now committed to the development project; namely, MOL (Hungary), OMV (Austria), Bulgargaz (Bulgaria), Transgaz (Romania), RWE (Germany), and BOTAS (Turkey), the Nabucco pipeline project is expected to reduce this region's dependence on Russian natural gas (World Bank Group, & Gerner, 2009).

Experts from the World Bank Group and Gerner have suggested that the Nabucco pipeline had the potential to begin operating as early as 2015. However, it has become obvious from news reports and academic literature that the online status of the project the Nabucco pipeline has been deactivated because the consortium countries, which include MOL (Hungary), Transgaz (Romania), OMV (Germany), BOTAS (Turkey) and Bulgargaz (Bulgaria) lack commitment (World Bank Group, & Garner, 2009). As a result, the involved countries have decided to consider opportunities in other energy pipeline projects.

Within in reviewed literature there are many arguments against the realization of the Nabucco pipeline. Götz suggests that the pipeline is problematic and alternative solutions should be implemented. By performing an in depth analysis of the pipeline, he argues that the success of the project is thrown into the realm of uncertainty because of political and economic competition. (Götz, 2009). He goes on to argue that construction of this pipeline would result in Turkey becoming an alternative hub of energy and lead to significant changes in the country's economy. Saban Kardas continues along this path of reasoning and suggests that if the Nabucco Pipeline is implemented, it would alter the geo-strategic dynamics of the country within the region. Furthermore, the European Union's diplomatic relations with Turkey would shift to a different level if Turkey were to obtain the prestigious status of 'energy hub' as a result of the realization of Nabucco (Kardas, 2011). Turkey's pending admission to the European Union is tightly interconnected with the implementation of Nabucco and this is why the completion of the project has been delayed longer than originally anticipated (Kardas, 2011). Götz and Kardas agree that Nabucco is charged with significant levels of geopolitical interests the prospect of it ever being fully realized has been put into doubt. Although less critical of Turkey, Ozkan holds a similar view but proposes that it is unlikely that Turkey will play the energy card since the country is fully aware of the negative consequences associated with shortages gas due to its own past experiences (Ozkan, 2011).

From an alternative point of view, it has also been claimed that the European Union would be wise to establish a common energy security policy in the near future (Rustamov, & Stergiopoulos, 2011). In their 2011 published article, they claim that the European Union should develop a strategic plan for managing the expansion of diversified sources directed from the Caspian basin towards Europe. As it is very well indicated in the 2015-2016 literature and newspaper articles, since the annexation of the Crimean Peninsula by the Russian Federation, the European Union has created the "Energy Union" in order to share a common policy on their energy security policy (Rafael, Juan, and Constantino, 2015). However, Rustamov and Stergiopulos even remarked on the alliance between Turkmenistan and Azerbaijan back in 2011 and they suggest that the two nations have become significant partners in the execution of a European diversification policy. The countries have offered support to Nabucco, as well as other projects, and suggest that any proposed project can potentially be realized with a common EU energy policy. (Rustamov, & Stergiopoulos, 2011). We see this with the implementation of the TANAP and TAP natural gas pipeline projects. However, they stress that it would be best to execute this policy as soon as possible due to the fact that the pipeline construction costs are expecting to rise significantly. However, it is likely that construction will be delayed, which will make the project even more expensive (Rustamov, & Stergiopoulos, 2011).

Fernandez offers an alternative point of view and states that "the Nabucco pipeline project poses a double challenge to Russia: it risks weakening both Russia's monopoly in Europe and its monopsony in Central Asia" (Fernandez, pg. 69, 2011). He argues that the reaction from Russia has demonstrated that its levels of competitiveness are increasing. This will encourage the realization of projects like Nabucco because the actions and approach of Moscow lead the countries of the European Union to act more decisively in regards to the security of their energy (Fernandez, 2011).

Nabucco's importance to the European Union has been very important and according to Fernandez, the project was motivated by the desire to increase the diversification of energy resources, particularly natural gas, in order to reduce the dependence on Russia (Fernandez, 2011) As such, Nabucco has endeavored to improve the connection of natural gas sources in the Caspian Sea and Middle East regions with the European Union. Rustamov and

Stergiopulos outline the idea that the construction of infrastructure capable of accessing these alternative gas sources could allow the Nabucco project to reduce the levels of reliance that the European Union has on exports of energy resources from Russia, which is the region's largest producer of natural gas (Rustamov; Stergiopulos, 2011). Arguing from the same position, Jarosiewicz states that Nabucco could also be used to reduce the interruptions of the energy supply as a preemptive tactic to lessen the likelihood of political disruptions like the Russian-Ukraine gas disputes in 2006 and 2009 (Jarosiewicz, 2012). The European Commission has stated that the consumption of gas in the European Union is predicted to increase and compared to the previous years, the role of Russia in the share of the percentage in supplying will remain at similar levels (Eurostat, 2015). Nabucco was once a source of hope in the efforts to reduce the percentage of the dependency, however, it has now become the victim of political challenges.

Political and economic issues related to the Nabucco project have challenged its implementation process. The Nabucco pipeline, in particular, has faced several obstacles driven by various agendas. The Chairman of Russia's State Duma's energy committee, Ivan Grachev, suggests that Nabucco unviable because it is a political play used to increase the economic pressure put on Russia (Barysch, 2010). Vladimir Putin, the Russian president, Nabucco is merely another effort to decrease the influence of Russia on the global stage. Russia has responded by terminating several deals to purchase natural gas from Azerbaijan and Turkmenistan. Other scholars have been critical of Nabucco and suggested that it is infeasible because it lacks the ability to guarantee that enough energy resources will be accessible from the sources it intends to link with the European energy market (Gotz, 2009). According to Gotz, meeting the quota of the 31 bcm has been put into doubt because at the point in time Azerbaijan has only offered to supply a relatively small portion of this volume. Furthermore, another confirmed company, Caspian Shah Deniz, has only confirmed that it can provide 8 bcm since its remaining production reserves have already been bought up by Russia (Kardas, 2011). Even though the Shah Deniz has rich reserves, it is still unknown whether these reserves are significant enough to live up to the expectations built into the proposal. Furthermore, Iran's foreign minister, Manouchehr Mottaki, made the following statement in relation to the proposed pipeline. "Speaking of Nabucco pipeline without Iran's participation would amount to nothing but a pipeline void of gas" (Luft, 2009).

Baev and Øverland examine the relevant pipeline literature and make a critical comparison between the Nabucco pipeline and the Russian proposed Southern Stream pipelines; both of these ventures are called "Mega projects" (Baev & Øverland, 2010). They suggest that the projects have been placed head-to-head in a development race, which has been complicated by various economic and geopolitical interests and agendas. They further highlight that the Southern Stream project has increased the competitiveness of Moscow, which is likely to become more strategic in its policy planning if other projects similar to Nabucco come to fruition (Baev & Øverland, 2010). Although the five mentioned countries have signed documents of commitment to the project, there has been no solid decision regarding its realization as of yet (Baev; Overland, 2010). As is now known, the final binding decision was announced and the implementation of the Nabucco project has been postponed. Even though the project has been given the approval from US and EU representatives, competition from other proposed projects and weak commitments from the Nabucco consortium have led TANAP and TAP to win over transportation of natural gas reserves from the Caspian basin towards the European energy market. According to Fackrell, unlike in the Nabucco project, Azerbaijan and Turkey have put forward their own natural gas pipeline project in which the TANAP project will become the main strategic link in the Southern Gas Corridor (Fackrell, 2013). Fackrell suggests that by choosing the TANAP project, Turkey and Azerbaijan have created a new energy Silk Road corridor. As he states in his article, Europe and Turkey will have an additional source of stable and secure gas resources via the TANAP project (Fackrell, 2013).

APPROACH OF THE REGIONAL COUNTRIES

Literature that exists in the field of European energy security also indicates many pieces of analysis and academic papers that concentrate on the role of the countries of Central Asia as well as Iran and Turkey. However, the most discussed country is the Russian Federation. This is mainly due to its important role in supplying the countries of the European Union with energy supplies. According to Tichy and Kratochvil, when looking at the basic approaches to the European Union and Russia's energy cooperation, it becomes visible that there are three main discourses of the energy relations (Tichý and Kratochvíl, 2014). The discourses of integration, liberalization, and diversification are the main three aspects that can be employed as a way of understanding Russian-EU energy relations. According to Tichy and Kratochvil, the diversification discourse is the most important and it emphasizes both the political and economic aspects of the cooperation. Security threats that the European Union faces in terms of its energy supplies and the diversification policy it chooses to follow have been understood by Moscow as a challenge. The authors state that "while the EU is trying to protect its distribution networks, Russia is seeking to get hold of them; whenever the EU is trying to expand its portfolio of supplier countries, Russia is bound to do whatever it can to prevent such a diversification."

(Tichý, Kratochvíl, 2014). From this statement, the authors clearly indicate that in order for both sides to continue productive cooperation with each other, the main legal document, which is known as the "Partnership and Cooperation Agreement", should be considered as the main field for new and renewed levels of cooperation. The European Union and Russia could clearly set the legal cooperation aspects and this would serve as a means for the European Union to demonstrate to Russia that it is one of the main energy suppliers and it could also demonstrate to Russia that it will implement a diversification strategy (Tichý, Kratochvíl, 2014). A similar argument is continued by Guney and Korkmaz, who state that the energy dialogue is of significant importance to both sides, especially when considering the abundance of changes that occur in global politics (Güney And Korkmaz, 2014). Both authors mention that even during the cold war period there was still dialogue and negotiation between Soviet Moscow and the West due to the necessity of natural gas sales. This same dialogue has continued during the post-soviet period, however, from that period time until the present time, natural gas has been very much politicized by both sides, especially from the European Union side's point of view. The authors mention that when reconsidering the 2006, 2009, and 2014 Crimean crises, both sides should try to understand the implications of their actions and accept both of their crucial roles in energy cooperation (Güney And Korkmaz, 2014). According to Urutchev, even the Crimean crisis will be resolved eventually so the question of the dependency of the European Union on Russian energy supplies needs to be considered and solutions need to be discovered in order to improve the security of the supplies (Urutchev, 2014). He proposes that the European Union should develop a strategy in which it combines its currently existing energy infrastructure while employing the support of the countries in the

Caspian basin for implementing energy pipelines with significantly larger capacities.

According to Yesevi and Tiftikcigil, Turkey and Azerbaijan has been recognized as allies in implementing their foreign policy interests from a regional approach. In their article, the authors mention that the factor of energy plays an important part in their relations and due to the implementation of the common energy projects the construction of the TANAP project has increased the level of their relations. Yesevi and Tiftikcigil indicate the role of Turkey as an important player in securing the energy security of Europe. Turkey's successful energy cooperation with Azerbaijan on the BTE and BTC natural gas pipeline, the involvement of Georgia as a transit country, and the realization of the Southern Gas Corridor bring the Turkish Republic to the forefront of the global energy trade. According to the authors, the relationship between Turkey and Azerbaijan defines the status of the European access to the Caspian basin, and therefore without these countries, the European Union would not have successful and stable energy access to the region (Yesevi And Tiftikcigil, 2015). According to Lashaki, Goudarzi and Lakani, who hold a similar position, the successful relationship between Azerbaijan and Turkey since 1991 has impacted on the formation of regional cooperative organizations, such as "The Organization of Black Sea Economic Cooperation (BSEC) and Transport Corridor Europe-Caucasus-Asia (TRACECA)" (Lashaki, Goudarzi and Lakani, 2015). They mention that these regional organizations support the corridor for European expansion all the way to the Chinese border via the Central Asian states. Via the TRACECA corridor, energy products are transported and this is stimulating the ongoing presence of the Turkish Republic and the European Union in the Caspian basin. However, the authors of this article pay specific attention to Turkish foreign policy in the South Caucasus and they particularly focus on and attempt to analyze the policy's impact on Azerbaijani and Iranian relations (Lashaki, Goudarzi and Lakani, 2015). According to Lashaki, Goudarzi, and Lakani, Turkey and Iran's interests have begun to confront one another in the South Caucasus region and rivalry between the two countries has caused political, ideological, and economic competition. This competition has demonstrated itself in the energy cooperation within the Caspian Sea, and despite Iran's attempt to block Western entrance into the region, Western companies have entered into the Caspian basin successfully nonetheless, largely due to the support of Azerbaijan. However, the authors state that all of these events have essentially become a reality especially due to Turkey's influence on the South Caucasus region (Lashaki, Goudarzi and Lakani, 2015).

The literature that exists concerning the European energy security policy not only concentrates highly on the Central Asian countries' roles in the process, but it also analyzes the role of the People's Republic of China and the Russian Federation in blocking their access towards the European gas market. Cobanli mentioned that after the fall of the Soviet Union, Central Asian states declared their independence and announced that their energy reserves were available to all countries and energy markets (Cobanli, 2014). He states that despite the visible ambition of the Central Asian countries and the economic interests of the Western countries, there has been very little interaction or dialogue between these parties, and as a result, no major energy infrastructure projects have been implemented to transport their natural gas reserves to the European gas market since 1991 (Cobanli, 2014). He continues by stating that this has resulted in China's successful entrance into the region, through the implementation of energy projects with Turkmenistan and Kazakhstan. However, the author goes on to suggest that European countries will be able to have access to Central Asia only under one condition, the support of

Turkey. According to Cobanli, all the Central Asian states, there are 5 in total, are Turkic states, and they share linguistic and religious similarities with Turkey. Therefore, most of the Central Asian countries see Turkey as the main guiding force leading the way towards building foreign policy cooperatively (Cobanli, 2014).

As established, when analyzing the recent literature, it becomes very visible that the European Union has set specific goals for the implementation of the "European Energy Union", which aims to make energy resources more secure, more stable, and more affordable to its members. According to Environmental Policy and Law, the European Union's main target is to reduce all the tools and countries that the European Union depends on from the energy framework (Environmental Policy and Law, 2015). According to the journal, the European Union's energy market has its own global importance, and its market is the largest importing energy market in the world, where it imports more than 50% of its needs for energy, simultaneously paying more than 400 billion euros per year. This situation has pushed the European Union to create the European Energy Union program (Environmental Policy and Law, 2015). The journal indicates the European Union's decision to secure the energy policy of the Union. The president of the European Commission, Jean-Claude Juncker, provides the following statement.

"For too long, energy has been exempt from the fundamental freedoms of our Union. Current events show the stakes, as many Europeans fear they may not have the energy needed to heat their homes. This is about Europe acting together, for the long term. I want the energy that underpins our economy to be resilient, reliable, secure and growingly renewable and sustainable" (Environmental Policy and Law, 2014).

When summarizing the European Energy Union's goals, it becomes visible that the implementation of the main energy infrastructure and diversification of the gas supplies to the European energy market is one of the main attempts to decrease the role of countries that create threats to their energy security policy. According to Urutchev, in order for the European Energy Union to become successful, it will need to fulfill the following conditions. The currently existing internal infrastructure needs to be united, new common policies must be accepted together with the implementation of the priority energy projects, and finally the countries within the Caspian basin must be supported so that they may properly build the necessary natural gas pipelines and accompanying infrastructure (Urutchev, 2014).

RESEARCH METHODOLOGY

This study's organization has been formed in the context of Azerbaijan's role in the energy security of the European Union. The study investigates already existing and newly infrastructure and describes the contemporary geopolitical and geo-economic situation in the region, with particular emphasis on the Caspian basin and how the proposed infrastructure could best be realized in the future so as to ensure the availability of alternative secure energy resources bound for Europe's energy market. My research seeks to drive and develop further research through the collection of data and information. Within this study, quantitative and qualitative data regarding the various pipelines have been collected and analyzed. Data have been collected through the performance of interviews, most of which were private. I have designed this thesis in order to research this particular area of the global energy trade and to obtain a narrative of the events and themes surrounding it. In this research, I have questioned and researched the articles and literature that relate to this field. I have researched the articles so as to answer the research question and explain the current circumstances surrounding the European Union's energy security and the part played by Azerbaijan in this policy's implementation. Specific attention has been given to the role of Azerbaijan in the planned pipeline projects, and also to the fact that those pipelines only travel through three countries before reaching their destination. Nevertheless, I decided not to limit my discussion and inspection to just the three countries, but rather to give an analysis of the role of the Islamic Republic of Iran, the Turkish Republic, the Russian Federation, as well as the Central Asian states, Turkmenistan and Kazakhstan in particular. In the process of discovering an answer to my research question, I have investigated the current situation of energy security in the European Union and it appears to be in need of multiple levels of diversification. Within this regional and global analysis approach, I have combined their roles and used the information to attempt to answer my research question of where Azerbaijan currently stands in this global and regional energy cooperation process.

The design of this study was organized based on my observations in the relevant literature. Data was gathered from primary and secondary sources, which were selected from a variety of articles, books, and journals relating to the European Union's energy security as well as Azerbaijan's role in its projected success. The majority of primary and secondary data was published after the fall of the Soviet Union when Azerbaijan gained independence. All of the abovementioned texts have been examined in order to gain an understanding of the circumstances surrounding this topic. However, despite the fact that most of the literature begins from the independence of Azerbaijan, I have nonetheless performed research and presented the broader energy history of Azerbaijan, not only to demonstrate Azerbaijan's current role in global energy but also to show how Azerbaijan as a country has been historically attached to the energy history of the world. Baku, being the oil capital of the world since the 19th century, has brought many changes to the development of the global energy sector. Therefore, I provide a wide historical background to the experience of Azerbaijan and explain how this historical experience now places Azerbaijani in a beneficial situation in which the nation can move forward in terms of implementing further energy diplomacy. I include reference to the infrastructure that has been constructed in Turkey, Georgia, and Azerbaijan since their collaboration has led to the following events. 1) It has facilitated cooperation starting with the completion of the Baku-Tbilisi-Ceyhan (BTC) and the Baku-Tbilisi-Erzurum (BTE) energy pipelines. 2) Through current infrastructure, the European Union has secured access to the South Caucasus region and Caspian Basin through the territories of Azerbaijan, Georgia, and Turkey. 3) The optimism and growth generated from this partnership have been the necessary catalysts for the realization of future energy pipeline projects within the Southern Gas Corridor. Within the aforementioned conceptual framework of my research, I present the currently proposed and constructed energy pipelines, such as the TANAP and TAP projects. Throughout the research, I have chosen to focus on these pipelines because they have been recommended as being able to potential diversifies energy directed towards European markets by both EU and Azerbaijani representatives. I analyzed these projects and used statistics as a means of demonstrating the capacity and security of each the pipelines.

The current EU energy policy and its strategy of diversification are focused on reducing the reliance of European countries on Russian energy imports. As a result, the majority of gathered literature has been separated into two sections, 1) publications that support non-Russian imports and 2) alternative routes that do not reduce Russia's market share of European energy imports. These opposing views have provided the chance to objectively debate the topic and organize varying perspectives into a transparent dialogue. While examining the role of Azerbaijan, current research has shown that the country will serve as a strategic resource for EU countries seeking alternatives to Russian imports and a diversified network of energy suppliers. The roles of Azerbaijan and other involved countries have been divided into several chapters. While providing the literature review and the data presentation analysis, I go further in my analysis of the countries from regional and global energy approaches. This wider analysis of Turkey, Iran, Russia, the European Union, and Central Asian countries gives me, as a researcher, the ability to understand the main implications and impacts of diplomacy and geopolitics on the energy politics in the region. To go further in my research, I take into account the regional conflicts, such as the war between Russia and Georgia in 2008, the annexation of the Crimean Peninsula by Russia in 2014, the Turkish-Russian coalition following the events of the jet crisis in Syria, because these events demonstrate how thoroughly the energy pipelines are covered within politics. As such, energy diplomacy will be analyzed within these developments. I have investigated Azerbaijani and EU government actions relating to the realization of transportation projects and the securitization of European energy security within the Southern Gas Corridor. The positions and commitments of various players and stakeholders have been examined and explained in order to discover and answer the research question.

CHAPTER THREE - PRESENTATION AND ANALYSIS

SOUTHERN GAS CORRIDOR

If the energy routes in the Southern Gas Corridor are adequately diversified, this will result in the assurance of stable and affordable imports with secured energy infrastructure. Therefore, the European Union, within the framework of its energy diversification policy, has identified and has supported new energy routes since the fall of the Berlin wall. This policy is mostly aimed at reducing the reliance of EU countries on a single energy supplier (Calanter, 2016). In the last two decades, natural gas reserves have become the main target of the European consumers. Due to many of its positive characteristics, the European Union has been following the policy of reaching new rich natural gas producing countries. The Caspian basin, Levant basin, and Middle Eastern regions have been at the center of attention within the agenda of expanding European natural gas imports. Eastern and central European Union countries are heavily dependent on a single natural gas supplier in high percentages (Calanter, 2016). Therefore, new natural gas corridors would not only help the European Union, but it would also provide other European countries with the opportunity to diversify their energy imports. The Southern Gas Corridor (SGC) aims to fulfill this policy of the EU countries and deliver natural gas reserves from the countries of the Caspian basin (Sevim, 2013). Currently, the SGC consists of one existing natural gas pipeline and in addition to this two natural gas pipelines have been further proposed and are currently under construction. The Baku-Tbilisi-Erzurum (BTE), also known as the South Caucasus Pipeline (SCP), is the already existing gas infrastructure that the SGC will use as its starting point. The TANAP and TAP projects are currently being constructed and they will be in their active phase of completing the project in less than a few years. At the completion of the first phase of the SGC, it will have the capacity to transport approximately 16 bcm of natural gas. When considering the potential supplies from the energy-rich Central Asian countries, it is likely that the SGC could easily increase the volume of the transported natural gas up to 80 bcm per year by 2019 (Sevim, 2013).

The European Union has developed a strategy to ensure the security of its energy imports through the SGC corridor in accordance with its diversification policy. The energy corridor is considered to be the most valuable alternative energy corridor for the EU gas market and provides an alternative route that bypasses Russia and also reduces the European Union's dependence on Russia's supplies (Sierra, 2010). All Western countries have supported this approach of the European Commission. The European Union's vision for this energy corridor has been to create a major access point into the regions containing Caspian natural gas reserves. However, the European Union considers the SGC not only to be the secured access corridor to Caspian gas, but also a very important mechanism by which to build strong relations with all of the countries along the corridor and negotiate their partnership in the European Union's energy policy (Dusciac, Popescu, and Parlicov, 2016). To some extent, this would create a common energy strategy on a multilateral level. This strategy has already begun to be implemented within the alliance of Azerbaijan, Georgia, and Turkey. The already existing energy pipelines that run between these countries has significantly helped to establish the experienced teamwork needed for further energy cooperation in the future. Azerbaijan, in collaboration with Turkey and Georgia, is already playing an active role in the EU's energy security because of its involvement in the BTC and BTE pipelines, which demonstrate the commitment of the country to facilitating future development in the Southern Gas Corridor (Rusnak, 2011).

Azerbaijan has the desire to see advancement of the Southern Gas Corridor because this will lead to the opportunity to secure energy exports and also strengthen its role in the energy security of Europe. However, Sek argues that the "EU's plan was always to stop the monopolistic roles of the suppliers and that's why diversified infrastructure especially in the gas sector, made this policy an important contribution and attention for the European energy security" (Sek, pg.1, 2012). It is further contended that step-by-step Europe is becoming closer to a level of infrastructure diversification in which security and certainty are assumed. On a final note, he says that the countries of Eastern Europe are the most concerned by the situation and are desperately striving to secure the future energy supplies entering their territory.

Jarosiewicz states that the Southern Gas Corridor will soon be the fourth most important of Europe's diversified gas routes. It is via this gas corridor that the EU energy market can access alternative energy sources from Kazakhstan and Turkmenistan via Azerbaijan (Jarosiewicz, 2012). It is also suggested that Turkey's relationship with the European Union's is going to be defined as a new kind of partnership in the context of the transit route. This will involve Turkey playing the role of an "energy bridge" between Azerbaijan and the European continent via Central Asia and the Caspian Sea. The implementation of the Southern Gas Corridor over the huge geographical distances is drawing the attentions of the European Union as well as the United States. The United States supports the energy route diversification policy of the European Union it is also showing an interest in the region as a result of economic, political, and social issues.

The Southern Gas Corridor has challenged the interests of Russia and the state company Gazprom. This is because Russia is afraid to lose its dominant position in the gas markets of Europe. Furthermore, the project is seen as a threat to the political interests that Russia has in the Caspian basin, South Caucasus, and Central Asian regions (Jarosiewicz, 2012). However, as a result of the crowded interest from various companies seeking to take part in the project, some countries have proposed their own pipeline projects. Examples of these include ITGI, TAP, TANAP, and the Trans-Caspian. As such, the European Union has decided to back any project under the condition that it satisfies the demands of Europe's energy security. The Nabucco consortium has agreed to propose Nabucco-West, which offers a shorter version of its original (Jarosiewicz, 2012).

In response to the abovementioned turn of events, Richard Morningstar, the previous US state department special envoy for Eurasian energy states that the Nabucco project is the most efficient form of infrastructure (Political Transcript Wire, 2009). Alternative options will only be considered if Nabucco is seen as commercially unviable. These other options include small pipelines, such as ITGI (Italy – Greece – Italy), TAP (Trans-Adriatic Pipeline), and TANAP (Trans-Anatolian Pipeline), which can be subsequently developed when gas volumes increase (Badalova, 2010). The commissioner of the European Union, Guenther Oettinger, indicates that Azerbaijan is going to be playing a pivotal role as both a transit country and a gas supplier. Within the geostrategic context of these 'gas games', it is believed that Azerbaijan's position is accurate. (Kostis, 2012).

A significant level of interest is also being given to the position of individual countries and their involvement in the Southern Gas Corridor. Some European countries have been negotiating on the specifics of pipeline projects directly with Azerbaijan, while the European Union and the United States assess the route in its entirety. As such, all projects are evaluated based on what they can provide for Azerbaijan's future. TAP, ITGI, Nabucco, Nabucco West, as well as other proposed pipelines have lodged proposals to carry natural gas to the European continent from Azerbaijan (Sierra, 2010).

EXISTING ENERGY PROJECTS - BTC (BAKU-TBILISI-CEYHAN)

There are number of rich oil reserves located off Azerbaijan's on the Caspian Sea's bed referred to as the Azeri-Chirag-Guneshli fields. There are also significant reserves of natural gas located here (Jain, 2005). However, there have been challenges associated with the transportation of energy products from the Caspian Sea because it has no access to open waters (Bahgat, 2006). Since the fall of the Soviet Union, there has a strong desire to provide access to the Caspian energy sources without relying on Russia. As a result, the implementation of the BTC pipeline has been put into effect without Russia's approval and cooperation. This project has been one of the initial energy pipelines to stretch from the energy markets in the West towards the Caspian. The crude oil pipeline has significantly altered the dynamics of economic and political relations between the countries involved (Erdemir, 2009). The BTC pipeline has become recognized as a symbol that represents the Azerbaijan's independence and his significantly enhanced growth and development in the country's post-Soviet history. The construction of the BTC crude oil pipeline has involved the political interests of many players throughout the region. This pipeline is also an example that illustrates the fact that in today's fast-paced world, the politics of pipelines are having an effect on the global geopolitics and they are transforming the nature of international politics into a new paradigm (Ermedir, 2009). Furthermore, the BTC pipeline was built during a period of significant political changes and maneuvers from the

Moscow and the West. It is therefore viewed as a success story in the Caspian region. These events have demonstrated to other nations the political strategies and tactics that are necessary for successfully playing the global energy games (Shaffer, 2005). Since the beginning construction of the BTC, it has provided the region with many benefits. As a consequence, multiple states with varying forms of governments and political agendas have worked together with the collective goal of achieving the objectives of energy security in the EU market (Carroll, 2012).

The BTC pipeline connects Baku with Tbilisi Ceyhan. It totals 1768km in length, making it the second longest pipeline for crude oil in the former Soviet Union. Its main role is to deliver crude oil to the Mediterranean Sea from the Caspian basin. Sophistication in communication and a vision for the long-term future was required during implementation. The engineering and technical parts of the project have also proven to be very challenging (Jain). A great deal of talks and negotiations took place in the context of the BTC pipeline and significant changes to contemporary oil politics (Erdemir, 2009). Having previously been a somewhat neglected region of the Eurasian continent, the South Caucasus is becoming a place of significant strategic importance. Some experts argue that the BTC could serve as a counterbalance to Russia and China's dominant hold over supplying oil and setting its price (Bahgat, 2006; Ermedir, 2009). Therefore, Western nations like the United States have developed business partnerships with Turkey, Georgia, and Azerbaijan (Carroll, 2012). Regional stability has been consolidated by the collaboration and investment of a number of governments and business that have helped to make the pipeline a reality. Another point worth mentioning is the fact that Turkey's East-West energy corridor is receiving a significant boost, which has increased the county's geopolitical importance (Peachey, 2011).

The construction of the BTC pipeline has also put Georgia at a significant advantage (Shaffer, 2005). One such benefit that came about due to Georgia's partnership was that it significantly boosted the process of the country's independence from Russia. This project has been viewed as an important breakthrough for the future of Georgia's political, social, and economic stability this shift in the political landscape was even recognized by Russia itself. The Russia Chairman of the State Duma Committee on Foreign Affairs, Konstantin Kosachev, stated that there have been many political benefits to the area as a result of these changes (Richard, 2007).

The construction of the BTC pipeline has provided the involved nations with a multitude of economic advantages. One notable example is the substantial increase in energy security (Peachey, 2011). Turkey, for instance, is prepared to take advantage of any opportunities given to it because of its strategic location in order for it to become a feasible part of the energy corridor through the connection of energy-producing countries and energy-consuming countries. Turkey has made commitments to invest in the development of Ceyhan so as to transform it into a hub for energy catering for multiple oil and gas importers (Erdemir, 2010). Turkey's long-term vision of developing itself as an energy hub is in accordance with the energy security priorities of Europe and equates to the establishment of a new energy market outside of the direct control of Russia (Carroll, 2012).

In addition to increasing European energy security, the pipeline is has been implemented on the basis that it will improve economic growth and development within the region. In the everyday functioning of society and the economy, oil is seen as an essential product. The consequence of the creation of this pipeline is the assurance of an increase in the supply of energy and this will also be significantly more dependable in regards to reducing the effect of disruptions from one source. Furthermore, the revenues generated by various partner governments will increase. Such income mainly comes from tariffs, sales, taxes, and employment. This income can then be used to improve living standards within the region through development initiatives (Peachey, 2011). Many local communities have benefited from the construction of the BTC because it has served as a significant means of employment in management, repairs, and maintenance (British Petroleum, 2009). Recent estimates have predicted that energy consumption in Europe will rise by around 60% by 2030 and this increase in demand can be met through the accomplishment of the BTC, which will transport crude oil in volumes of approximately 50 million tons per year (Carroll, 2012).

Although the BTC pipeline cost over 3 billion USD to implement, it currently transports about a million barrels of crude oil daily, which has deemed it a significantly worthwhile investment (Carrol, 2012). The key rationale behind the project has been to grant the global energy market access to the vast energy reserves of the Caspian Sea. This goal has now been reached and European energy consumers now have an alternative to the current suppliers. The pipeline itself is relatively long and has overcome many geographical obstacles and in hospitable terrains. The promotion of stability, improved interregional communications, and the provision of employment to local workers have been positive byproducts within the process of construction and management. As such, the BTC project has achieved the goal of benefiting participating states' economies and societies (Erdemir, 2009).

The demand of the BTC pipeline is predicted to increase due to the fact that it is the most cost-effective and inexpensive means of transporting energy resources. All of the countries that benefit from the pipeline appreciate the positive effects of the pipeline, which has unfortunately not received the level of global acclaim that it deserves (Richard, 2009). It is important to emphasize that at the time of its proposal in 1994, the BTC project was widely thought to be unfeasible (Jain, 2005). Nonetheless, Turkey, Georgia, and Azerbaijan pooled their collective resources and in order to make this project a success (Shaffer, 2005). Critics of the project forecasted that rather than facilitating economic cooperation, the BTC project would conflict with the national interests of the Russian Federation and lead to chaos in the region. This, however, has not occurred and rather than hostility, the project has allowed for a level of greater collaboration between member states, healthy competition, and the establishment of a means by which to promote prosperity and peace between these nations (Ermedir, 2009). This project was initially adopted by an international consortium comprising of over ten stakeholders, namely: SOCAR (State Oil Company of Azerbaijan), TPAO, Itochu, Statoil, Eni, TotalFinalElf, ConocoPhilips, and the largest participant, BP (British Petroleum, 2009). The fact that such a significant amount of stakeholders have decided to become involved in the BTC project confirms its potential and optimism.

In terms of political advantages, the politics of pipelines is quickly changing the dynamics of the world. The BTC pipeline added a great deal of value to the countries involved, in terms of development, employment, and infrastructure, and is expected to provide the South Caucasus region with increased economic stability (Carroll, 2012). Another political advantage of this project is that it has brought together various governments to work together as a team in order to accomplish their social and economic goals (Peachey, 2011). As a result, there has been an increase in the levels of peaceful co-existence between the different member states and also the client countries who are receiving much needs supplies of energy products as a consequence of the projects success (British Petroleum, 2009).

BTE (BAKU-TBILISI-ERZURUM) NATURAL GAS PIPELINE

The Baku-Tbilisi-Erzurum (BTE), also known as the South Caucasus Pipeline (SCP), is used to transport natural gas to via Georgia to Turkey from Azerbaijan's Shah Deniz gas fields. For the majority of its distance, the pipeline travels parallel with the BTC crude oil pipeline but its final destination is Erzurum, Turkey. Here it links up with a pre-existing distribution network that transports gas to further locations (Souleimanov and Kraus, 2012). Most European countries predominately import natural gas and crude oil as their main energy sources. It is for this reason that the BTC and BTE were given top priority and implemented as a single construction project. A further reason as to why the two projects were laid in parallel was to reduce both the environmental and social impacts within the countries through which they travel, effectively containing the infrastructure within a controlled zone. Construction was undertaken by the South Caucasus Pipeline Company, which is a joint venture corporation made up of several companies and led by BP and Statoil, the largest shareholders. (Rustamov and Stergiopoulos, 2011). During the main construction works of these pipelines, over twenty thousand people were employed to build the pipelines within the corridor (Youngs, 2009).

This pipeline stretches for a distance of 691km. Its diameter is 42 inches and it has an annual capacity of 7 bcm of natural gas (Energy Information Administration, 2010). A large part of the project also includes the construction of an intermediate pigging station, two compressor stations in Azerbaijan and Georgia, and eleven little valves. The supply of natural gas to Turkey and Georgia is another major goal of the BTE project. Because the pipeline travels through Georgia, the country has the right to receive 5% of the total volume of gas that is carried though its territory (Efe, 2011). In addition, the country has been given the right to buy half a billion cubic meters of natural gas annually at a discounted rate.

It is also predicted that this pipeline will supply Eastern European Union countries with Caspian-region natural gas via TANAP and TAP through the pipelines linking Azerbaijan to the Turkish-EU border. After linking Greece to Italy, it is expected that further pipelines are going to be in a project that will be discussed in the near future (Papava and Tokmazishvili, 2010). The BTE project has also helped to provide several political and economic advantages (Marketos, 2009). The primary benefits have been the local and national levels of economic growth that participating countries have experienced. Particularly in Europe, natural gas is quickly becoming more popular than other fossil fuels. It is for this reason that there have been a significantly increased number of opportunities to become involved in natural gas pipelines. Due to the rising level of subsequent development, the citizens of the respective countries will inevitably appreciate some of the associated improvements of this (Richard, 2009).

A further advantage to come about because of the BTE project is the promotion of natural gas consumption as a more reliable, cost-effective, and secure energy source that is comparatively cleaner than oil or coal (Draghicescu, 2011). This encourages consumers to use gas as a replacement for other energy sources that are more costly, bulky, unreliable, and unclean (Draghicescu, 2011). It is believed that compared to other fossil fuels, such as coal and oil, natural gas is the cleanest (Paliwal, 2017).

Natural gas has also been used as a replacement for fuels that for driving turbines in power stations. This shift will consequently decrease the levels of greenhouse gas that are emitted into the Earth's atmosphere and serve to reduce the effects of climate change (Paliwal, 2017). The streamlining of the natural gas distribution will mean that many power generators are going to have the opportunity the convert to a cleaner and cheaper fuel source, which will potentially reduce our environmental impact, particularly due to the fact that air pollution will decline (Paliwal, 2017). There are also a number of political consequences of this project, such as the resulting political stability in member states as well as the fact that it promotes various communities composed of a multitude of ethnic groups to peacefully co-exist, which is one of the reasons why there has been such a high level of collaboration between states within the construction period (Efe, 2011). When different groups of people work together on a common goal their differences become less apparent and their agendas become aligned, which has the effect of reducing regional tensions while promoting long-term peace and stability.

The BTE project has become very popular due to the fact that it is the first pipeline to stretch from the Caspian basin to Turkey. It has also encouraged investors to capitalize their wealth in Azerbaijan's other natural gas fields. This implemented natural gas energy pipeline has incentivized the proposal and construction of additional pipelines aimed at supplying Europe with the vast Caspian gas reserves. Therefore, the BTE natural gas project has effectively raised the hopes of energy consumers in Europe and served as a stimulus for newly proposed natural gas projects (Papava, Tokmazishvili, 2010). The establishment and active status of the BTE and SCP pipelines have in a way laid down the foundations of the energy corridor for European countries, especially from the perspective of the effective transportation of the natural gas that the SCP brought for the proposal of the Southern Gas Corridor. The SCP natural gas pipeline paved the way for other projects to transport gas products from the Caspian region to Europe in larger volumes. Due to the fact that it is widely believed and accepted that natural gas is the most environmentally friendly fossil fuel and due to the European Union's strict policy regarding emissions, the fuel source is quickly gaining prominence and attracting investors (Draghicescu, 2011). Therefore, the BTE project has also demonstrated to the countries of the European Union that Azerbaijan can transport environmental friendly natural gas reserves from the Caspian Sea towards the European energy market. On the other hand, the SCP natural gas pipeline has given Azerbaijan the important experience of working with and cooperating with European energy consumers, especially in the field of exporting natural gas resources to the European gas markets. Therefore, with the implementation of the SCP pipeline, Azerbaijan has gained larger ambitions with more advanced pipelines to transport its gas reserves to the European market.

PROPOSED INFRASTRUCTURE

When looking at the successful implementation of the BTC crude oil and SCP natural gas pipelines, it becomes clear why the same energy corridor has received so many pipeline proposals to bring more natural gas reserves from the Caspian basin (Dagdemir, 2008). Azerbaijan has been the main player in the Caspian basin region to contribute to the European Union's energy diversification policy and since 2011 it has received many proposals to select from as means of transporting its natural gas reserves. Currently, Azerbaijan, with its Shah Deniz Stage II, plans to become one of the main contributors for the European Union's energy diversification strategy (Kim and Blank, 2012). Natural gas, which will be produced from the second stage of the Shah Deniz field in the Caspian Sea, will travel more than 3500 km in distance to reach the European gas market. This 3500 km long journey is called the Southern Gas Corridor and it is expected that with the enhancement of the existing energy infrastructure and construction of the new pipelines, this corridor will contribute to the security of European energy (Khatinoglu, 2016). The Southern Gas Corridor consists of several proposed energy pipelines and as such involves a lot of stakeholders and interests. Today, a major goal of the Southern Gas Corridor is to enhance the existing natural gas South Caucasus Pipeline (SCP), in order to complete the TANAP and TAP natural gas pipelines. All of these developments in total have the involvement of 7 countries and 11 international energy companies, each possessing the desire to reach the goal of the successful implementation of the Southern Gas Corridor (Azerbaijan Oil & Gas Report, 2015). Therefore, within the data presentation, it is important to analyze the current projects taking place within the Southern Gas Corridor and look at their current future status of implementation.

THE TRANS-CASPIAN PIPELINE PROJECT

The Trans-Caspian Pipeline is a proposal to construct a submarine pipeline to carry natural gas between Baku in Azerbaijan to Turkmenbashy in Turkmenistan (Arinc and Elik, 2010). From Baku, the pipeline would then link up with the BTE pipeline. Azerbaijan would serve as a transit country in this project (Swanström, 2012). This pipeline also has the potential to link up with Kazakhstan's Tengiz field. The Trans-Caspian Pipeline project has received a lot of attention and researchers, therefore, have access to an abundance of diversified information. This increased interest is because this pipeline would be the first to link the Central Asian region with the South Caucasus region, which is viewed as the gateway between Asia and Europe. Both Azerbaijan and Turkmenistan have the potential to play important roles in diversifying the energy security of the European Union (Pomfret, 2012). According to Arinc and Elik, "an assessment of Turkmenistan's natural gas and of the transit country of Azerbaijan indicates that the risks of disruption to supply and transportation could be minimized". They go on to argue that "Turkmenistan as a natural gas supplier and Azerbaijan as a transit country also clarify the role of Turkey as an energy hub country in the Eurasian energy environment" (Arinç and Elik, 2010). Turkmenistan, having one of the richest natural gas reserves, has the potential to take on a significant role in the strengthening of energy security in Europe and reduces Europe's reliance of Russia. As a part of the Southern Gas Corridor, the proposed project satisfies the agenda of the European Union (Arinç & Elik, 2010).

Turkmenistan is also paying close attention to the proposed pipeline because it has the potential to reduce the country's dependence on the Russian gas distributors to transport their energy supplies. It has also been argued that the Trans-Caspian project would strongly support the Southern Gas Corridor and further bind of the geopolitics and economies of the countries of the Black Sea and the Caspian Sea (Costel, 2011). The region surrounding the Black Sea is seen as having strategic significance to pipelines such as this and development of the pipeline infrastructure there would bring the South Caucasus much closer to the European Union. Furthermore, the construction of the Trans-Caspian pipeline will lead to rising levels of cooperation between Central Asia, the South Caucasus region and the European Union whilst integrating the surrounding regions as well as further enhancing relations towards the Western world (Guliyev & Akhrarkhodjaeva, 2009). Just like the abandoned Nabucco pipeline, the Trans-Caspian is predicted to decrease the reliance of the Europe on Russian gas. For most of history, the Central European region has been supplied with natural gas exclusively by Russia (World Bank Group, & Gerner, 2009). If the project is successfully finished, the pipeline has the potential to transport gas to Central Europe from Kazakhstan and Turkmenistan and it will reduce Europe's susceptibility to recurrent supply interruptions (Guliyev and Akhrarkhodjaeva, 2009). The project had been put on hold following an unsettled disagreement regarding the Caspian Sea's territorial borders, which was sparked by Iran and Russia (Raczka, 2000). However, the gas dispute between Ukraine and Russia recharged the optimism about the realization of the Trans-Caspian Gas Pipeline. Because this pipeline would not enter Russia, it could potentially lead to a permanent solution to the interruptions caused by disagreements between Ukraine and Russia (Arine and Elik, 2010).

Although the Trans-Caspian project has been debated and discussed thoroughly, several challenges still stand in the way of its implementation. The still unsettled legal status of the Caspian Sea has made it very difficult make a start on the project (Raczka, 2000). According to Raczka "the Caspian Sea's location and its oil-rich resources put it in the middle of a heated political debate for its status" (Raczka, 2000). It is because of the Caspian's unclear status that Iran has stopped negotiating and prevented all infrastructures proposed. The country is using the Caspian's status to block Europe from entering Central Asia through this sea. If realized, then the pipeline would subsequently decrease Iran's influence over the Central Asian states, which would thus have an effect on the relationship between Iran and the European Union (Moradi, 2006). As a result of the staunch positions of Russia and Iran, there has been very little development towards the implementation of this project (Oil and Energy Trends, 2007).

Iran and Russia are staunchly opposed to the project because it serves as a threat to their international influence and they have used tactics to prevent its completion. It is thought that Russia and Iran proposed a gas cartel along with gas producing countries from Central Asia in 1999 (Raczka, 2000). In the following year, Russia and Iran took matters to court and renewed the territorial disputes regarding Caspian borders (Raczka, 2000). This attempt to slow down the project had the desired effect and the project was subsequently put on hold for a few years. Then in 2006, an interest in the Trans-Caspian pipeline was re-sparked due to the gas dispute. However, the project was again obstructed in 2007 when Russia, Turkmenistan, and Kazakhstan agreed to rebuild and expand the Central Asia Center Gas Pipeline System's western branch (Oil and Energy Trends, 2007). The agreement takes energy products that were supposed to be carried by the Trans-Caspian pipeline and instead serves as a replacement and carries the Central Asian gas to Europe (Marketos, 2009). A further instance of a political maneuver was Moscow's claim that the Trans-Caspian project has too many technical and environmental risks that will cause too much disruption if a political resolution is not sought first (Swanström, 2012).

More recently, the escalation of Iran and Russia's opposition to the project has led the two governments to invoke the 1921 and 1940 treaties, arguing that any gas or oil project in the Caspian should need the consent of each of the five littoral countries, namely, Russia, Iran, Kazakhstan, Turkmenistan, and Azerbaijan (Costel, 2011). Russia and Iran maintain the stand that the proposed project is illegal. There is also the issue of growing concerns in Western countries that if they continue to cooperate with Georgia and Azerbaijan, then Armenia will be driven towards Russia and Iran (Cornell, 2011). This anxiety has compromised the support of the Trans-Caspian project. However, an advantage of the pipelines construction is that it offers the opportunity to stabilize volatile energy prices (World Bank Group and Gerner, 2009). This is because it is the shortest of the currently available options (Arinc and Elik, 2010).

Not only has the project been attacked by Iran and Russia due to environmental concerns, but it would also reduce the incomes of the two countries and keep energy prices low, which would further decrease their earnings (Marketos, 2009). Finally, in the end, the research shows the key reason for the resistance to the Trans-Caspian Pipeline's realization is actually caused by forces outside of the region, where the agendas of Iran, China, Russia, the United States, and the European Union come into conflict. It is said that because the Caspian Sea is located in Eurasia's heartland, whoever holds control of the area would have power over the whole region (Marketos, 2009). An alliance between China, Russia, and Iran against the European Union and the United States could lead to significant issues relating to the construction of any energy projects, not just the Trans-Caspian project.

TANAP – TRANS ANATOLIAN GAS PIPELINE

As mentioned earlier in the research, there have been many proposed energy pipelines and, in some respect, these pipelines have been competing against each other to transport the natural gas reserves from the Caspian basin. All of these proposed pipelines differ widely from each other in terms of their characteristics, which include varying levels of capacity, the routes through the countries that they pass, and also in their prices. This is the reason why when considering which of the pipelines to select the countries involved must calculate the entire outcome of the decision that would be taken when choosing the proposed pipeline. Starting from 2011, the Southern Gas Corridor has received pipeline proposals, such as the Nabucco, AGRI, ITGI, TANAP, and TAP projects. Despite all of the promotion of the quite famous Nabucco pipeline, due to weak commitments of the European energy companies, the project was delayed and in the end, it was cancelled (Shiriyev and Davies, 2013). European energy companies have tried to shorten and upgrade the proposal under the Nabucco gas pipeline project, however, this was not enough for Azerbaijan to select the Nabucco gas pipeline project.

Instead, the TANAP project decided on in June 2012 with the purpose of linking gas fields in Azerbaijan to energy markets in Europe (Umbach, 2012). Scholars predict that the cost of the project will total about 9.3 billion USD (Global Data, 2017). The pipeline will stretch 1841 km from Azerbaijan's Shah Deniz 2, through Turkey, and on to Europe (Umbach, 2012). It is estimated that the initial stages of the pipeline will be able to transport 16 bcm of natural gas and of this, the Turkish Republic will use 6 bcm and the remainder will be sent to Europe (Global Data, 2017). In subsequent stages, it is believed that this volume could double or even triple depending on future demand. By 2023, TANAP's total capacity could reach 23 bcm and by 2026, this number is expected to reach 31 bcm. The project was originally inspired by the Azerbaijani desire to have a direct pipeline to Europe (Umbach, 2012). The country's state oil company, SOCAR, is in possession of a 58% share of the pipeline, while the Turkish energy company BOTAS holds 30 percent and the BP energy company holds the remaining 12 percent. This share demonstrates Azerbaijan's objective to regulate the TANAP project and transport it energy products the Turkish-European borders with its own pipeline (Business Monitor International, 2013). Moreover, many countries have announced their interest in the construction and implementation of the TANAP pipeline project. This suggests that the project has already received international attention and as encouraged Eastern European nations to make investments into the pipeline. In 2017, SOCAR is planning to attract more than 4 billion US dollars to further the construction of the TANAP pipeline (Report, 2016). The president of the State Oil Company of Azerbaijan, Rovnaq Abdullayev, has made the following statement concerning their future role in the TANAP project.

"We continue talking with foreign banks for continuation of foreign funding of TANAP. We expect that we will be able to attract 4 bln USD for the project in this stage. We continue negotiations with International Reconstruction and Development Bank, the member of World Bank Group, Multilateral Investment Guarantee Agency, Asian Infrastructure Investment Bank, European Investment Bank and European Reconstruction and Development Bank for funding the project." (Report, URL, 2016).

This statement clearly demonstrates that despite the significant fall in the prices of oil and the consequential negative impacts on the Azerbaijani economy, SOCAR is willing to complete the project as soon as possible in order to bring back the economic benefits that TANAP provides.

Since Azerbaijan's independence, Turkey has entered the South Caucasus and developed a tactical relationship with the country and this has improved the opportunity for Turkey to create a bridge to access Central Asian Turkic countries (Vardaryildiz, 2012). Also, Azerbaijan and Turkey's relationship has helped both nations to integrate into the Western world, especially in the framework of energy cooperation. This collaboration has led to a successful social, political, and economic partnership between the two countries. Their continued cooperation throughout the last 20 years has become very significant in the South Caucasus region and has allowed them to develop further relations with the whole Eurasian continent. The political relationship between Azerbaijan and Turkey has helped to establish the energy corridor between the Caspian basin and Europe. With the construction of the BTE and BTC pipelines the two nations have demonstrated that collaboration in the field of energy has the potential to develop even further (Vardaryildiz, 2012). The proposed agreement to construct the TANAP project has shown that Azerbaijan and Turkey are prepared to work together to provide the European Union with an alternative to Russian energy supplies.

By taking on the duty of implementing TANAP, Azerbaijan has achieved what European countries could not, as demonstrated by the abovementioned Nabucco project (Socor, 2012). Socor also states that "the TANAP project shows that Azerbaijan will become a connecting link between Europe and Asia in several aspects: transit of oil, gas and rail with the Baku-Tbilisi-Kars railway. This gas project demonstrates that nothing is possible in the region without Azerbaijan" (Socor, 2012). In the eyes of the European Union, Azerbaijan, which has traditional been viewed as solely an oil producing nation, will now also been known as a natural gas exporter. Azerbaijan is fully committed to the supply of its energy gas reserves to the European Union and TANAP will serve as a significant instrument to achieving energy security in Europe when it becomes fully active in 2018. Turkey is also becoming very influential in the Caspian Sea region, particularly due to the signing of the TANAP agreement. Officials from Turkey have put a lot of attention into bringing Central Asian countries closer to this project as well. In this respect, Turkmenistan is one of the main goals in terms of accessing the Central Asian gas reserves and in buying their natural gas for the subsequent transportation via the TANAP natural gas pipeline (Vardaryildiz, 2012).

The projected size and capacity of the TANAP pipeline has been criticized by scholars who argue that the project will not even be able to satisfy Turkey's demand for natural gas (Kaya, 2012). This project is not expected to serve the needs of Turkey since its energy needs exceed the TANAP pipeline's 16-bcm capacity (Kaya, 2012). Turkey is still highly dependent on the Russian and Iranian natural gas imports and this situation will continue until projects like TANAP become fully operational and open new opportunities for its expansion and motivation for other projects, such as the Trans-Caspian natural gas pipeline. It is widely believed that Russian supplies to Turkey will fall as soon as the second phase of the project is put into motion. Once this occurs, Turkey and countries of the eastern European Union will be in a position in which they are much less dependent of Russian supplies and thus their energy security will have increased substantially. In the future, the capacity of TANAP is expected to rise to around 40 bcm, which would certainly put Turkey in a much more secure position. The TANAP has also provided Azerbaijan with a significant chance to improve economic strength, as is made clear in the following statement given by Kaya.

"The realization of the Trans-Anatolian Project by 2018 will strengthen Azerbaijan in strategic terms, offering it a direct route to the world markets in the place of one that would be controlled by Russia. From Moscow's point of view, the realization of TANAP is a strategic setback" (Kaya, URL, 2012).

It has been shown that the TANAP pipeline provides a huge opportunity and its objectives are likely to be officially realized in 2018. Currently, this pipeline is under construction and according to the officials, the pipeline is in a state of successful implementation. At the end of 2016, a TANAP consortium announced that construction work on the pipeline is running ahead of its planned schedule and half of the construction of the pipeline has already been completed. In a statement given by TANAP's General manager, Duzyol Saltuk, "more than half of the project, or 55 percent, of its construction was completed at the end of November and we are ahead of schedule" (Hurriyet Daily News, URL, 2016). Successful construction of the TANAP pipeline project and the important role it will play once it becomes operational will attract other natural gas producing countries. These countries will include Israel, Iraq, Iran, and Turkmenistan. Turkmenistan has already indicated its interest in diversifying its routes of energy exports but understands that this would be a difficult task to implement without the

Trans-Caspian or any other Central Asian and South Caucasus connecting pipelines. The same situation follows with Tehran in the Islamic Republic of Iran, which, after the lifting of the sanctions, is willing to cooperate with Azerbaijan and transport some of its natural gas reserves to the EU gas market via the TANAP gas pipeline project (Karimov, 2015). Despite the fact that Middle Eastern countries, such as Iraq, are struggling with internal war, they have also indicated some interest in joining the TANAP gas pipeline project (Rufiz, 2015). According to Iraq's minister of Oil, Adil Abdul-Mahdi, "SOCAR have cooperated with Iraq for many years, and we have a commercial agreement. If the SOCAR can work in Iraq, any other companies from other countries will be able to work too." (Trend bib: 140, 2015). Being one of the history's important energy players of the world, Iraq is seriously considering the TANAP project as well as the transportation of energy reserves, especially natural gas reserves, to the European energy market. Therefore, the Iraqi government, together with Turkey, is planning to develop a new gas project between Turkey and Iraq to ensure stable and secured access to the EU gas market via the TANAP gas pipeline project (Rufiz, 2015).

TAP – TRANS ADRIATIC PIPELINE

The Southern Gas Corridor (SGC) is geopolitically and geo-economically the most complicated of the proposed natural gas pipelines. The SCP and TANAP project would carry natural gas all the way to the Turkish border and on to the European Union, reaching the Greek border. Therefore, the third pipeline would be Trans-Adriatic Pipeline (TAP) that would begin carrying Caspian resources to the EU gas market for the very first time. The energy resources of Azerbaijan's Shah Deniz gas field would go on a 3500 km journey on the SGC to reach its destination (Khatinoglu, 2016). In general, the main aim of the TAP project is to transport Caspian gas reserves to the European gas market. This pipeline will connect with the TANAP pipeline at the EU-Turkey border and cross the Albia and Adriatic Seas to reach the shores of the Italian region of Apulia (Ozdemir, 2014). Once the TAP becomes fully operational, it will connect to the Italian natural gas network in order to diversify the internal EU natural gas needs. The length of the TAP pipeline project is 878 km and it has a total capacity of 10 bcm (Progressive Media Group, 2016). Since 2016, the TAP has been under construction and the pipeline project is expected to be complete by the end of 2019. The pipeline will then become fully operational and the first gas reserves will start passing through the TAP pipeline in 2020. SOCAR, Snam, BP, Fluxys, Axpo, and Enagas are the shareholders of the pipeline project (Progressive Media Group, 2016). The European Bank for Reconstruction and Development (EBRD), the European Investment Bank, as well as the involved states and other credit agencies and financial institutions are currently engaged in the construction of the pipeline. The European Investment Bank has already made the decision to invest €2 billion euros into the TAP natural gas pipeline project (BankWatch, 2016). Also, due to the strict environmental laws and regulations in the European Union, the TAP project is being built using new technological innovations as a way to minimize the negative environmental impacts (Paliwal, 2017). Also, one of the unique characteristics of the TAP pipeline project is that the pipeline is integrated with a specific design so that in the future the volume of the transported gas could potentially be increased. As it was mentioned before, with the current capacity of 10 bcm and accelerating construction works, the TAP pipeline has the potential to transport more than 20 bcm in additional natural gas reserves (Mena Report, 2015). Under the interconnection framework, the TAP pipeline could also provide an important option for connecting with existing and proposed projects, such as with the Interconnector Greece-Bulgaria (IBG) and the Ionian Adriatic Pipelines (IAP) (Greece Oil & Gas Report, 2016). The European Commission vice-president, Maros Sefcovic, discusses the TAP and other connected proposed natural gas pipelines and makes the following statement.

"It's a project which is built in a super-strategic area, very rich in hydrocarbons, very close to Turkmenistan, Iran, northern Iraq… I am sure that the guys who are developing Israeli, Egyptian or Cyprus gas fields are looking at the pipe as a potential delivery route" (Financial Times, URL, 2016). Therefore, the European Commission has selected TAP project as one of the "Projects of Common Interests", which would serve the goal of decreasing the reliance on Russian natural supplies.

In many ways, the TAP pipeline project together with the TANAP pipeline project are considered to be the evolution of the abandoned Nabucco pipeline project. In 2013, when the Nabucco proposal was cancelled due to weak political support, a number of projects, such as TAP and TANAP were proposed as alternatives to reaching the Caspian basin gas fields and to contribute to the diversification process of the European energy policy (Talus, 2017). Unlike Nabucco, which was highly politicized, the TANAP and TAP projects were competing with the Russian proposal of the South Stream gas pipeline project. However, TANAP and TAP overlapped in many ways with Nabucco's length and goals to reach the gas markets of the European Union (Stefanova, 2012). Specifically, the TAP project took on the role of the western portion of the abandoned Nabucco gas pipeline project. Therefore, in 2013, the Shah Deniz II consortium decided to choose the TAP project as the main gas pipeline project to carry the Caspian gas reserves. It is also important to mention that the TAP pipeline was 500 km shorter than the

Nabucco's western portion and therefore, it would cost significantly less money to construct the project (Mustafayev, 2016). All of these characteristics became the reason for the cancellation of the Nabucco project and subsequently the TANAP and TAP projects emerged together as the main streams of the Southern Gas Corridor. In a way, the cancellation of the Nabucco pipeline project resulted in a positive outcome for the Russian strategy to maintain its dominant role in the European gas market in the face of the TANAP and TAP projects. It is important to note that during the period between 2013 and 2014, the European Commission had paid detailed attention to the implementation of the Southern Gas Corridor and therefore this has generated many challenges to the Russian gas strategy (Mustafayev, 2016). In particular, the impact of the Crimean annexation has led to significant changes in the European Union's energy strategy against the Russian Federation. As a result, in 2015 the European Union declared the creation of the Energy Union and a new strategy was announced that had the primary goal of reducing dependency on the gas exports from Russia.

For the European Union, the TAP project provides another important tool, which is that this pipeline directly connects Greece to Italy. One of the main targets of the Energy Union of the European Union is to develop and increase the infrastructure network within the European Union's borders. Therefore, TAP would, in a way, significantly contribute to the southern energy network of the European energy infrastructure and fill in the "missing link" between Greece and Italy (Dreyer, 2013). This project would also involve Albania and connect this countries network to a single European gas network. Therefore, as well as its important role in carrying Azerbaijani gas from the Caspian basin, it will increase the capacity of the European energy infrastructure system. The TAP project will also increase the energy infrastructure of the Balkan states, in particular, the energy security of Albania (Dreyer, 2013).

According to the deputy minister of Energy and Resources of Albania, Ilir Bejtja, "this is the opportunity for gasification of the country. Albania will have three connection points for natural gas and this will give us the opportunity to play a key role for supplying Balkan states" (CC Law Office, URL, 2015). As it is very visible from the statements of the government officials, the TAP project, in general, will bear economic benefits not only to the involved states and their citizens but also to the surrounding regions of the pipeline route. As a result, the Balkan states, as well as the EU member countries, will have joint and connecting energy infrastructure (CC Law Office, URL, 2015).

The TAP pipeline is the final leg of the SGC project and its completion means a lot for the implementation of the alternative gas corridor for the EU gas market. However, this pipeline is also facing some challenging obstacles largely due to its important role in developing the diversified European energy strategy. First of all, due to delays in Italy, the construction works of the TAP projects have slowed down. The local opposition in Italy and protests against the TAP project has caused a significant threat to its implementation (Progressive Media Group, 2016). According to the claims of the protesters, the TAP pipeline could destroy the Italian environment, despite the fact that in 2015 the central Italian government has approved the implementation of the project. Also, SOCAR's failure over the DESFA (Greek National Gas Company) deal in late 2016 has raised significant concerns and fears over the implementation of the TAP project. This disappointing result concerning the DESFA deal could have a significant negative impact on the Azerbaijani and Greek relations, especially in terms of their energy cooperation framework, and this state of affairs puts the successful completion of the project of TAP at serious risk. However, despite all of the negative events that have occurred over the course of the TAP project, Azerbaijan has announced that the country will continue to support the implementation of the TAP project. The ex-minister of energy of the Republic of Azerbaijan, Natiq Aliyev, made the following statement. "The cancellation of the transaction on privatization of Greek operator DESFA by the State Oil Company of Azerbaijan (SOCAR) and the results of the referendum in Italy are unable to have negative impact on the construction of export gas pipeline TAP" (ABC, URL, 2016). However, he also added that these kinds of political and economic issues needs to be addressed together with all of the involved countries so that the SGC could be implemented successfully (ABC, 2016).

CHAPTER FOUR – GLOBAL AND REGIONAL APPROACH

INTRODUCTION

Hydrocarbon resources have become one the key elements that are essential to gaining political influence. The uncertainty of their continued supply can be viewed as an economic weakness for many countries. Therefore, this situation has caused many countries to either implement their interests and gains economic prosperity or become dependent and vulnerable due to the instability of their energy security (Bradshaw, 2010). This case is especially visible on the Eurasian continent, where energy resource rich countries and energy dependent countries meet and implement different kinds of strategies and policies in an attempt to secure their economic and political interests. This energy relationship between energy-producing and energy-consuming countries has created such a dynamic geopolitical situation that it has brought major changes in the policies of many countries. Energy resources have become the most strategic tool in determining the foreign policy of all of these countries. However, it is another matter to analyze which countries have been successful and which have been unsuccessful in the implementation of a successful energy security policy because challenges exist and they are always changing due to constant shifts in world politics (Bahgat, 2014). There are several key issues that have brought new challenges to global energy diplomacy. These include current energy relations between Russia and the European Union, Iran's re-entrance into energy markets after the lifting of sanctions, the rapid growth of Asian countries' demand for energy resources, and most importantly, China and Turkey's entrance into global energy politics. Therefore, when analyzing energy diplomacy, it is important to consider regional as well as global approaches to these abovementioned countries. Analyses of domestic and international interests regarding these countries within the energy diplomacy framework can provide an important understating of their foreign policy building strategy. The production of crude oil and natural gas also brings about geopolitical and geo-economic interests that affect not only the global energy market, but also create security concerns which cover social, economic, and political areas of every country on the planet (Dannreuther, 2015).

Currently, there are many changes that are taking place in the security of global energy. New obstacles and challenges to energy security have emerged. These include increasing demand for energy resources in newly emerging markets, military conflicts, as well as social and political instability in many regions of the world. Global politics has been affected by the increased share of the developing economies' consumption of resources from the global energy market. This has generally shifted the geographic focus of energy demand from the Western world to the Eastern world (Radu, 2015). The emergence of new countries with the capability of producing crude oil and natural gas since the fall of the Soviet Union as well as the implementation of new energy projects have created many geopolitical problems for the traditional energy-producing countries. Given the fact that emerging markets are constantly increasing the role of newly established energy-producing countries becomes more critical. Since 1991, South Caucasus and Central Asian countries in the Caspian basin region have very quickly entered into the global energy market with ambitious investment plans for their energy infrastructure. As a result, energy collaboration between the Western world, particularly with EU countries, as well as ex-Soviet countries has reached an active phase in terms of negotiations and the implementation of proposed crude oil and natural gas pipelines (Sharipov,

2016). However, since energy fields are quite likely to involve political confrontations, this energy collaboration has brought many challenges both to the European Union and Caspian basin countries. These challenges include Russia's increased and dominant role in the European energy market, the entrance of Iran into the global energy market with the lifting of sanctions, China's entrance into the Central Asian region and its subsequent implementation of the new energy pipelines, Turkey's increased role in becoming a new energy hub linking the East and the West, the still undefined legal status of the Caspian Sea, and finally the military and political conflicts in the region that surrounds the proposed western energy pipeline projects (Richardson, Ronny et al, 2016).

To understand the regional and global approaches towards the implementation of the pro-western energy projects, it is important to analyze the geopolitical approaches of Iran, Turkey, Russia, the European Union, and Caspian basin countries. Challenges that EU countries face within this energy security framework have to be understood from the perspective of the above-mentioned countries. Therefore, in order to understand the competition between these countries, it is very important to discuss Russia, Iran, Turkey, and Central Asian countries' geopolitical and geo-economic role in the energy security policy of the EU countries. EU countries' access to the Caspian basin, and the currently existing energy pipelines that reach the EU energy market, mainly from Azerbaijan, such as the BTE and BTC, create an important example of how challenges could be overcome to achieve the implementation of new natural gas projects. Through an understanding of the geopolitical interests, together with strong commitments, the realization of the diversified energy sources could become a reality. So far, European countries have been successful in the implementation of such a policy in the South Caucasus, largely due to the strong commitments of the Republic of

Azerbaijan. However, the volume of the energy sources that are transported to the EU energy market doesn't currently meet the criteria of the European energy policy. Therefore, accessing the Central Asian rich energy sources via the South Caucasus, mainly through Azerbaijan, is the current challenge that the European Union is facing. The TANAP and TAP projects that are presently being built under the Southern Gas Corridor create an important base for further implementation of access to Central Asian countries in terms of increasing the total volume of energy sources. It is also visible that Central Asian countries have shown significant interest in joining the policy that promotes the transportation of their own energy resources towards the European energy market. This also gives Central Asian countries a huge advantage because they can decrease their dependency on one route and diversify their energy export routes towards new markets. This is why this policy, which decreases the role of Russia and China in the Central Asian region, also generates a lot of political pressure from these countries (Christoffersen, 2016). Furthermore, Iran's return to the global energy market because of the lifting of sanctions increases the vulnerability of traditional oil and gas producing countries. However, in the near future, it will not affect Russia, due to the outdated energy infrastructure that Iran possesses (Davenport, 2016). Therefore, the Caspian basin corridor, together with the Republic of Turkey, is currently the primary route for EU countries to build their energy policy on and show great commitments to the implementation of such projects in order to diversify their energy imports.

IRAN ISLAMIC REPUBLIC

The events that occurred after 1979 resulted in serious consequences for the new Islamic regime known as the Islamic Republic of Iran. In particular, US-Iranian relations have suffered significantly since the Iran-United States hostage crisis involving 60 American diplomats in the US Embassy in Tehran, the capital of Iran. As a result, the event halted all relations between the two countries and concluded with the isolation of Iran in the international arena. This isolation started with the embargo, which covered not only political but also economic and social spheres of development. Overall, when we look at the history of the policy of isolation directed against Iran, we see a periodic and chronological worsening of the sanctions. Such events include actions in 1979 when the United States froze all Iranian financial assets, in 1995 when the United States prohibited all forms of trading with the Islamic Republic of Iran, and finally in 1996 when the United States expanded the range of its sanctions on Iran by blocking any company investing in Iran (Rafique, 2013). The European community also joined this isolation policy in regards to Iran in 2012, and this generally affected the geopolitical and geo-economic situation in the Eurasian region, especially in the Middle East (Bahgat, 2013). The US policy of isolation towards Iran lasted for more than 30 years, until 2016, when Iran was finally allowed back on the international stage again as a result of nuclear reconciliation. An agreement in January 2016 at a Vienna meeting has resulted in the Euro-Atlantic community's decision to lift the economic sanctions on Iran and Iran's decision to release roughly 100 billion US dollars of its frozen assets (Davenport, 2016). According to some researchers, Iran will take the opportunity in this nuclear deal to invite all the potential Western investor companies, and as a result, this process could potentially lead to the rapid growth of the economy. According to recent estimates given by Iranian officials, within the next 10 years, the country's current economic strength will experience a rapid increase in magnitude and its GDP will reach between 300 billion US Dollars and 1 trillion US Dollars (Javed, 2016). Once again, this will depend on how effective Tehran is in creating and facilitating a positive economic atmosphere for investors and countries interested in future investment opportunities.

During the sanction period, the most negatively affected area of the country was its economic sector and as a result, the energy sector of Iran has suffered significantly not only due to the oil and gas export embargo on Euro-Atlantic countries but also through a lack of technological investment in Iran's energy infrastructure. It is important to take into consideration that Iran has one of the largest crude oil and natural gas reserves in the world (Bhat, 2014). With such vast quantities of valuable energy reserves, Iran has lost many opportunities to develop its energy infrastructure and to grow its economy throughout the sanction period. When we look at the current energy outlook of Iran, the country has 21.7 billion tons of proven crude oil reserves, which accounts for 9.3% of the estimated global total, as well as 34 trillion cubic meters of proven natural gas reserves, accounting for 18.2% of the predicted global total (Iran Power Report, 2016). Integration of Iran into the world energy market with such proven energy reserves would, without a doubt, alter the dynamics of the energy security of many countries. Now that Iran is a sanction-free country, as well as being one of the leading members of the Organization of Petroleum Exporting Countries (OPEC) and the Gas Exporting Countries Forum (GECF), it will provide momentum to the country's integration into the wider international energy trading community. But for that integration to occur effectively, Iran would need to create adequate and modern export capacities as well as infrastructure for exporting its energy resources, especially its natural gas reserves. As a result of its constant increase in natural gas demand, Iran has been blocked from becoming a major key player in the international gas market. To give an example, Iran holds 18.2% of the world's total natural gas reserves but because of its weak infrastructure capacity, the country has failed to reach the wider global energy market (Iran Power Report, 2016). This discrepancy in the efficient distribution of global resources has the potential to be significantly improved by increasing the involvement of Iran in the global energy market.

Iran's rapid integration into the global energy market in a short time period and the country becoming one of the major key energy players is dependent upon just a few important factors. First of all, Iran would need to invite the global energy companies to develop the country's natural gas and crude oil production facilities with new technological advances which the country currently lacks. The gas industry of Iran will require a massive volume of investment and an effective development policy in order to meet the ever-increasing requirements and demands of the energy market (Rafique, 2013). It is very important to mention that when Iran was subject to international sanctions many natural gas fields were left undeveloped due to a lack of modern technologies and economic problems. After the nuclear agreement with P5+1 states, and with the lifting of the sanctions, Tehran has become very enthusiastic to implement all the necessary reforms required to attract major oil and gas companies. To summarize, Tehran's primary goal is to supply European and Asian energy markets with huge amounts of energy resources as soon as possible. For Iran to become an important player in the energy field, it must first take crucial steps in the very near future in order to secure its own prosperity. Those steps cover the development of energy infrastructure, the development of potential crude oil and natural gas fields, and the discovery of new energy markets. Creating new pipeline projects and selling natural gas resources to India, Pakistan, Japan, South Korea, and EU countries would promote an even more significant development of its energy fields and increase the quantity of its energy resources (Tantau and Khorshidi, 2016). In light of this information, Iran currently plans to construct 6 LNG (liquefied natural gas) terminals. These terminals have a capacity of 70 million tons in total and as such would serve Iran's desire to reach Japanese and South Korean energy markets. However, the county would also be transporting a portion of the LNG towards the EU market (Houshisadat, 2015).

The prospect of Iran reaching the EU energy market in large quantities has prompted the country to begin development on newer pipeline projects. However, the proposed construction of the 1800km long natural gas pipeline via Turkish territory to reach the EU market has created global concerns over Iran (Kunu and Hopoglu, 2016). Due to the expensive construction of the pipeline via Turkish territory and lower gas prices in the EU energy market, the decision-making process of the Iranian officials has been negatively affected. Iran currently exports around 10 bcm of natural gas to Turkey via the Tabriz-Ankara gas pipeline with a capacity of approximately 14 bcm per year. According to Cohen the "existing Iran-Turkey pipeline, with its 14 billion cubic meters per year capacity, would be the first line of supply of Iranian gas to Europe, capable of providing up to 7 billion cubic meters per year" (Kosolapova, 2016). The planned improvement of the pipeline is expected to double the capacity of the quantity of the natural gas flow. Since the lifting of the sanctions, Iranian officials have also started to take into consideration the TANAP and TAP projects, which are expected to reach the European gas market. Therefore, Iran can transport an extra 10 bcm of natural gas resources via the Tabriz-Ankara pipeline and then on to the EU countries via the TANAP and the TAP (Yesevi and Tiftikcigil, 2015).

AZERBAIJAN AND IRAN

One of the important actors in the South Caucasus region and Central Asia is the Islamic Republic of Iran. With the collapse of the Union of Soviet Socialist Republics (USSR), the Islamic Republic of Iran became a neighbor to the newly established South Caucasus states. Azerbaijan, being one of the states in the South Caucasus with newly regained independence, has received particularly special attention from Tehran. This attention provided an important opportunity for Tehran because the Republic of Azerbaijan in the South Caucasus is considered to be the only state that shares historical and religious cohesion with Iranian state. Also, the large Azerbaijani minority in the northern region of Iran does create an important cohesion and harmony between the two countries. Within the South Caucasus and Caspian regions, Baku has been an important spot for Iran's foreign policy building. However, this relationship has not been very successful over the last two decades despite the fact that the two countries share many things in common. Iran's failure in its attempts to have an influence over the newly established independent South Caucasus states has resulted in the entrance of Turkey, the US, Israel, and several EU countries into the region. Because of the fall of the USSR, Iran and the Euro-Atlantic community took the opportunity to have an influence over political and economic spheres in the South Caucasus region. Tehran's struggle to negotiate with the Euro-Atlantic community, as well as its ambitions to influence the South Caucasus region and to replace Moscow after the fall of the Soviet Union, has failed. This failure was primarily caused by the United States' staunch opposition to granting Iran entrance into the region. Since the South Caucasus and the Caspian basin are rich in oil and gas fields, this has attracted regional and global players to invest in the region. As a result of this, oil and gas reserves have played a key role in geopolitical and geo-economic struggles. In particular, the United States' opposition to Iran's engagement in Azerbaijan's oil and gas industry, under the international sanctions on Iranian energy companies, has blocked Tehran's expansion into the region. On the other hand, Russia's strategy to weaken the presence of Euro-Atlantic countries, such as the United States, Turkey, Israel, and EU member states, in South Caucasus region has pushed Moscow to significantly improve its relations with the Islamic Republic of Iran. According to Grinberg, Russia and Iran's improved relations unite mainly under the anti-American spirit that they both share (Grinberg, 2015). According to him, when analyzing the circumstances, it is very important to take into consideration that both countries consider the South Caucasus region as their own backyard (Grinberg, 2015).

In this context, regional and global power's presence in the region has made it very difficult for South Caucasus countries to maneuver and operate. Thus far, Azerbaijan is the only South Caucasus country that has been able to create a balanced policy with all the regional and global players (Abilov and Isayev, 2015). In particular, Azerbaijan's very sensitive relations with its neighbors have made the country the most politically and economically stable in the region. Since its independence, Azerbaijan has implemented a policy to gain significantly improved access to the European Union, in accordance with creating a balanced policy between Tehran and Moscow. This has helped Azerbaijan in the formation of a "multi-vector" policy and under this policy Azerbaijan has maintained relatively normal and healthy relations with Tehran, even during the sanction period. As the Iran deal with P5+1 over nuclear deal took place in 2016, Azerbaijan used its reputation during the sanction period to demonstrate to Iran that Azerbaijan is always welcoming of economic and political strategic development between the two countries (Shokri Kalehsar, 2016). On the 23rd of February 2016, the President of the Republic of Azerbaijan paid a one-day official visit to Iran, and for many observers and researchers this visit turned out to be a very strategic move for ensuring the continued cooperation between the two countries. Azerbaijan's well thought out policy during the sanction period on Iran, as well as its decision to not support the sanctions, has boosted the ties between the two countries. As a result of this action, during president Aliyev's visit to Tehran, many important documents were agreed upon and signed. This documents covered significant political, economic, and social fields of cooperation between both countries (Trend Capital, 2016).

ENERGY BASED RELATIONS

Azerbaijan is positioned in an extremely strategic location on the crossroads of the energy transportation routes. Because of its unique position, it has succeeded in becoming one of the major energy trading hubs on the Eurasian continent. Azerbaijan's ability to extract, refine, and transport through a diversified range of pipelines and to negotiate the trade of its national energy resources with the European energy market has guaranteed not only the economic growth and stability of the country but also its continued political independence (Agayeva, 2012). The development of oil and gas infrastructure in its territory has allowed Azerbaijan to maintain itself in a very advantageous position in the regional and global energy markets. Due to Azerbaijan's "multi-vector" policy, energy companies from European countries, the United States, Turkey, Israel, China, India, Russia, and many other countries have invested in the Azerbaijani energy industry (Khan, 2016). While keeping its strategic independence, Azerbaijan is consistently pursuing closer relations with partnering countries. In particular, the result of Iran's nuclear deals with P5+1 formatted countries would provide Azerbaijan with an important opportunity to create an energy alliance with Tehran. With the removal of these political barriers, Iran's ambitions will improve and the country will become even more capable of entering the European energy market via the Caspian basin countries, especially via Azerbaijan's existing and proposed energy infrastructure. It is very critical to mention that the nuclear agreement will also provide Tehran with an important new role in the European Union's energy security. Both Iran and the European Union's ambitions over the construction of new energy projects bring to the fore the important role of Azerbaijan and the first step in this role would be for Iran to join the currently constructed TANAP (Trans-Anatolian natural gas pipeline) project. As a consequence of the TANAP project, Iran would be able to export its natural gas reserves directly to the European energy market. Since global gas markets need a constant flow of energy sources, Iran needs to have short, direct, and stable gas pipelines and terminals. For such flow of gas to be made possible, Tehran, in allegiance with Western companies, needs to devote not only its financial capital but also its commitment to fulfilling long-term obligations (Kosolapova, 2016). Together with important political decisions, the process of exporting natural gas from Iran to the European energy market would play an important role in the development of cooperation between the two sides.

The European Union's main goal in energy security is the diversification of a variety of energy resources to its market from multiple sources. Baku and Tehran are both endowed with enormous natural gas reserves. As such, they are both potential candidates in the supply of huge amounts of energy resources to the European energy market. Since Azerbaijan possesses a strong history of experience in working together with the European energy consumers, this would also help Tehran in building similar such cooperation in reaching the European gas market. According to many analysts, Iran's involvement in the TANAP and TAP gas pipeline projects would result in an automatic invitation to the foreign companies to invest in the Iranian energy sector (Bajrektarevic and Posega, 2016). This is a great opportunity in the post-sanctions era for Iran to recover its economic growth and develop its energy infrastructure as soon as possible. It is very important to mention that over the past two decades Azerbaijani companies have also had the important opportunity to practice investing in foreign countries and Iran could potentially become a desirable destination for Azerbaijani companies to invest their capital. Azerbaijani companies' investment in the Iranian energy sector would provide greater knowledge and technology to the Iranian region of the Caspian basin. When president Aliyev paid an official visit to Tehran in February 2016, both countries signed 11 memorandums of understanding (MoU) in different fields of cooperation and one of the signed documents concerned the memorandum of understanding signed between the State Oil Company of Azerbaijan (SOCAR) and the National Iranian Oil Company. This document became an important declaration of both countries' determination to cooperate with one another in the energy field (Mehdi, 2016). As the president of the Islamic Republic of Iran, Hassan Rouhani, stated during a joint press conference with president Aliyev, it was clearly indicated that both countries have firmly committed to working together in the Caspian basin gas and oil fields and playing an important stabilizing role in reaching the European energy market with increased volumes (Mehdi, 2016).

Currently, Iran and Azerbaijan have established infrastructure for a gas swap agreement, whereby Tehran supplies the gas demands of the Nakhchivan Autonomous Republic, an exclave of the Republic of Azerbaijan, while Baku, on its part, supplies fuel to the northern provinces of Iran (BBC Monitoring Middle East, 2013). Furthermore, both countries have been extensively involved in working together on several oil and gas projects, and Azerbaijan's giant Shah Deniz gas field in the Caspian basin is an example of this cooperation. But the undefined legal status of the Caspian Sea, over the past two decades, has created disagreements between the two countries. For many observers, president Aliyev's visit to Iran and the agreement to work together will lead to an agreement on the legal status of the Caspian Sea in the near future. As Baku and Tehran boost their trade relations, more difficulties will be unraveled and as a result, energy relations between the two countries and Baku's assistance to Tehran in accessing the European gas market will promote the further development and general harmony of energy security in the entire region.

In this context, Iran would need to pay special attention to pipeline geopolitics. Since the lifting of the economic sanctions, Tehran has started to consider the prospect of joining other countries in strategic regional and global projects. As the TANAP gas pipeline project is currently being constructed, Tehran has already started to show interest in joining the project when it is fully operational. According to Iran's ambassador to Azerbaijan, Mohsen Pak, Tehran is ready to participate in all the regional and global projects that have favorable outcomes for the country. The TANAP and TAP developments are very strategic gas pipeline projects connecting the Caspian basin to the European energy market. As such, they serve to lure the interests of Iran in supplying natural gas via this energy corridor. Azerbaijani officials have already invited Iran to join the TANAP project. In his meeting with Iran's Oil Minister, Bijan Zangenehin, the Minister of the Economy for the Republic of Azerbaijan, Sahin Mustafayev, stated that "Iran can use Azerbaijan's infrastructure, especially the Baku-Tbilisi-Ceyhan (BTC) pipeline to export its oil" (IENE, 2016). Mustafayev not only invited Iran to use the oil and gas pipelines, but he also invited him to use the Azerbaijanı gas storage facilities and proposed to build further cooperation in oil and gas engineering. These actions will consequently lead to the promotion of joint production of natural gas and crude oil equipment and technologies (IENE, 2016). Additionally, Turkish officials have also announced that Turkey is very welcoming of any possibility that furthers the prospect of Iran joining the TANAP gas pipeline project. During his visit to Tehran on March 2016, the previous Turkish Prime Minister, Ahmet Davutoglu, met with the Iranian president, Hassan Rouhani, to discuss the supply of Iranian natural gas to the European gas market via the TANAP pipeline. With the lifting of the sanctions, it is becoming very obvious that all of the regional countries are heavily involved in building new energy alliances within the context of recent geopolitical shifts in the region. With enormous energy reserves, Iran is currently involved in a vital decision-making process period. When analyzing the current geopolitical and geo-economic status of the region, Iran's integration into the Euro-Atlantic community is extremely dependent upon its continued cooperation and negotiation with both Turkey and Azerbaijan. Due to Azerbaijan's extensive political and economic experience with the European market and Turkey's geographically strategic location, Iran is put in a position in which it has no other option but to cooperate. The historical experience that Turkey and Azerbaijan hold will be a very important factor for Iran to consider when the time comes to build new relations with the European countries.

According to an official representative from the Iranian National Gas Company (NIGC), Azizolla Ramezani, the work that his company has been engaging in during the post-sanctions period will help Iran to export more than 40 bcm of natural gas in the very near future. He stated that by 2021, the amount of exported natural gas would reach 68 – 80 bcm annually. According to A. Ramezani, as the capacity of exports increases, wider regions will become continually connected to Iranian natural gas reserves. He stated the following: "Notwithstanding Iran's large natural gas reservoirs, it is not a key player in gas exports yet... Iran can turn into a global energy trade zone, given its special geopolitical position and massive hydrocarbon reserves." (Financial Tribune, URL, 2016). Therefore, Iran's strategic plan in energy security is to involve all the regions of Eurasia, such as European, Turkish, Indian, and Chinese gas markets. In particular, Iran intends to increase the volume of exports to the Islamic Republic of Turkey. However, since the lifting of the sanctions, Ankara and Tehran haven't completely agreed on the price of Iranian natural gas supplies. Both countries would need to address the gas price issue and from there Turkey will increase its volume of imports from Iran. Aside from the agreement on the price of gas, the two countries are experiencing problems with the stability of supplies. A lack of modern energy infrastructure and outdated transportation pipelines have prompted Iran to refrain from increasing its gas exports due to continued increases in its domestic consumption. However, if we look at the Turkey's total natural gas imports during the period of the first half of 2016, the Iranian share covers 17% of these imports (Iran Power Report, 2016). This number demonstrates very clearly that no matter how poor Iranian energy infrastructure is, it plays an important role in providing Turkish energy demands, and therefore once the investments into Iranian infrastructure are completed, Iran's export share of Turkish imports would automatically increase. As a result, energy cooperation between the two countries would reach a strategic level, and this level will serve the interests of European countries. This is because the development of modern energy infrastructure between Iran and Turkey will mean larger and more stable transportation of natural gas to the EU energy market (Ayman, 2014).

The construction of the TANAP gas pipeline project is in its active phase, and both Baku and Ankara are working extremely hard to have the construction of the pipeline completed as soon as possible. The recent official announcements by both countries have demonstrated that Azerbaijan and Turkey have come to an agreement to speed up the construction time of the TANAP project, which was originally supposed to be completed by the end of 2018 (Erkan, 2016). The sooner the project is completed, the faster the supplies will reach the European gas market. Therefore, Iran will have direct access to the EU gas market and will have shorter and newer pipeline routes for its gas supplies. Azerbaijan has already begun to discover new advanced methods and procedures to prepare transportation of Iranian natural gas towards the European market via the TANAP pipeline (Interfax: Ukraine Business Daily, 2016). Azerbaijan has such an excellent system of energy infrastructure that there are many options that can be implemented not only for Iranian gas but also for Iraqi natural gas intended for transporting via Azerbaijan towards the European gas market. When considering the currently connected existing energy infrastructure between Iraq and Iran, Iraqi gas via Iran could reach Azerbaijani soil and from there it could be transported to the EU gas market via the TANAP (Interfax: Ukraine Business Daily, 2016).

IRAN'S ENERGY STRATEGY

According to some other statements, Iran could consider the option of expanding its exports of gas supplies towards the East rather than the European gas market due to lower prices and falling demand (IENE, 2016). However, Iran is not presently in a situation to fully expand its attention towards the eastern gas market. This is because the Euro-Atlantic community remains the group that holds the status of having the world's best energy infrastructure development and technology. Given their positive reputation, Iran will not squander the opportunity to invite Euro-Atlantic countries to invest in its energy sector. Since the European countries are striving to expand on the diversification of their incoming energy sources, it is obvious that these countries won't invest in Iran's energy sector without the confirmation that Iranian gas flow is guaranteed to reach the European gas market in a safe and timely manner. As a result of this, it is in the mutual interests of both sides to create long lasting political and economic cooperation with each other. For Iran, that cooperation could only be beneficial if it involves teamwork with its neighboring countries, such as with Azerbaijan and with Turkey. Therefore, while Azerbaijan and Turkey are building a new energy pipeline corridor to the European gas market, it is definitely in the interest of Iran to join the pipeline corridor in order to attract more European investment in its energy infrastructure as soon as possible. In addition to this, the political integration towards the Euro-Atlantic community is of great importance to Iran after such a long period of sanctions. According to the Deputy Oil Minister for International Affairs, Amir Hossein Zamaninia, Iran is willing to sell its natural gas reserves to the European gas market even if it is not economically viable due to the lower price of gas in these countries compared to the eastern gas market. He states, "this is because we want to use our economic relations to create some political cohesion," (Azernews, URL, 2015). This means that Iran is planning to use the energy cooperation with the Euro-Atlantic countries to form a sense of political unity in order to reduce the likelihood of future disagreements and tensions. Economic dependency on one another, if nothing else, ensures that political divergences and instability are maintained at low levels and furthermore, it forces the involved countries to sit down at the negotiating table to form compromises. As Zamaninia states in regards to Iran's new policy towards the Euro-Atlantic community, "We want to have relations not only with the southern Persian Gulf littoral countries but also with Western countries. When economic relations grow and political disagreements diminish it reduces the chances of having sanctions brought back." (Azernews, URL, 2015). From these words, it is very evident that Iran is not looking forward to enduring another period of sanctions in the near future and because of this, Iran is attempting to claim a greater share of the European gas market even with the initial unprofitable short-term economic prospects. Thus, the current energy infrastructure from Azerbaijan via Georgia and Turkey towards the European Union is the quickest and most direct option for Iran to access the European gas market, even with a relatively small volume.

The Turkish Republic offers the geographically shortest route for the Islamic Republic of Iran to export its natural gas reserves to the European market. Long before the sanctions, Tehran had always envisaged the building of a major pipeline project in order to access the lucrative European market. However, due to historical events and sanctions, the realization of such a project has been continually postponed. Today Iran, finally able to operate free from sanctions, wants to use this opportunity to access the global energy market. However, the present lack of pipelines and energy infrastructure in conjunction with the availability of the Turkish territory provides an important opportunity for Tehran to finally get back on track. It is obvious that the first phase of the TANAP project will not be game changing for Iran due to its relatively small capacity of gas supply. However, the TANAP gas pipeline project at its final phase of completion will reach a total capacity of 31 bcm in 2026 and this will provide a strategic opportunity for Iran to export its gas to a significantly wider market (Hurriyet Daily News, 2016). At the present time, Iran is obliged to work with Turkey towards the upgrade of the Tabriz-Ankara gas pipeline to join the TANAP project with higher volumes, a minimum of 10 bcm. This will not only provide a tactical opportunity for Tehran to reach the EU gas market, but it will also allow for the export of even more gas to the Turkish market. On a visit to Tehran in 2016, previous

Turkish Prime Minister, Ahmet Davutoglu, stated that "Iran is an important gas supplier and Turkey is an important market," (Gastechnews, 2016). During the period when Ankara's relations with Moscow deteriorated, Turkey began to consider importing Iranian natural gas supplies in larger volumes. The ongoing diplomatic relations between Turkey and Iran, evident from Turkish official visits to Tehran, and vice versa, clearly indicated that both Iran and Turkey are in favor of not only developing their energy cooperation but also in creating major regional and global energy projects. These projects are expected to play an important role in European energy security policy.

The main goal of the European Union is the diversification of energy supplies coming into its energy market. Therefore, the Republic of Azerbaijan and the Islamic Republic of Iran have the potential to become two of the most important energy suppliers of natural gas to the European energy market. With the current lifting of sanctions, Iran may involve itself through the TANAP and TAP gas pipeline projects when these pipelines become operational. Iran's involvements in these pipeline projects will automatically push and hasten foreign companies to invest in the energy sector of the country during the post-sanctions era. Azerbaijan alone, with its properly established energy companies, is seen as a very attractive opportunity for Iran to develop economic relations with. The country offers the potential for investment from a closer geographical location. The country also possesses greater knowledge and experience in working closely with the European countries. This close cooperation will not only serve the security of the flow of energy, but it will also create a sense of political unity amongst the participating countries. Azerbaijan, Turkey, and Iran have the opportunity to work together in an endeavor to change the entire geopolitical paradigm of the surrounding region, which would, in turn, serve to further the prosperity and development of the area. Iran's plan to restore the country's economy and develop its energy infrastructure will push the country to take part in the energy infrastructure development, which is currently being built by Azerbaijan and Turkey. When Iran officially becomes a partner in the TANAP gas pipeline project, Tehran will ensure secure transportation of its gas supplies with minimum investment costs and it will drive the country to play a strategic role in European energy security policy. Likewise, Iran's entrance into the European energy market would not only play an important role in the diversification of pipeline routes and supplies for the European countries, but it would also create sufficient competition of prices in the European gas market.

Overall, due to the lack of energy infrastructure and high domestic natural gas demand, Iranian gas exports to the European gas market in high volumes are not predicted to begin until 2018. The Southern Gas Corridor is the most attractive project for Tehran to join and employ as a transport method for its natural gas supplies to the European gas market.

REPUBLIC OF TURKEY

Throughout the last two decades, the Republic of Turkey has been experiencing impressive economic growth and development. As a result of this significant improvement, the country is currently ranked as the 16th largest economy in the world (Unay, 2016). Turkey's geographical location has played an important role in connecting the East to the West and the North to the South. Since the fall of the Ottoman Empire, Turkey has undergone political, social, and economic transformations. Turkey's strategic geographical location also formed a strong base for the economic development of various industries. Since the country has seen outstanding economic growth developments in recent years, the demand for energy sources has increased significantly. This development has motivated Turkey to create secure and reliable energy routes to its energy market. Turkey is now ranked as one of the largest energy consumers, and this consumption constantly continues to increase. Turkey currently depends on imported natural gas resources for 98% of its total consumption, which is supplied by Russia, Iran, Azerbaijan, etc. Turkey's accepted state program 2023, indicates the country's vision to become part of the top 10 economies in the world, and within the bounds of such a target, Turkey's demand for energy resources will increase even more in volume (Yasar, 2016). The Turkish Republic has been very much aware of these situations and as such the country has used its unique geographic location to play an important role in implementing its energy strategy. As a result, the government has created a stable and encouraging investment environment for all players who wish to invest in its energy strategy program. As a consequence of this, a country located at the crossroad between Asia and Europe has begun to structure its energy diplomacy. Turkey has been using its valuable location to implement such energy based geopolitical policies and due to this, the country is fast becoming one of the main energy routes for hydrocarbon resources from the Caspian basin and the Middle East to the European energy market. Turkey's energy diplomacy has reached these goals with the implementation of the BTC crude oil and BTE natural gas pipelines. These pipelines have helped Turkey to create close economic ties with Azerbaijan and Georgia, and most importantly to access the Caspian energy resources. The successful operation of the existing energy infrastructure has pushed the proposal for the new energy projects and Turkey's active participation in the Southern Gas Corridor (SGC) has allowed new projects to be implemented and realized quickly. The construction of the TANAP gas pipeline project and the development of SGC will not only promote Turkey to become a strategic transit country and an influential player in the European energy market, but it will also motivate other gas-rich countries, such as Iran, Iraq, Turkmenistan, and Kazakhstan to join the project in delivering their gas reserves to the European energy market (Winrow, 2013).

During the period when relations between Russia and Turkey worsened over the jet crisis, Russia suspended the Turkish Stream Project and imposed a number of economic sanctions. Turkey's energy imports from Russia are estimated to be around $400 per tcm of natural gas and due to worsening relations, Russia could implement further energy sanctions by increasing the price of energy resources, or even by cutting off 100% of energy supplies to Turkey, such as during the period when relations between Russia and Turkey worsened over the jet crisis (Yanik, 2015). Therefore, Turkey's strategy to diversify its imports and to build alternative energy supplies to its economy has empowered the strategic importance of the SGC project. As a result, the role of Azerbaijan in the diversification of energy resources has increased, and building much better energy security has become a vital policy for Turkey. Under the SGC project, Turkey would not only build diversified energy routes but also receive extra gas resources through TANAP, which would promote competition in the energy market and increase the pressure on other suppliers to both reduce the prices for gas and deter any chances of energy sanctions in future.

The Turkish republic is situated strategically between Asian, European, and Middle Eastern regions. As such, the country aspires to be an important energy transit corridor and energy hub with key access to energy pipelines. Furthermore, in order to secure its energy supplies, the country has diversified its gas and oil supplies and expanded its storage facilities. Turkey has signed agreements with the European Union to secure transit supplies and diversify European energy security. European dependency on Russian gas supplies, expensive gas prices, and the conflict between Russia and Ukraine has seriously threatened European energy security (Journal of European Studies, 2015). This has resulted in the implementation of a new strategy for European Union countries to develop innovative gas supply security policies. One of the major strategies of this policy is the European Commission's decision to fully support the Southern Gas Corridor project's implementation. The European Commission's 2020 Energy Strategy program stated clearly that energy cooperation and construction of the TANAP and TAP gas pipeline projects under the SGC project would be supported (Floridan, 2013). In this strategy of the European Union, the SGC project has been seen as a potential link in reaching Caspian basin and Middle Eastern countries, such as Iran and Iraq. Since the sanctions on Iran have been lifted, it is expected that Iran, through the SGC project, will contribute to the European Union's energy market. Azerbaijan and Turkey's role in the implementation of such a strategy is very crucial and both of these countries have encouraged the surrounding gas-rich countries to join the SGC project. It is obvious that the SGC project will not result in a drastic decline in Russian natural gas imports in the near future. However, it will help in securing further demand for the energy security in Europe.

Surrounding energy-producing countries from the Caspian basin and Middle Eastern regions are seeking to reach the European energy market. They understand that Turkey will play a strategic role in the future and most are willing to take Turkish energy interests into consideration. Turkey wants to replace Ukraine's position and plans to become one of the major European energy transit countries (Schubert, Pollak and Brutschin, 2014). Natural gas resources from Russia, Iran, Azerbaijan, Kazakhstan, Turkmenistan, and other countries would travel through Turkish territory to reach the stable European energy market. So far, Turkey is one of the best solutions to the European energy security concerns, and the country has started to play an active role in building a comfortable political climate for Iran and the Caspian basin countries to consider forging such an energy alliance. It is important to mention that Turkey also built the same political climate for Russia to reach the European energy market via its territory. The Turkish Stream natural gas pipeline project was an important project for Russia to construct an alternative transit route to the European market, bypassing the Ukraine (Karagol and Kizilkaya, 2015). But during the jet crisis between Ankara and Moscow, the implementation of the Turkish Stream pipeline was postponed and as a result, Russia's plan to build an alternative pipeline through Ukrainian territory has temporarily come to a standstill. Turkey, being well aware of its key positioning for gas pipeline projects, wants to guarantee its demand for natural gas reserves. Turkey has been lobbying its interests in energy security to the European Union and the country wants to involve as many energy-rich countries to participate in regional energy projects as possible. As a result, with the exception of the White Stream project, all the remaining planned energy projects will pass through the Turkish Republic. Since the nuclear deal between the Euro-Atlantic community and the Islamic Republic of Iran, Turkey has started promoting the supply of natural gas from Iran. This support is certainly related to the ambition of Turkey to become the main corridor for the flow of Iranian natural gas imports. In general, Turkey with its energy policy strategy will become the center stage in the energy battle between the East-West and North-South energy cooperation crossroads (Souleimanov and Kraus, 2012).

TURKEY AND AZERBAIJAN

During the Soviet Union period, Turkey had no opportunities to build strong economic relationships with the rest of the Turkic states. Despite the ethnic and linguistic similarities between Turkey and the Turkic states, the communist regimes operating in the Turkic states proved to be a huge obstacle in the advancement of economic relations with Turkey (Ruseckas, 2000). Since the fall of the Soviet Union, Turkey has entered the region and has started to build relations with Azerbaijan, Kazakhstan, Turkmenistan, Uzbekistan, and Kyrgyzstan. But out of all the Turkic states, Azerbaijan obtained a unique country status for the Turkish Republic due to its geographic location in accessing Central Asian Turkic states via the Caspian Sea. Also, due to ethnic and linguistic affiliations, Azerbaijan automatically became the main platform in building such relationships. When Azerbaijan gained its independence in 1991, Turkey became the first country to officially recognize their sovereignty (Ruseckas, 2000). The development of political and economic relations between the two countries has been conducted with the slogan of "one nation, two states" and until this period, relations have been on a constant increase. Under this motto, the two countries have created common energy projects and developed a strategy to create an alternative energy corridor between Asia and Europe.

In the last decade, both countries have experienced significant economic development. Currently, when looking at GNPs for 2016, Turkey ranked as the 16th and Azerbaijan ranked as the 65th largest economy in the world (Unay, 2016). The two countries have facilitated strong economic bases for trade relations and companies from both countries have invested significantly into each other's economies. The main areas of trade between Azerbaijan and Turkey range from the energy industry to retail, construction, and technological sectors. There are over 3000 Turkish companies operating in Azerbaijan and until today, together with energy investments, Turkish companies have exceeded over 6 billion USD in investment (Kirisci, 2013). The operational status of the existing BTC and the BTE energy pipelines has been instrumental in attracting greater investment from companies. Completion of the construction of the Baku-Tbilisi-Kars railway by the end of 2016 will promote a direct ground connection between the two countries and as a result, economic relations between the two countries will develop even further. According to the Turkish minister of Customs and Trade, Nurettin Canikli, the positive relations between the two countries have created a unique model for economic bilateral relations. As Canikli states "the exceptional development of bilateral relations in so many areas could serve as a role model for the entire international community." (Canikli, URL, 2015). From Canikli's statement, it is clearly seen that both Azerbaijan and Turkey have enjoyed the establishment of the Supreme Council on Strategic Partnership and this strategic cooperation will further assist in the development of strong relations. Currently, Turkey is the largest investor in Azerbaijan's non-oil sector, estimated to be around 4 billion USD per year, and by 2023 it is expected to triple (Canikli, 2015). During the visit of the Azerbaijani President, Ilham Aliyev, to Turkey on March in 2016 for the fifth meeting of the Turkey-Azerbaijan High-Level Strategic Cooperation Council, it was indicated that the strategic partnership would reach higher levels in the near future. Turkey has globally expressed its position in supporting Azerbaijan on a number of occasions (Azvision, 2016). Turkey's invitation of Azerbaijan to the 2016 G20 annual summit, and the participation of Azerbaijan in such an important event, is a great example of how both countries are supportive of each other on the international stage. Turkey has supported Azerbaijan's position in the Azerbaijani-Armenian Nagorno-

Karabakh conflict and requests the international community to resolve the conflict under the territorial integrity of the Republic of Azerbaijan. In support of Azerbaijan, Turkey has closed its borders with Armenia and announced that the borders will reopen under one condition: the complete withdrawal of all Armenian troops from the internationally recognized territory of Azerbaijan (Koolaee and Goodarzi, 2015).

In general, Turkish-Azerbaijani relations in the last two decades have gone through major developments. Political, economic, and social areas have received important attention from both countries and this has provided the opportunity for the development of energy cooperation. This cooperation generally attracted regional and global countries' attention to the region. Being an energy supplier and transit country for Central Asian states and Turkey, Azerbaijan is assisting in the realization of energy projects that promote the energy security of European countries. The South-Caucasus and Central-Asian countries are seeking a policy, which grants them access to the European energy market and for that reason they understand Turkey's importance in the realization of such a policy. Azerbaijan, together with Turkey, understands this policy very well and has announced to the world that both of the countries are ready to help all regional and non-regional countries in joining the Southern Gas Corridor project. For this reason, the implementation of such an energy project and the construction of the TAP and TANAP projects indicate the importance of the alliance between Azerbaijan and Turkey.

TURKEY AND CENTRAL ASIA

When the countries in Central Asia gained their independence from the Soviet Union in 1991, Turkey started to build strong diplomatic relations as soon as possible. This strategy was followed by the integration of the central

Asian states, namely Kazakhstan, Turkmenistan, Uzbekistan, and Kyrgyzstan towards the Turkish Republic via the South Caucasus, mainly through Azerbaijan (Feller, 1997). In the last two decades, because of ethnic and linguistic similarities, Turkey was able to invest in most of the political, economic, and social spheres of central Asian states without any major obstacles (Esen, 2016). It should not be forgotten that since the Central Asian republics' independence, Russian, Iranian, Chinese, and Euro-Atlantic communities' interests in the region have become very evident. Turkey's wide presence in the region has provoked the above-mentioned players to challenge Turkish integration in the region. For Central Asian republics, the presence of Turkey is also very vital because Turkey provides new economic opportunities, alternative trade routes, and energy markets to the region. However, for every Central Asian nation, as well as Turkey, the establishment of strong relationships with one another is viewed not just as business and new market opportunities, but also as an opportunity to build strategic alliances with countries who share common ethnic and cultural roots. Turkey's usage of its soft power in Central Asian states has been promoted through educational, cultural, business, and pop culture spheres. For this reason, common history, language, religious beliefs, and traditions have helped to not only deepen the partnerships on a bilateral level but also at a wider regional level with the involvement of the entire central Asian region. The establishment of multilateral institutions and organizations, such as the International Organization of Turkic Culture, founded in 1993, the Parliamentary Assembly of Turkic-Speaking Countries, founded in 2008, and the Turkic Council, founded in 2009, has promoted cooperation in social and political fields in strengthening historical ties. Currently, there are many academies, TV channels, and radio stations that operate with the intention of stimulating the creation of a common Turkic language (Kaplan, Yuvaci and Amanov, 2015).

Regional and global projects in all spheres would serve to facilitate the development of economic cooperation and integration. Boosting the relationship between Turkey and Central Asian states highly depends on the implementation of a diverse range of regional projects. The Silk Road project, which aims to boost trade and transportation routes by restoring the ancient Silk Road, which linked Europe with Asia, will eventually promote positive economic development on the entire continent. Turkey's presence in the region and its various projects will be affected by the involvement of China, Iran, Russia, as well as other significant players (Marketos, 2009). Therefore, both for the Turkish Republic and for Central Asian countries, cooperation in the energy sector and improvements in transportation routes, together with the political coalition, have become some of the most important policies to focus on. There is huge potential for Turkey and for Central Asian countries in developing their energy sectors together with the involvement of Azerbaijan and European countries. Due to Azerbaijan's geographic location and the constantly growing status of the country in economic and political spheres, Turkey together with Azerbaijan, have all the necessary requirements for becoming major partners with the central Asian states. But out of all the strategic partnership initiatives, potential cooperation in energy spheres and proven rich hydrocarbon resources in Central Asian states are the main factors for the implementation of this huge economic project. Turkmenistan has a proven 18,000-bcm natural gas reserves, which means that it is ranked 4th place globally. The country has been very ambitious in expanding and diversifying its energy routes over the last 10 years (Kolb, 2012). At present, the country only exports uncertain volumes of its energy resources to China, Iran, Russia, and Afghanistan. However, the country currently lacks any alternative routes toward European countries and therefore the country is highly dependent on the already existing infrastructure. This situation hinders the implementation of a strategy regarding the diversification of the energy routes. The same problem occurs with Kazakhstan, which mostly exports its hydrocarbon resources to the Russian Federation and the People's Republic of China (Khalid, Hashmi, and Ahmed, 2016). Kazakhstan is very eager to build and diversify its energy routes in reaching new energy markets, especially the European energy market. This is where Turkey's increasing demand for natural gas reserves come to the forefront in implementing such a policy in Central Asian states. If we consider the high volume of natural gas exports from Kazakhstan and Turkmenistan to Turkey, these countries would not only reach the energy demanding and developing Turkish gas market, but they would also be provided with an opportunity to access the stable European energy market. Furthermore, the European Union is highly interested in receiving high volumes of natural gas into its energy market from Turkmenistan and Kazakhstan. Currently, the countries involved are continuing negotiations to deliver the central Asian gas reserves to Europe. Besides the implementation of the Southern Gas Corridor (TANAP and TAP gas pipeline projects), the construction of the Trans-Caspian natural gas pipeline project is also one of the major proposed pipelines in accessing Turkmen gas for exporting to Europe via Azerbaijan, Georgia, and Turkey, effectively bypassing the Russian Federation and the Islamic Republic of Iran. Azerbaijan has welcomed the initiatives of the European Union and Turkey in supporting the construction of the Trans-Caspian pipeline. Turkey also announced that the country is ready to import natural gas not only as a consumer but also as a supplier to countries within the transit corridor for transportation of their energy resources. When Turkmenistan's president, Gurbanguly

Berdimuhamedow, paid an official visit to Turkey in 2015, he stated that Turkmenistan is ready to create a mechanism with Azerbaijan and Turkey for the development of the Trans-Caspian pipeline project (Yeni Safak, 2015). Due to some disagreements between Azerbaijan and Turkmenistan over the ownership of certain energy fields in the Caspian Sea, the implementation of the Trans-Caspian gas pipeline project has been postponed until further notice. Turkey has also been attempting to mediate between Azerbaijan and Turkmenistan over the disputed oil and gas fields in the Caspian Sea. Westward transportation of natural gas reserves requires agreement and settlement of the issues and claims between Azerbaijan and Turkmenistan. Therefore, the European Commission and Turkey's contribution to resolving the disagreements have been playing an important role. If the negotiations conclude with an agreement, the Trans-Caspian pipeline will be used to supply natural gas from Turkmenistan to Azerbaijan and to Europe via Turkey.

THE RUSSIAN FEDERATION AND TURKEY

When conflict erupted between Turkey and Russia with the downing of a Russian SU-24 plane by a Turkish F-16 fighter jet in November of 2015, Ankara and Moscow froze their relations and each side started a blame campaign against the other (Tanrisever, 2016). Prior to this conflict, both countries' positions were united in many global events, and therefore Ankara had refused to join the Western sanctions against Russia when the Crimean conflict broke out. However, after the shooting down of a Russian SU-24 plane, their relations changed for the worst. The freezing of all economic and political relations resulted in Russian sanctions against Turkey and all of the planned energy, economic, social, and other projects had been postponed. Also, the proposed construction of the Turkish Stream natural gas pipeline had been postponed. In addition, the tension between the two countries negatively affected the surrounding regions including the Central Asian and South Caucasus regions. It was highly unlikely that countries in the region would choose a side in supporting either state. Moreover, all the surrounding countries did share a common interest – the improvement of the relations between both Moscow and Ankara. For example, the president of Kazakhstan, Nursultan Nazarbayev, announced his concern over the Russian-Turkish confrontation and said, "From the first days of our sovereignty, we have been making every effort to bring closer our brotherly people. Turkey means much for Kazakhstan and we will never give up the policy of cooperation. For us, the crisis in the relationship between Turkey and Russia has become a big problem. Both Countries are our important partners and allies" (Fedorenko, 2016). Also, the president of the Republic of Azerbaijan has stated, "Azerbaijan has had close ties with both Turkey and Russia, and that it regrets and is concerned about tension between the two countries" (CommonSpace, URL, 2015). He added that Azerbaijan is willing to do everything within its power to reduce the tension between Moscow and Ankara.

Before the jet crisis between Turkey and Russia, various economic projects were planned to implement, and the Turkish Stream gas pipeline project was one of them. The Turkish Stream gas pipeline was a proposed project that would run across the Black Sea connecting Russia to Turkey and then on to Greek territory. The Turkish Stream project, with its offshore and onshore pipeline parts, planned to have a capacity of 63 billion cubic meters of natural gas annually (Karagol and Kizilkaya, 2015). This project would not only supply the European Union countries, but it also intends to deliver gas to the Turkish market as well. However, after the jet crisis, Russia announced that the Turkish Stream gas pipeline project had been suspended and in the future, if the relationship between Moscow and Ankara recovers, there will be a possibility for the project to resume. As a fast-developing country, Turkey is highly interested in diversifying its routes for energy demands. Because of this, Russia plays a very important role in Turkey meeting that demand. Turkey is likewise important to Russia in accessing and building new transit routes that reach the energy market of the European Union. In general, both countries need each other to develop important energy cooperation in accordance with meeting each other's demands.

Turkey wants to create a safe energy corridor between energy-producing countries and energy-consuming countries. The country is located near the wealthiest energy-rich countries of the world – Russia, the Caspian basin, and the Middle East – and has created its energy policy to play a dual role in this strategy, as a consumer and as a transit country. In this context, Turkey is interested in making agreements with all the energy-producing countries in developing that energy strategy. The main goal of the Turkish republic is to eliminate all possible threats to supply security and to reduce the energy supply deficiency. Russia is, without a doubt, one of the main countries that threaten Turkey's energy policy implementation objectives. Being 70% dependent on external energy resources, Turkey has been receiving most of its natural gas imports (60%) from the Russian federation and this figure clearly shows how Turkey is desperate to not only continue to receive Russian imports but also to diversify and build alternatives to Russian imports (Tunc, 2012). Considering the previous tension between the two countries, the impact on energy supply security has not created any problems for Turkey but it is expected that in the long run if the jet crisis continues, it would have a contrary effect on the Russian economy. When considering the situation in the Russian economy, for its energy exports, Turkey paid around 12.8 billion USD in 2014 (Kunu, 2016). Turkish dependence on Russian energy supplies has resulted in Turkey becoming the second largest natural gas market for the Russian Federation.

Turkey has now become the largest gas buyer on the European continent. Due to rapid economic development, Turkey's demand for natural gas supplies has recently increased to more than 48.7 billion cubic meters (Arinc and Ozgul, 2015). Due to increased industrial and urban gas consumption, Turkey is considering all possible routes in diversifying resources from Azerbaijan, Central Asia, and the Middle East. In the long run, if the beginning of 2016 did not normalize Russia's relations with Turkey, Russia could have decreased its share in the Turkish gas market. The completion of the TANAP gas pipeline project in 2018 and the agreement between Turkey and Iran in April of 2016 to renovate the existing energy pipeline to increase the gas flow to Turkey would encourage Russia to increase its supplies and decrease the price of gas exports (Alipour, 2015). Also, due to the normalization of Turkish-Israeli relations and the discovery of huge oil and gas fields in the Mediterranean Sea, Israel will export gas to Turkey and this will further weaken the Russian position in the Turkish gas market. According to some analysts, if Turkey and Israel make an agreement on the construction of a pipeline, Israel could initially export around 5 bcm by the end of 2019 (Sales, 2016). Also, it is very important to mention that Turkish and Iraqi sides have also agreed to negotiate on cooperation in the energy sector. The Iraqi representative has announced that around 10 bcm will be exported to Turkey annually if the agreement is established between the two countries (Efe, 2011). Taking into consideration the various options for Turkey, the country will be better off diversifying its portfolio instead of being dependent on the high cost of Russian gas in the long run. This policy of Turkey will definitely prompt Russia to reevaluate its dominant position in the Turkish gas market. The jet crisis period between Moscow and Ankara has not had such a negative effect on the energy field since the energy sector constitutes one of the main parts of the economic relationship between the two countries. Both countries had no other realistic option but to cooperate and rebuild their relations. As a result, in the beginning of 2016, both countries took the path to normalize the relations and bring back the previous relations, including the implementation of the energy pipeline project – South Stream natural gas pipeline.

In the next three to four years, when new energy projects (TANAP, TAP, and others) become operational, the risks in terms of energy supply security for Turkey will be eliminated. All of the new energy-rich countries and new alternative energy projects would guarantee that Turkey ensures the security of its supplies and diversifies its energy routes, while also serving as a transit country for the energy market supplies of the European Union. Under these circumstances, Russia could have potentially lost billions of dollars if the jet crisis had continued. The jet crisis could have resulted in Russia losing 50% of its share in Turkey's gas market (Tunc, 2012). It is clearly evident that Russia's stance during the jet crisis period could not only have hurt its energy exports to the Turkish energy market in the long run, but its stance could have also canceled the implementation of the Turkish Stream gas pipeline, which was supposed to transport upwards of 60 bcm of natural gas via Turkey to the European energy market (Karagol and Kizilkaya, 2015). As a result of the above-mentioned claims, recent events indicated clearly that leaders of the two countries understand the importance of the strong relationship between their two nations. In June 2016, the Turkish president, Recep Tayyip Erdogan, wrote a letter to the Russian president, Vladimir Putin, apologizing for the incident involving the downing of the Russian Su-24 Jet, and his deep sympathy and condolences for the deaths of the pilots. In his letter, President Erdogan stated, "We never had a desire or a deliberate intention to down an aircraft belonging to Russia" (Asharq Alawsat, 2016). He went on to describe Russia as "a friend and a strategic partner" of the Turkish Republic and requested to rebuild political and economic relations between the two countries. On its side, Russia has accepted the Turkish apology and welcomed the normalization of relations between the two nations. For many analysts, this positive Turkish move will not only lead to the restoration of relations but will also contribute to peace in the Middle East. As many analysists believe, the normalization process between Turkey and Russia will restart talks and negotiations on the EU gas pipeline. The Turkish Stream gas pipeline, which starts in Russia, runs under the Black Sea via Turkey to Greece and from there towards the EU energy market, is of vital importance to both sides. For Russia, The Turkish Stream pipeline is the alternative proposal to the South Stream pipeline, which was to run from Russia to Bulgaria (Karagol and Kizilkaya, 2015). Due to EU competition law and the Crimean conflict between the EU and Russia, Moscow has been pushed to propose the Turkish Stream gas pipeline (Bebler, 2017). It is expected that the normalization process will continue until when a number of Russian-imposed sanctions against Turkey will be completely lifted. Once Gazprom receives confirmation from Moscow, the talks and negotiations on the implementation of the Turkish Stream will recommence.

THE EUROPEAN UNION AND TURKEY

The Turkish Republic is considered to be an important energy hub country. Currently, a large volume of crude oil and natural gas resources are being transported via the BTC and BTE pipelines. This includes gas transported via the Turkish straits by tankers to the European energy market. Since the secured and continuous flow of energy is the main aspect of energy security, Turkey, with its stability and commitments, is seen as one of the primary countries involved in European Energy security policy. EU member states are seeking a policy, which offers diversification of their energy imports, and Turkey, with its strategic geographical location, is one of the most viable alternatives in the EU's diversification policy. Turkey already has existing regional pipeline infrastructure and has demonstrated that it will contribute even more to the proposed energy projects. Therefore, geopolitical and economic concerns that are related to the implementation of the energy projects have to be addressed to Turkey as an energy hub country. The status of Turkey is considered to be a "central country" as the previous Prime Minister, Ahmet Davutoglu, stated (Anadolu Agency, 2012). He argued that Turkey is in the center of the crossroads between Asia and Europe and major energy producing and energy-consuming countries would need to come to terms with Turkey on energy security issues. From the Caspian basin and the Middle East to the Balkans and other European countries, Turkey is considered by many to be the primary energy-trading center in long-term policy building projects.

The European Union has been developing a strategic energy security policy, particularly due to the fear of being dependent on Russian natural gas imports. As such, European countries have strengthened their ties between the southeastern regions of the continent. Strategically located between the largest energy producing and consuming states, Turkey has received significant attention from the European, South Caucasus, Central Asian, and Middle Eastern countries due to its energy pipeline project. Under the current circumstances, Turkey holds an important position in the diversification of the European Union's energy imports. Adding to this the Russia-Ukraine tension over the Crimean conflict, Turkey is going to become the country to replace Ukrainian territory as the European energy transit country in the transportation of Russian gas resources. However, worsening relations between Russia and Turkey over the shooting of a Russian military jet have postponed the implementation of the proposed Turkish Stream gas pipeline project. Despite the tension between the two countries, they have nonetheless announced that they have frozen energy relations. While Turkey remains open to all the energy-producing countries, it has implemented special energy policies seeking to target the European energy market with the Caspian basin and the Middle Eastern energy resources (Yesevi and Tiftikcigil, 2015). Turkey is well positioned to supply energy resources from Iran, Azerbaijan, Turkmenistan, and other energy-producing countries to the European energy market. The European Union also takes heed of Turkey's capacity to become an energy hub because of its energy diversification routes. For this reason, Turkey and the European Union have created a strategic energy partnership program for energy cooperation. In this regard, the interests of both sides overlap with each other in finding ways to secure natural gas supplies. This determination became clear after the events of 2006 when the Russia-Ukraine tension erupted over the Russian natural gas prices (Ugur, 2016). Since the cut-off of supplies to the Ukraine for three days, this has pushed the European Union to seek alternative ways of avoiding dependence on one producer. One of the main active scenarios in building such a strategy became visible with the support of the Southern Gas Corridor (SGC). Turkey holds an important position in the SGC project and the European Union understands that a strategic partnership with Turkey would be very beneficial. In 2012, Turkey and the European Union created an agenda in building a strategic alliance for energy security policy. In this regard, Turkey and the European Union's positive agenda acts as an important road map for energy cooperation and includes: strong evaluations on the development of common energy infrastructure and the promotion of energy efficiency and technologies (Aktar, 2012). Under this Agenda and proposed energy pipeline projects,

Turkey would become a major part of a southern energy route. The European Commission's 2020 Energy Strategy is a great example of the significant role that Turkey would be playing in strengthening European energy security (Floridan, 2013). The SGC project in the 2020 Energy Strategy has been pointed out as not only a way of accessing the Caspian basin energy reserves, but also as a potential connection to Middle Eastern energy-producing countries. Especially with the lifting of the sanctions, Iran would be in a position in which it can join the SCG project and bring its huge natural gas reserves to the global stage. Turkish-Iranian cooperation would eventually promote the security of the energy policy of the European countries. The availability of South Caucasus, Central Asian, and Middle Eastern countries' energy resources, as well as an increasing demand from the European countries, would lead many proposed projects to run through Turkey en route to Europe.

It is also very important to mention that Turkey and Israel have recently restarted their diplomatic relations after a 6-year break due to the Gaza flotilla raid in 2010 (Kirshner, 2011). In 2016 diplomatic relations between the two countries started to warm again and the main reason behind this attitude change was economic, humanitarian, and political interests. The Israeli Prime minister, Benjamin Netanyahu, has accepted the Turkish claims and therefore he has not only apologized to Turkey but has also paid 20 million USD in compensation to the families of the dead aid workers during the incident of the Gaza flotilla raid in 2010 (TCA Regional News, 2016). These two important countries of the Middle East will not be able to continue ignoring each other when many disagreements and conflicts of interest need to be discussed and resolved. From an economic point of view, in 2010 Israel discovered a large natural gas field in the Levant basin. For Israel, it was not only important to develop this gas field solely because of its own energy demands, but also as a means to transport the produced gas resources to the European market. This is because for Turkey it is all about becoming the energy hub for Europe, and Israeli gas would increase its importance further and give greater influence in relation to EU energy policy. The Turkish Republic, with its foreign policy, understands that Israeli gas reserves and new energy pipelines would help the country to have geostrategic influence in relation to EU strategy in the Middle East (Dagoumas, 2017). The 'under construction' status of the TANAP gas pipeline project and the restarting of negotiations on the construction of the Turkish Stream gas pipeline project after the normalization of Turkish-Russian relations has encouraged Turkey to involve Israeli gas reserves in its energy interests. So far, Turkey has been considering investing in Israeli gas infrastructure. Since there are already existing energy interests in Israel, the Turkish Republic will contribute more political and financial efforts to construct the potential gas pipeline project from the Levant basin. Of course, Israel now has the opportunity to export its natural gas reserves to neighboring Jordan and Egypt, but the ability to send its gas to the European energy market would make the country much more vital to the European Union (Siddig and Grethe, 2013). Therefore, Turkey's role in reaching the European gas market has become very strategic for Israel. On the other hand, when looking at the facts, it is obvious that natural gas transportation from Israel would contribute to the reduction of European countries' dependence on Russian natural gas. Therefore, this will decrease Russia's influence on the European energy market. From a geopolitical point of view, Israel needs to consider Cyprus's position since the planned pipeline will run through its territorial waters. Therefore, due to the conflict in Northern Cyprus in 1978, Cyprus and Turkey will need to put aside political tensions and reap the benefits of economic cooperation (Jensehaugen, 2014). It is important to mention that in the Levant basin, Cyprus has also discovered its own gas field, which it has named Aphrodite. This gas field could also add additional natural gas to the planned pipeline between Israel and Turkey. This energy cooperation in the Levant basin would make the energy pipeline much more significant. Lastly, it is crucial to understand that the planned pipeline from Israel to Turkey would serve the interests of the Western world, and therefore Moscow and Tehran will be observing any developments concerning the construction of the pipeline between Israel and Turkey. The Israeli-Turkish energy alliance is a win for Western countries because it would allow for the implementation of pro-western pipeline cooperation in the Middle East. This situation is changing European energy dynamics in positive developments and is further contributing to the diversification of the energy routes.

Turkey is currently the key country for Europe's energy diversification policy. European demand for energy resources and Turkey's geographical access to the Caspian basin and the Middle Eastern energy-rich countries has promoted the implementation of the energy diversification program. Turkey's role in bridging the European energy market with the Caspian and Middle Eastern regions will significantly increase the importance of the country. It is very obvious that Turkey is the solution for the diversification strategy of the energy supplies and therefore, all the existing and proposed pipelines will be implemented only with Turkey's support and desire. There has been a global shift in energy consumption from crude oil to natural gas resources, which initially stimulated the construction of the abovementioned pipelines. As such, most of the natural gas reserves from Central Asia, South Caucasus, and Middle East countries will have to be transported via gas pipelines in large volumes.

EUROPEAN UNION

For the countries of the European Union, energy security is one of the most important goals to strive towards. Energy security is defined as "the uninterrupted availability of energy sources at an affordable price" (Kocaslan, page 735, 2014). So far, maintaining a situation that is in line with this definition has been an issue for European countries throughout the history of modern energy, especially when the Middle East Oil Crisis took place in the 1970s. It was at this time that all the developed economies realized that natural energy resources have become a major element in the growth and development of their economies. Since the European countries recognized this reality, "energy diversification" has become the main strategy in foreign policy for energy matters (Aalto and Temel, 2014). The European countries' strategy to prevent the formation of a monopoly involving just a single or a few countries, such as Russia, over the energy resources has been the driving force behind the creation of a common energy policy. However, as of yet, the European Union hasn't achieved its goal of implementing a common energy policy. Currently, the European Union is taking great lengths to achieve a well-created policy of energy diversification and to ensure the stable and constant flow of energy resources to its energy market. All the efforts of the European countries in building such an excellent energy security policy have so far been unsuccessful due to the geopolitical dynamics of the region, which is surrounded by economic and political interests (Jacob, 2015). Europe, being a developed economic region, has been struggling with the geopolitical subtleties of its energy security. Europe also fully comprehends the fact that if energy supplies were to be abruptly stopped for any reason, the economy of the continent would not be able to continue to operate at its current levels and this would result in major social and financial problems. If there were to be an economic collapse due to energy cut-offs, then European countries would definitely face national crises since a nation's economy is highly tied to its strength. Because of this reality, the continent continues to struggle through a very difficult geopolitical situation. Particularly with the decline of its indigenous crude oil and natural gas production, European countries have been driven to rely on neighboring countries, such as the Russian Federation. Russian domination over the supply of both crude oil and natural gas has created an unstable energy security policy in Europe and the EU countries in particular (Irine, 2014). Despite all of the efforts of the European Union, most of the member states have a heavy dependence on energy imports. Continuous threats to its energy security and the necessity to find solutions to the problems of energy dependence have driven the European Union to create a more rigorous policy concerning the diversification of energy supplies towards the European energy market. Policies that diminish the heavy dependency on Russian energy exports have forced the European Union to analyze and accept a common energy policy within the current geopolitical context. This is because the energy sector is deeply intertwined with political interests and agendas. As such, in order for the European Union to be successful in such a secured energy diversification, it will need to thoroughly evaluate any geopolitical implications of its actions. Furthermore, it will be necessary for European geopolitical energy policy to create and maintain the flow of long-term effective energy products from a variety of diversified routes.

Since its creation, the European Union Commission has always considered the security of energy resources and due to the constant increase in demand for energy supplies, it is becoming ever more difficult for the commission to create a strategically designed plan aimed at decreasing the current energy dependency status. However, it is important to have a complete and thorough understanding of the current energy dependency situation within the European Union countries themselves. First of all, not all of the EU states are equally dependent on energy supplies. The variations become particularly evident when comparing the significant differences between eastern EU countries and western EU countries, and also the stark differences between northern EU countries and southern EU countries (Rocco, 2013). Especially since the end of the Cold War, ex-communist EU countries with new industrial capitalist developments and investments, such as Hungary, Eastern Germany, the Czech Republic, Slovakia, Poland, the Baltic States, and Balkan countries, have become high- energy-consuming countries (Groszkowski, 2013). On the other hand, developed economies of European Union, such as Germany, France, and the United Kingdom, have shown little increase in their demands for energy consumption. The energy dependency difference becomes even more visible when comparing individual countries within the European Union. For example, the Baltic States, such as Estonia and Lithuania, as well as Eastern EU states, such as Poland and Hungary, are heavily dependent on a single energy supply source. This single dependency can reach up to 80% of total consumption in some eastern EU countries (Yildirim and Yasa, 2014). This is because most of the eastern part of the European Union lacks the proper diversification of energy resources. On the other hand, some Balkan states and most of the western EU countries have, for the most part, succeeded in creating a diversified network of energy resources. From an energy security perspective, we can, therefore, divide states within the European Union into two separate categories, namely; 1) energy secure countries and 2) energy non-secure countries. Energy non-secure countries within the European Union face huge problems in terms of constant changes in the prices of various energy resources and, most importantly, changes in the volumes of energy supplies. These issues have had a significant effect on the economies of those countries. Therefore, energy security in the current geopolitical context is synonymous with economic security and any countries that are dependent on energy resources in high volumes face serious economic threats. As a result of this, the main concern of the European Commission is to promptly solve the problem of energy dependency, to improve the security of supplies, to develop the internal energy market, to ensure better prices for energy resources, and most importantly to create competitiveness with diversified energy routes. All of the above-mentioned goals of the EU commission clearly demonstrate the importance of the European energy policy. Of course, finding solutions and improving the European Union's energy security is not a trivial task when one considers the geopolitical tensions in the greater Eurasian region. Also, when considering the fact that the European Union still lacks a common foreign policy on energy security, the current situation does not fully permit the EU commission to establish any policies (Teixeira, 2014).

In 2006, the European Union faced its first serious energy security threat when Russia, for the first time, cut the volume of the gas after the territorial dispute between the Russian Federation and Ukraine (Schubert, Pollak and Brutschin, 2014). The diversification of energy routes and sources became the number one priority of EU policy makers. Until this time, there had been a growing dependence of the EU states on Russian energy supplies, in particular, natural gas, which had reached almost 40% of total imports (Marie-Claire Aoun et al, 2014). This drove the European Union to immediately search out additional alternative energy-rich regions for its energy supplies. This is at a time when the Middle East and the Caspian Regions are becoming the main agenda of the European energy security policy. The significance of the new energy actors in the Caspian region since the descent and subsequent collapse of the Soviet Union in the diversification policy of energy supplies, particularly natural gas reserves, has become very important for European policy makers. The rich resources of the Caspian region and the volumes of these energy reserves indicate clearly that if the European Union facilitates access to such reserves, it will have a huge influence over the European energy market. If one considers countries such as Azerbaijan, Kazakhstan, and Turkmenistan, the diversified energy supplies from these countries would be an important tool for EU countries and would also help to further negotiations with Moscow on the concerns of the energy supplies from Russia. So far, since the fall of the Soviet Union, it is only the Republic of Azerbaijan that has transported energy resources to the European energy market. These resources were transported in small volumes via the BTE, also known as the South Caucasus Pipeline, which is a natural gas pipeline, and the BTC, which is a crude oil pipeline. The existing BTE gas pipeline, starting from Azerbaijan and continuing via Georgia to Turkey and then finally to Greece, is planned to be expanded further in both volume and in length. The planned task of the BTE is to extend it with the TANAP project. At present, the TANAP pipeline is under construction, however, its eventual aim is to make possible the transportation of gas reserves from the Shah Deniz (King of Sea) energy field of Azerbaijan towards the heart of the European Union. The TANAP's increase in capacity in subsequent development phases will reach 24 bcm per year by 2023 and the final capacity of 31 bcm per year will be reached by 2026 (Sevim, 2013).

Although the majority of the energy that is demanded by European markets will be supplied by Azerbaijan, Turkmenistan also plans to utilize the energy infrastructure for the transportation of its own natural gas reserves. With these rich natural gas reserves, Turkmenistan offers a strategic alternative for the European gas market in terms of the total amount of reserves and the security of its transportation. Developers have already proposed an energy project that would connect Turkmenistan to Azerbaijan via the Caspian Sea, which is known as the Trans-Caspian pipeline (Guliyev and Akhrarkhodjaeva, 2009). If this plan were to be realized, the proposed pipeline project would definitely secure the implementation of the diversification policy of the European Commission. Nevertheless, the EU Commission must also win over the support of Turkmenistan because of its current interest in exporting natural gas to Russia and China. The Russian energy company, Gazprom, is also attempting to acquire the operation of several key natural gas fields in the Caspian basin. Furthermore, Gazprom is offering to purchase the gas recourses at European price rates so that Caspian region countries' energy resources will not reach the European gas market directly. In the process of buying marked up resources, Moscow is developing a policy, which aims to obtain most of the energy recourses directed towards the European gas market via multiple directions in an attempt to deprive Europe of viable alternative trading partners and consequently block the European diversification policy. Russia is currently buying large volumes of natural gas from Turkmenistan and Kazakhstan, which is helping to support the Russian monopoly in the European gas market (Spassov, 2014).

EU AND THE RUSSIAN FEDERATION

For much of recorded history, the European continent has been a region in which many global players have played an important role in political, social, and economic developments. Such developments have been drastically accelerated throughout the last century. During the Cold War period when there was a global conflict between communism and capitalism, Europe's relations with the Soviet Union remained extremely tense for several decades. After the fall of the Soviet Union, the tensions between Russia and the

European countries have persisted and this has made it very difficult for both sides to build fully functional cooperative relations (Dale, 1999). For Europe, Russia is an important country because of its energy interests and the fact that Russia is Europe's largest natural gas and crude oil supplier. In particular, natural gas resources are especially crucial for European countries and Russia happens to control most of the gas pipelines that supply the EU gas market. Furthermore, the Caspian basin countries, such as Turkmenistan and Kazakhstan, export their natural gas reserves via Russia's already existing gas pipeline infrastructure in order to access the European gas market (Gidadhubli, 2015). As a result, Russia has been forced into becoming one of the central players in the European gas supply market. Therefore, the European Union's dependency on the key element, natural energy resources, as well as Russia's dominating role has pushed the European Union to find a proper solution to the current situation. Over the last two decades, the European Union has been implementing new energy strategies that are mainly focused on energy security and its diversification. When Russia increased the price of natural gas by more than 40% to Ukraine in 2014, European countries faced an immediate energy security threat (Oguz, 2015). Ukraine's inability to pay for Russia's expensive gas and the abrupt interruption of Russian gas flow developed into an energy crisis for EU countries. The implementation of a new energy policy and the gaining of access to new energy-rich countries in the South Caucasus region, Central Asia, and the Middle East would significantly help most of the European countries to source alternatives to Russian-dominated natural gas supply. The current Russian annexation of Crimea, the conflict in the Donbas region, and the EU sanctions on Russia are all helping to prolong the tensions across the continent and are continuing to threaten the security of the energy policy of European countries now and for the foreseeable future. When the gas supply to Ukraine was cut-off for two weeks in 2009, it was an obvious warning sign to European countries indicating that they need to diversify their sources of energy. The Commissioner for Climate Action and Energy, Miguel Arias Cañete, stated the following during his speech in Brussels in 2006 at the European commission meeting.

"After the gas crises of 2006 and 2009 that left many millions out in the cold, we said: 'Never again'. But the stress tests of 2014 showed we are still far too vulnerable to major disruption of gas supplies. And the political tensions on our borders are sharp reminders that this problem is will not just go away. Today's proposals are about a reliable, competitive and flexible system in which energy flows across borders and consumers reap the benefits. They are about standing together to protect the most vulnerable. And they are about securing our clean energy future: I can assure that our commitment to a clean energy transition is irreversible and non-negotiable." (EU Commission Press Release, URL, 2016)

The South Caucasus, Middle Eastern, and Central Asian countries present themselves as new options for EU countries to be able to diversify the flow of their energy sources. Therefore, in order to have secure access to such alternative regions, European countries will have to forge stronger geopolitical and economic relations with those countries. Because of this reason, when understanding the current situation of European energy security, it is not only enough to analyze the European perspective but it is also necessary to focus on the geopolitical and geo-economic aspects of the partnering countries. In the last two decades, Russia has played the leading role in being Europe's natural gas supplier. This has not only provided a huge economic benefit to Russia but it has also endowed Russia with the ability to powerfully influence the foreign geopolitics of the region.

The European Union, with a consumption volume of 520 billion cubic meters of natural gas per year, is the second largest natural gas-consuming region on the planet after the United States of America (Doukas, Harris et al, 2013). Russia may not be the only natural gas supplier to the European Union energy market however it is definitely the most important gas exporter to Europe. Around 33% of the EU imported natural gas is of Russian origin (Belyayev, 2013). Back in 2009 when Russia cut-off its gas exports to Ukraine for two weeks, the European Union faced a serious security threat and as a result, for the sake of its energy security, the EU has accepted action plans and policy roadmaps in order to have a more secure and stable flow of energy, and also to diversify the portfolio to different energy sources. The action plans and policies that the European Union has created serve only one main interest and this is clearly mentioned in Energy Roadmap 2050 of the European Union (Hey, 2012). It states the following:

"There will be no compromise on safety and security for either traditional or new energy sources. The EU must continue to strengthen the safety and security framework and lead international efforts in this field" (Eur-Lex, URL, 2011).

Currently, the European Union is trying to create a mechanism to implement a multilateral energy security policy and therefore the European Union is working very hard within the limits of its multilateral policy in order to reduce Russia's influence on the European energy market. Although Europe will not be able to totally eliminate the Russian influence in the energy market, with access to Azerbaijan and Turkmenistan's natural gas resources in the Caspian basin as well as Iranian, Israeli, and Iraqi natural gas resources in the Middle Eastern regions, the dependency on Russian energy supplies will ultimately decrease in the long-term and therefore promote the energy security policy of the European countries.

The development and discoveries of new hydrocarbon reserves in the Middle East, such as Israel and Cyprus, as well as Iran and Iraq in the Levant basin, the South Caucasus, Azerbaijan, and the Central Asian countries of Turkmenistan and Kazakhstan have presented new options for European countries to have the chance to diversify their energy imports; particularly their natural gas resources (Dagoumas, 2017). In order to be able to make its energy policy possible with the above-mentioned countries, the European Union needs to analyze and understand the geopolitical implications of the regions of those countries. This is very important because the energy diversification policy of the European Union will eventually decrease the amount of Russian gas supply to the EU energy market in the long run and this will automatically provoke Moscow's geopolitical interests. This means that Moscow will put in extra effort in its attempts to stop the European Union's entrance into the Caspian Basin region with mega energy projects. However, the European Union's staunch commitment and its thorough action plans aimed at diversifying energy supply routes would likely lead to the creation of important mechanisms for the implementation of the multilateral energy security policy. Still, no matter how much the European Union tries to reduce Russian influence on its energy market, it is most likely that it will never be able completely rid itself of this reality. Nevertheless, throughout these new strategies and policies, the European Union will succeed in bringing additional energy routes and eventually this will lead to an increase in the total volume of natural gas reaching EU energy market.

The new routes from the Caspian basin and the Middle East serve the interests of all the players with the exception of Moscow, which is highly vulnerable in maintaining its prominent position in the current state of the European energy supply market. In some of the European countries, Russian natural gas supply has reached up to 100% of total imported gas and, as a result, these countries have become economically and developmentally dependent on Russian exports (Dusciac, Popescu, and Parlicov, 2016). As a consequence, energy dependency for economic development results in political dependency on the supplier and it is for this reason that Russia's energy relationship with the European Union has created this security warning to member countries. The European Union clearly understands that an energy monopoly or the complete dependency on foreign imports in one region or country gives the supplier a chance to indirectly influence the economic and political state of affairs within the other countries. The European Union sees this as a very risky threat to its own security and it is because of this reason that all new energy policies and action plans serve the main goal of diversifying its energy partners as much as it can. The ultimate goal of these actions is to secure a future in which none of the energy partnering countries has the ability to become so dominant. The European Union's energy diversification plan not only requires new stable suppliers but this plan also requires stable and secure transit countries in which energy pipelines will be able to run through securely without any major interruptions. The reason that the European Union is so concerned with this matter is because of the important lessons that it learned during the 2009 and 2014 Ukraine energy crisis and conflicts (Gümüscedil and Yasin, 2015). On both occasions, the flow of gas through pipelines was interrupted during the transit between Ukraine and Russia to the European Union's energy market. In light of these incidents, any additional stable energy suppliers, together with secure transit countries, would only contribute to the European Union's current energy security policy efforts.

The European Union's natural gas consumption relies heavily on its imports from Russia, Norway, and Algeria. These three countries combined provide up to 81% of the European Union's total natural gas supplies. Natural gas is the second most used energy source after crude oil, with a current gross consumption of 24%, versus 34% of crude oil (Patterson, 2013). This indicates the vital role that natural gas plays in European energy security. Moscow has been provided with a significant economic advantage by playing the role of the European Union's biggest natural gas supplier, and throughout this domination, it has gained important tools through which it can increase its foreign levels of influence. Thus, for Moscow, losing or decreasing its shares in the European gas market does mean losing or decreasing its foreign influence. Russia, as a supplier, and the European Union, as a consumer, would both need to maintain relatively strong and stable energy partnership relations in order to maintain economic stability. However, due to all the geopolitical events and conflicts, together with the clash of international interests, this has resulted in an extended delay in the implementation of much larger energy projects. EU sanctions against Russia relating to the Crimean crisis are not included in the energy sector, and this has therefore demonstrated how much the European Union still stands dependent on Russian gas sources. However, it is also argued that "without Europe as a customer, the Russian economy would collapse", and that both sides would lose if there were to be any such gas interruptions (Patterson, pg. 11, 2013). Since the European Union is Russia's biggest customer, the result of losing such a purchaser would lead to a significant economic crisis. Therefore, since a large portion of Russia's economy is based on energy exports, it would bring about enormous damage to the Russian Federation. Because of these threats to its economic wellbeing, Moscow has been using a different strategy as a means to affect the EU energy diversification program. This strategy goes beyond the relationship between the European Union and Russia and therefore covers regional geopolitical implications, such as the use of the state-owned company, Gazprom, for influencing the energy market. Gazprom has been working very hard to influence to the EU gas market and force out all the other neighboring energy-rich countries from the gas market. However, even though Gazprom has an influence on the EU gas market, with a share of 39% in natural gas supplies, it is not able to sway as much influence over the energy-rich neighboring regions, such as the South Caucasus, Central Asia, the Balkans, and the Middle East (Luciani, 2015). These regions are rich in fossil fuels, including vast amounts of natural gas reverses, and therefore the European Union has shown a lot of interest in these regions and the potential to help diversify their energy market gas supplies. The European Union sees these countries as an important opportunity to build several natural gas pipeline projects and therefore to establish a long-term energy partnership over the hydrocarbon reserves.

EU DIVERSIFICATION POLICY

Before discussing Europe's imported energy resources, it is important to explain that Europe does indeed have its own indigenous gas reserves, which it can rely upon to a certain extent. Several European countries are endowed with natural gas resources. Norway and the Netherlands are the major regional producers. With Norway's 110 bcm and the Netherlands' 69 bcm, together these countries account for approximately 70% of Europe's indigenous production (Norway Oil and Gas Report, 2016). However, the volume of Europe's natural gas production will begin to decrease towards the 2030s. Also, the shale gas reserves on the European continent are expected to reach around 16bcm (Holgate and Wagner, 2013). However, the various European countries differ widely on the most appropriate drilling and fracking techniques and also in their views on how these actions might have a potentially negative impact on the environment. This has brought about serious difficulties for the implementation and development of the industry. Shale gas production is a technique that involves fracking of the underground and is achieved by the injection of chemicals into the soil together with water. According to many researchers, recovered water from fracking operations includes radioactive materials, which could heavily damage the environmental ecosystems of adjacent areas (Lu and Gao, 2014). Potential threats include the contamination of local ground water reservoirs. Therefore, EU environmental regulations and other obstacles will have to limit the shale gas production in European countries. As a result, the need for more natural gas reserves will lead to a greater increase in energy imports. The European gas market, which is heavily dominated by Russian gas imports, is implementing and building projects in the hope of succeeding in the energy diversification policy. When analyzing the policy on possible alternative suppliers, it is important to understand the geopolitics from regional and continental approaches.

North Africa currently has a share of 15% of total European gas imports and holds the rank of the European Union's 2nd largest supplier of gas (Gheorghe, 2013). Over the last 10 years, this percentage had the potential to increase significantly in volume and could have even surpassed Russia. However, due to the Arab spring and the subsequent domino effect of revolutions in North African states, most of the established energy cooperation networks and infrastructure has been damaged or completely destroyed (Voskopoulos, 2015). Therefore, the current likelihood of an increase in natural gas exports from North African states towards the European gas market is extremely unlikely. Factors such as political and economic instability, outdated energy infrastructure, and the decline in the production of natural gas, as well as increases in domestic demand have all served to prevent North African states from exporting a meaningful amount of their natural gas reserves to the European gas market. If we consider the fact that Algeria holds the world's 4th largest shale gas reserves, this indicates that North African countries have a huge opportunity to increase their natural gas exports (Gheorghe, 2013). In the future, there is a likely possibility that North African countries, such as Algeria, Libya, and even Egypt will increase their LNG gas exports. However, according to many economists, the current political and economic instabilities in North African states will continue for a long period of time and this will inevitably serve to prolong the European Union's dependence on Russian gas (Voskopoulos, 2015).

On the other hand, the Levant basin, which is estimated to have huge natural gas reserves, is considered to be a viable source of alternative energy to the European energy market. Recent natural gas discoveries in the Levant basin, especially in the territories of Israel, Cyprus, and Lebanon, have brought about new implications in terms of energy security. This is because countries in the Levant basin have been 100% dependent on importing energy fuels, and these new discoveries would now provide an attractive opportunity to these countries to not only become energy self-sufficient but also to export their produced natural gas reserves (Dagoumas, 2017). In general, these countries would eventually develop the Levant basin region into an energy hub for the European energy market. There are many challenges that must be faced in order to ensure that this region is to become an energy hub in terms of developing those fields and building the necessary energy infrastructure. For this reason, throughout the development of the discovered natural gas fields, it is crucial for the Levant basin countries to work together with countries who have had experience in building and managing similar such energy infrastructure. Israel and Cyrus are working hard to create the required technological advancements and it is for that reason, along with support from other international energy companies, that the energy fields will be available for both domestic needs and for global exports. As mentioned previously in the research, Turkey will play an important role in making it possible for the Levant basin countries to export their natural gas reserves to the European gas market. If the Levant basin countries, especially Cyprus and Israel, demonstrate a commitment to becoming part of European energy security, then it will require access to the Turkish energy infrastructure, such as TANAP and Turkish Stream natural gas pipeline. Accessing Turkish energy infrastructure means easy access to the European gas market at a reasonable price because the Turkish route is currently the closest in terms of reaching the market. Also, when considering how expensive investments in energy infrastructure building are, Turkey, with existing advanced energy pipelines, offers the best option for countries of the Levant basin. However, geopolitical uncertainty in the Middle East and historical tensions between Greek Cypriots and Turkey bring challenges for European countries concerning the construction of such energy transit infrastructure to promote the diversification policy of European energy security. European countries should find a way to promote energy cooperation between Cyrus and Turkey so that in the long term it can have stable access to the Levant basin's energy reserves (Jensehaugen, 2014).

In 2015, the European Commission launched a new program called the 'Energy Union', which focuses on building better energy security for the European Union (Papatulica, 2016). This Energy Union is specifically designed to guide and help member countries in ensuring that "secure, affordable and climate-friendly energy" reaches their economy. The framework of the Energy Union is designed to enhance energy security and aims to address demand, supply, and transportation whilst actively supporting sustainable climate-friendly energy development. It also seeks to unite the various energy markets and systems of each member state country and develop external energy policy relations with its various neighboring regions. The Energy Union's main strategy is to transform the European Union's current unstable energy dependency into a more secure and uninterrupted supply of energy. The Vice-President of the Energy Union, Maros Sefcovic, stated the following during his meeting in Brussels in 2016.

"The Energy Union Strategy, launched one year ago, promised to provide all Europeans with energy which is secure, sustainable, and competitive. Today's package focuses on the security of our supply, but touches upon all three overarching goals. By reducing our energy demand, and better managing our supply from external sources we are delivering on our promise and enhancing the stability of Europe's energy market" (Asia News Monitor, URL, 2016).

The European Union's cooperation with the Caspian and Levant basin countries and its strengthening energy relations with countries such as Azerbaijan, Turkmenistan, and Israel would help to implement the strategies of the Energy Union. When we take into consideration that the European Union has already established energy cooperation with countries such as Azerbaijan, it makes it much more viable to implement significantly larger energy projects. The previous BTC and BTE pipelines have proven that Azerbaijan and the European Union have the ability to work cooperatively together and engage in stable energy collaboration. It is for this reason that under the Southern Gas Corridor (SGC) project, two proposed pipelines, namely TANAP and TAP, became one of the major steps in building a diversified route for the European gas market. These two projects under the

SGC have been identified in the European Union Commission as the 'projects of common interests' (PCI) and referred to the SGC as the priority corridor. Therefore, pipeline projects under the Southern Gas Corridor, such as TANAP and TAP have become the European Union's primary PCIs. Vice-president, Maros Sefcovic, stated the following in regards to his views on the SGC's pipeline projects.

"Once complete, TAP will be a major asset in European energy security tool box. By opening up access to gas from Azerbaijan, TAP will allow many countries. including in Central and South East Europe to diversify their sources of gas. Southern Gas Corridor will be vital for reaching the Energy Union objectives of diversification of sources, routes and energy security. Therefore, timely completion is crucial so that gas from the new suppliers can flow to Europe by 2020" (Badalova, URL, 2016).

According to Sefcovic, when considering the potential of the Caspian and Levant basins' future supply, the European Union is willing to work very closely with these countries in an attempt to increase the volume of their gas flows in the long-term. In 2016, Istanbul held a High-Level Dialogue between the European Union and Turkey. The Minister for Energy and Natural Resources of Turkey, Berat Albayrak, as well as the European Union Commissioner for Climate Action and Energy, was involved in discussions. During the High-Level Dialogue, both sides of the debate on the cooperation in the energy sector also discussed the importance of the SGC, which is in the list of PCIs. When looking at the joint press statement of the High-Level Energy Dialogue, the following is stated.

"Both sides underlined the importance of Turkey as a key country for EU's energy security and as a regional energy hub, and they re-affirmed their joint commitment to the successful implementation of the Southern Gas Corridor. Its timely completion is critical so as to allow gas flowing to Europe by 2020. In this regard, Turkey will continue to play an active role in the Southern Gas Corridor Advisory Council which will convene for a second meeting shortly. This Advisory Council meets on a regular basis to politically strengthen the development of the Southern Gas Corridor by bringing together all the countries and stakeholders involved" (Natural Gas Asia, URL, 2016).

In the statement, it was also mentioned that both sides would continue discussing the availability of natural gas reserves in the South Caucasus region and Turkmenistan. As such, there will be continued dialogue to ensure additional natural gas resources from the Caspian basin are added to the SGC.

It is very important to mention that the European Union created the Eastern Partnership (EaP) program in 2009 and the goal of the program was to strengthen relations between the European Union and six eastern neighboring countries, namely Azerbaijan, Armenia, Belarus, Ukraine, Georgia, and Moldova (Journal of European Studies, 2015). One of the main goals of the EaP is to bring the involved countries together and promote the energy security of the European Union. EaP provides an important platform for discussing the building of energy infrastructure. Within the European Union's EaP energy security strategy, Azerbaijan has been the key country, not only due to its huge energy reserves but also due to its strategic location. It is situated between Russia and Iran and has access to Central Asian countries via the Caspian Sea. This country's commitment, from such a strategic geographical location and with its ongoing contribution to the European energy security diversification policy, demonstrates clearly that Azerbaijan is a reliable partner. During his speech at the Global Energy Congress, which was held in Istanbul, the president of the Republic of Azerbaijan, Ilham Aliyev, stated the following.

"We took the first step for the Trans-Anatolian Natural Gas Pipeline (TANAP) in 2012 in Turkey, which is a significant part of the South Gas Corridor, under the leadership of Azerbaijan and Turkey. TANAP is an important agreement and many countries might become a part of this project" (Euractiv, URL, 2016).

President Aliyev clearly indicated Azerbaijan's commitment to providing the EU energy market with stable and secure energy reserves for the foreseeable future. He further underlined the importance of the TANAP and TAP projects and said that natural gas from Azerbaijan will be supplied to global energy markets under the Southern Gas Corridor route.

THE RUSSIAN FEDERATION

The Russian Federation's energy history began in the late 18th century. However, a lack of technological advancements and a very weak energy industry in Tsarist Russia led to very slow progress and development in the field (Mikail, 2010). Consequently, the leaders of Tsarist Russia soon realized that the only way to develop the energy industry was to remove the tough restrictions on the majority of foreign investors. The country subsequently invited Western companies to assist in the building and development of a technologically well-equipped energy industry. It was at that time in history when European and US energy companies were invited to take part in the development of the oil fields, in particular, those found in Baku (Johnson, 2010). This cooperation with Western companies during the

Tsarist Russia period facilitated a more cordial relationship between the two sides. This improvement in relations had brought such a great deal of cooperation that Russia was eventually transformed into an enormous oil producing country. By the end of the 19th century, Tsarist Russia had dominated global crude oil exports, supplying around 30 percent of the world oil demand (Johnson, 2010). Russia's economically beneficial situation continued into the 20th century. During the Soviet Union period, the energy industry was at the center of Russia's attention. However, Soviet Moscow had started using energy resources for a variety of different reasons, especially since the end of WWII when Europe was effectively divided into a Communist East and a Capitalist West. Moscow soon became the dominant power in the global crude oil export industry. By the middle of the 20th century, the Soviet Union had doubled the oil production and effectively transformed the union into the primary supplier of crude oil to European countries, both communist and capitalist countries. Since the fall of the Soviet Union, the Russian Federation has suffered significantly with the drop of production levels of crude oil and this resulted in an energy sector crisis (Mikail, 2010).

Since the year 2000, the country has paid a lot of attention to reforms in the energy sector. As a consequence of this, stabilization of the energy sector has become implemented under state control. Moscow took control of the energy industry by nationalizing most of the existing energy companies, the most prominent of which are Gazprom and Rosneft (Belyi, Nappert, and Pogoretsky, 2011). As a result, Moscow was placed in a position whereby it could play the energy card on not only its European Union customers, but also on the newly born ex-Soviet countries. Since the end of the Cold War when ex-Soviet countries secured their independence, Moscow has successfully managed to raise the price of energy supplies through tough negotiations and bargaining. Even though European countries have had some opportunities to temporarily use other energy resources to maintain Russian pressure on the supply of energy and prices, ex-soviet countries did not have that same chance and due to a lack of energy infrastructure and organization, these countries have subsequently become fully dependent on Russian energy supplies (Mikail, 2010). Starting from the year 2000, this policy of Moscow has helped Russia to manage the country's energy industry and this has resulted in the stable and prosperous development of the energy industry once again. The particularly high crude oil and natural gas prices have meant that Moscow has received huge amounts of funds and this has therefore provided Moscow with the opportunity to develop the Russian economy on all spheres of the country's development. The energy policy that Moscow has been following has also helped the country to influence ex-soviet countries that were dependent on energy supplies. However, both the devastation of the 2008 global financial crisis as well as the drastic fall in oil prices in 2016 has caused great concern to the Russian Federation (Fiedorczuk and Grabowiecki, 2016). The fall of oil prices, which began in 2015, is an especially dire situation for Russia when one takes into consideration that approximately half of the budget of the country is generated from the sale of crude oil and natural gas. It has been suggested that the decline in global oil prices has directly affected the economy of Russia in an extremely negative and detrimental way. Currently, Russia's total energy revenues are made up of 80% crude oil and 20% natural gas exports (Fiedorczuk and Grabowiecki, 2016). Because oil contributes to the majority of total energy exports, the significant fall in oil prices has drastically reduced the previously huge amount of income that was pouring into the Russian economy.

Being the largest oil producing country in the world, the Russian Federation has become heavily dependent on its energy exports over the last two decades. These exports, which account for 70% of its total export revenues, have made Russia one of the most significant players relying on the global energy trade (Patterson, 2013). Nevertheless, the Western sanctions against Moscow over the Crimean conflict have further contributed to the negative effect on the economy of the country. The economy of the country shrank by up to 4 percent and it is expected that this situation will continue to remain the same so long as low oil prices and sanctions are a reality. Since 2014, Western economic sanctions have directly targeted many Russian companies and, together with low oil prices and poor management of the economy, have become the main factors contributing to the decline of the Russian economy (Bebler, 2017). According to Ben Judah, "Putin looks strong now, but his Kremlin is built on the one thing in Russia he doesn't control: the price of oil" and he continues by claiming that "eventually, the money is going to run out, and then he will find himself in the same position Soviet leaders were in by the late 1980s, forced to confront political and economic crises while trying to hold the country together" (Matthews, pg. 15, 2014). Like Ben Judah, many critics with a similar opinion about Moscow's energy diplomacy believe that a country with an oil based economy will inevitably collapse sooner or later, just as the Soviet Union did in the late 1980s. Weak economic development of the economy and the staunchly aggressive foreign policy of Russia have brought about more obstacles in the creation of a mutually beneficial strategic energy partnership between the European Union and Russia. However, it is a fact that with or without such a strategic energy partnership deal, energy resources are the main key to forging closer links between the European Union and the Russian Federation. In fact, when looking at recent figures concerning Russian energy exports, it becomes very obvious that the two sides are highly dependent on one another; the European Union being dependent on crucial Russian energy exports, and Russia being dependent on income from EU energy purchases. The energy exports of Russia to the European Union make up approximately 30% of the European Union's energy import share. According to 2013 figures, the European Union imported 154 million tons of crude oil and 140 bcm of gas from Russia (Patterson, 2013). These energy exports of Russia to Europe make up the vast majority of its total energy exports. As such, a delicate situation exists in which Russia and Europe are forced to cooperate in order to ensure continued growth and development.

Moscow's uncooperative policy due to the sanctions placed upon it has also raised questions for Russia about perhaps building and facilitating more diversified markets for Russian exports of energy supplies. The tension between Russia and the West has not only pushed EU countries to consider implementing a better energy security policy, but the Russian Federation has also made the decision to implement a policy designed to broaden its energy markets. Moscow's ambition to increase its energy share in Asia's energy market is one of the main targets of the Kremlin (Mankoff, 2015). This target would not only help Moscow to diversify its energy markets for the sale of its energy supplies, but it would also help Moscow to reduce its own unsustainable dependency on the sale of energy to EU energy markets. Russia's natural gas and crude oil deals with China and the construction of new energy pipeline infrastructure has indicated the extent to which Russia is willing to expand its fossil fuel exports to the Asian energy market. In 2016, when the Russian President, Vladimir Putin, attended the World Energy Congress in Turkey, Istanbul, he made the following statement.

"We intend to actively expand exports of hydrocarbons in the east – China, Japan, India. Together with our partners from other countries we are developing our energy and transport capabilities: we are expanding LNG production, implementing a number of other large infrastructure projects on the delivery of hydrocarbons to the traditional and new markets, including the 'Eastern Siberia – Pacific Ocean', 'Power of Siberia' pipelines as well as the corresponding future supplies to China" (RBTH, URL, 2016).

As he made it clear in his statement, Moscow is working towards modernizing and rebuilding its own energy infrastructure as well as investing in the energy sector together with energy terminals in seaports in Asia. According to many experts, Western sanctions have driven Russia to build tighter relations with China and other Asian countries. This cooperation between the two countries, especially in the energy sector, is one of the main geopolitical interests that they both share. It is also very important to mention that Moscow and Beijing are the co-founders of the Shanghai Cooperation Organization (SCO). It is for this reason that these two countries consider themselves as the main two powers in Eurasia in accordance with the SCO framework. In Putin's statement at the World Energy Congress in Turkey, Istanbul, it is clearly stated that Russia intends to increase its energy exports not only to China, but also to India, Pakistan, Japan, and other major economies of Asia. In late 2016, Russia's oil company, Rosneft, entered into the Indian energy market and made a deal with the Energy Company of Essar Oil (DailyMail, 2016). Rosneft made an agreement with Essar Oil to purchase 49 percent of its shares. The fact that Essar Oil is in possession of one of the largest energy refineries in India would provide an important opportunity to the Russian Oil Company. As Igor Sechin, head of Rosneft, stated, "Rosneft is entering one of the most promising and fast-growing world markets" (Indian Express, URL, 2016). He continues by mentioning that this enormous refinery would allow for the Russian company, Rosneft, to export its energy reserves to Asia-Pacific countries. According to many analysts, this agreement aims to send a message to Western countries that

Moscow has a number of opportunities to which it could diversify its energy exporting markets. The policy of diversifying energy markets for exports seems to be very realistic for Moscow because EU demand for energy resources is constantly decreasing whereas demand is currently increasing in developing Asian countries. Therefore, during the sanctions period, there has been an opportunity for the Russian Federation to consider expanding its fossil fuel exports (Tichy and Kratochvil, 2014).

On the other hand, the Western countries' nuclear deal (Joint Comprehensive Plan of Action) with the Islamic Republic of Iran at the end of 2015 and proposals to lift the sanctions pose a legitimate concern for most of the oil producing countries, including the Russian Federation (Popova and Rasoulinezhad, 2016). Iran's ambition to increase its oil exports after the lifting of sanctions has put more fear in other countries, particularly during the period of low oil prices. However, all oil producing countries, including the Islamic Republic of Iran, realize that it is better to limit crude oil production. It can be inferred that Iran's decision was not only related to its solidarity with OPEC countries but also due to the fact that the country underwent long years of sanctions. Furthermore, due to a lack of modern energy infrastructure, the country is not able to significantly increase its production in the short-term. As such, Iran is in favor of oil prices remaining at high levels for the foreseeable future (Davenport, 2015). Moscow is very much aware of this situation and understands that in the short-term future Iran will not be able to threaten the Russian Federation's interests in the European gas market or the global oil markets. According to Viktor Katona, who is an energy expert in Russian International Affairs Council, "the competition between Iran and Russia did certainly take place, but it is far from being a full-scale scrap. For the most part, Iran reclaimed its traditional European market, primarily Italy and Greece, whilst elsewhere its return was less palpable, leaving Russia more space" (Khlebnikov, 2016). However, when considering European energy policy, and the diversification of its energy imports, Iran will remain one of the key opportunities for the European Union to help decrease its dependence on the Russian energy resources. When one also considers that the European Union's energy market will not grow significantly in the near future, Tehran's comeback will remain very important in terms of decreasing Russia's share of the European energy market (Trenin, 2016).

When considering all of the above-mentioned geopolitical aspects of Russia's role in the European energy market, it becomes very visible that challenges for both sides are substantial and in this situation, the building of policies becomes the most difficult task for all of the players. In regards to energy security policy building in the Russian Federation and the European Union, it is very clear that both sides are heavily reliant on each other. The question of energy dependency is the toughest challenge for the European Union countries however it will also be a critical challenge for Moscow to maintain its role as being the dominant energy supplier to the European energy market. When considering the scope of the entire crisis, including the surrounding regions, as well as the transformation of security issues, the future will hold new and challenging problems for Western countries and also for Russia. The economic and financial crisis in the European Union, the events of the Arab Spring in Egypt, Tunis, and Libya, the refugee crisis, terrorist attacks, the ongoing war in Syria, Iraq, and Ukraine, and Western sanctions on the Russian Federation are all having a negative effect on the development and shaping of energy security policy. Therefore, both for the European Union and for Russia, these global crises have dominated and shaped the policy building agenda.

EU – RUSSIA ENERGY STRATEGY

After the end of the cold war, with the fall of the Berlin wall and with the subsequent fall of the Soviet Union, EU countries have made the decision to bring Russia closer to the European community and this policy resulted in the signing of the 1994 European Union – Russian Federation Partnership and Cooperation Agreement (Poyraz, 2011). This agreement became the platform for uniting and developing cooperation in economic and political sectors. For the European Union, it became a primary objective to create a common strategy with Moscow. This agreement is aimed at developing activities that serve in the promotion of stability, energy security, and partnership between the European Union and Moscow. The successful integration of the Russian Federation towards the European Union community would result in the implementation of the main security goal, which is, as mentioned in the European Union's Security Strategy, "a major factor in our security and prosperity" (European Security Strategy, 2003). This approach automatically affected the extensive bilateral relationships on the trade, energy, and integration of economic areas in the global economic system. However, many major direct conflicts, such as the Russo-Georgia war in 2008, the Orange Revolution in Ukraine in 2004, NATO's closer cooperation with post-Soviet countries, and finally the European Union's Eastern Partnership Program (EaP) and European Neighborhood Policy (ENP) have been negatively affecting Russia's partnership with the European Union leading up to this period. Finally, the recent war in Ukraine and Russia's intervention and annexation of Crimea from Ukraine became the final straw in the breakdown of relations between the European Union and Russia. The abovementioned result and failure in the Russia-EU normalization period have also increased the levels of tension in all of the surrounding regions. As a result, the Ukrainian conflict culminated with the European Union imposing sanctions

166

on the Russian Federation. However, Russia responded to these sanctions by placing a variety of its own sanctions on EU countries as a form of political retaliation. Although these sanctions did not cover any areas of energy cooperation, the subsequent unpopularity of Moscow brought forth statements from EU countries calling for a sharp reduction in energy imports, especially natural gas imports from the Russian Federation. This position of the European countries was a clear indication that, these countries, particularly Eastern and Central European Union countries that are supported by Brussels, made the formal decision to minimize their energy dependency on Russian imports. However, the current energy dependency on Russian energy exports, as well as the uncertain nature of the European Union's energy strategy, has clearly demonstrated that a policy of sanctions and isolation towards the EU countries, and also within the EEP that is aimed at bringing Ukraine closer to the European community, would only result in deeper and deeper tensions.

In general, the conflict between Russia and Ukraine and its effects on trade has had enormous consequences for the energy security of Brussels. The main reason for this tension is the geographical location of the country. Ukraine is situated on the main juncture between Moscow and Brussels. Therefore, most of the pipelines that go from Russia to European countries pass directly through Ukrainian territory. Approximately 40% of the energy resources that are imported into the EU energy market currently travel through Ukraine (Sotolongo, 2014). Therefore, Ukraine's strategic transit role in European energy security and its conflict with Russia has put the European Union in a situation in which it is very vulnerable to disruptive events. This was especially the case when Russia used its energy 'weapon' as a tool to put pressure not only on EU countries but also on Ukraine in 2006, 2009, and again in 2014. The 2009 event, in which Russia cut-off gas supplies to

Ukraine for 2 weeks in the middle of winter, resulted in major problems to European countries (McLaughlin and Mock, 2009). The two-week cut-off resulted in the closure of numerous factories, resulting in a significant slowdown in production and economic growth. In addition to this, millions of citizens living within EU countries were left completely without working heating systems, freezing in their houses in January at the peak of the cold European winter. In 2015, according to the Russian president, Vladimir Putin, if Ukraine doesn't agree with its natural gas payment demands, then the gas supplies will be cut-off completely. He stated "this may create a threat to transit to Europe, to our European partners. We hope that gas supplies will not be interrupted. But this does not depend only on us, it depends on the financial discipline of our Ukrainian partners" (Independent, 2015). If this is indeed the case, then in order for the European Union to challenge this situation, it is necessary to take measures towards reducing the EU countries' vulnerability to Russian gas supplies being suddenly and unexpected turned off. The Energy Union was created by EU countries and aimed to synchronize EU domestic energy networks and diversifies energy routes. The 2014 natural gas transit cut-off through Ukraine became the last warning to the EU countries (Independent, 2015). In regards to this matter, Russia has taken measures, which ignore the creation of the Energy Union of the EU countries. It is clear that Moscow believes that the notion of EU countries building a common energy policy is impossible. Therefore, even if EU countries are successful in securing such a common energy policy, this dependency could not be majorly reduced in the foreseeable future. In 2016 Miguel Canete, who is the EU commissioner for climate action and energy, stated, "we are still far too vulnerable [to a disruption of gas supplies]. With political tensions on our borders still on a knife edge, this is a sharp reminder that this problem is not just going to go away" (CFR, URL, 2016). Even before 2014, when there was a two-week Russian cut-off of natural gas to several European countries in 2009, the United States and the European Union successfully cooperated in the formation of a joint energy council. The energy council has been working towards the common goal of decreasing the EU countries' dependency on Russian energy supplies. In 2014, at the G7 summit in Brussels, the United States announced that a new energy policy would be created to finally put an end to the EU countries' dependence on Russian exports and stop Moscow from using its 'energy weapon' as a means of implementing its foreign interests. During the 2014 G7 summit, ex-US president Barack Obama stated that "the use of energy supplies as a means of political coercion or as a threat to security is unacceptable" and continued by saying that "the crisis in Ukraine makes plain that energy security must be at the center of our collective agenda" (Time, URL, 2014). Also, the former president of the European Commission, Jose Manuel Barroso, stated "it was utterly unacceptable that European gas consumers were held hostage to this dispute between Russia and Ukraine" (Time, 2014).

After a 40-year prohibition on the export of its own energy reserves, the United States finally lifted its ban and the country began to export crude oil and natural gas, especially to European countries (Egan, 2016). The central aim of the United States has been to facilitate a positive relationship with EU countries by assisting in the reduction of their dependence on natural gas and crude oil exports from Russia. However, current estimates suggest that it would take the United States at least 10 years to reach the export numbers required to surpass Russia's energy exports to the EU energy market (Egan, 2016). Nevertheless, Washington is generally continuing to build a common energy policy with Brussels in an attempt to put a stop to Russian domination. As Amos Hochstein states, "energy security and economic security in Europe is directly linked to our concerns [U.S.] national security, and we are committed to that." (CFR, 2016). In the long term, European countries have encouraged big interest US companies to take part in European energy security and export more natural gas reserves to the European energy market. However, according to Keth Crane, who is an energy expert, "we would never approach what the Russians have been. We'd still be a marginal supplier" (Time, 2016). As has been seen from all the statements, European energy security will still remain under significant Russian influence. Therefore, Moscow's new energy policy, the implementation of new energy projects, and the diversification of transit routes are putting European countries and neighboring transit countries in a much more difficult and challenging situation.

THE RUSSIAN FEDERATION'S ENERGY POLICY

The Russian federation currently has several key natural gas pipelines that provide EU countries with gas supplies that are seen as essential for economic prosperity. When looking at the list of natural gas pipelines, the Gazela, Megal, Nord Stream, Brotherood, and Yamal-Europe gas pipelines play the most strategic network role (Papava and Tokmazishvili, 2010). These pipelines carry the large bulk of Russian natural gas towards the European gas market. For the most part, these existing natural gas pipelines pass through Ukraine and Belarus, with the exception of the Nord Stream (Luciani, 2015). All of these pipelines are operational and Moscow is, therefore, utilizing the full capacity of this infrastructure as a means to sell as much gas as it possibly can. There are also a number of proposed natural gas pipelines that are currently being put into active phases by the Russian Federation in an attempt to implement further interests of the country in relation to European energy security policy. There are a few proposed gas pipelines to the EU energy market that Russia is considering and, despite ongoing pressure from the European Commission and the Eastern European Union countries, Russia is planning to implement said pipelines in a timely manner.

One of the examples of this proposal is the German favored Nord Stream 2 natural gas pipeline (Talus, 2017). As with the previous Nord Stream gas pipeline, the second proposed Nord Stream would also run through the Baltic Sea, bypassing Poland and reaching Germany. The proposed pipeline would carry 55 bcm per year and therefore provide a greater capacity than its previous Nord stream pipeline (Banciu, 2016). The Nord Stream 2 would not only give Moscow the chance to increase its natural gas exports to the European Union, but it would also provide Germany with an opportunity to boost its status as the center of distribution to the Western European countries. However, most of the Eastern EU countries stand firmly against this proposed gas pipeline. Countries that opposed the Nord Stream pipeline from its initial proposal have also put forward claims that Moscow should not be permitted to expand the Nord Stream into the Nord Stream 2 and consequently double the capacity of the current gas pipeline infrastructure. Countries like Poland, Ukraine, Belarus, the Czech Republic, and other Eastern EU countries have voiced their concerns regarding the political aspects of the Nord Stream 2 gas pipeline project (Banciu, 2016). These countries also happen to be the traditional transit countries that almost all of the existing gas pipelines currently travel through. These former eastern bloc countries fear that the Nord Stream 2 would render the European Union even more dependent on Russian gas supplies. However, Russia has already started work on the Nord Stream 2 project. In accordance with the project plan, parallel twin gas pipelines are currently being constructed along the Baltic Sea route. The Russian construction company, OMK, has already started to deliver steel pipelines for the Nord Stream 2 since the middle of 2016.

Western European energy companies such as Shell, OMV, Uniper, etc. have each taken part in the building of the Nord Stream two pipeline project. Many EU countries have voiced their criticism in regards to these energy companies and have stated their desires to maintain their solidarity with the European Union's energy strategy (Fatima, 2016). The Energy Union of The European Union, which was created in 2014, created 5 main objectives that established the fundamental pillars of the Energy security policy. These pillars are 1) supply security, 2) a fully integrated internal energy market, 3) improved energy efficiency, 4) emission reduction, and 5) research and innovation. Out of these 5 pillars, the Nord Stream 2 pipeline has to meet above-mentioned criteria's. Maros Sefcovic, who is currently the vice-president of the European Commission on Energy Union, has also demonstrated the same position. Sefcovic mentioned that the Nord Stream 2 gas pipeline would significantly decrease the chances of the diversification of routes and sources towards the EU gas market (Ukraine Business Daily, 2016). As it is seen from most of the statements from the EU officials, the proposed Nord Stream 2 gas pipeline will face enormous challenges in the process of its eventual implementation. However, the European Commission hasn't yet announced that the proposed natural gas pipeline has been suspended as it did in the case of the South Stream Gas pipeline project.

The Russian gas company, Gazprom, originally created the South Stream natural gas pipeline. It would have bypassed Ukrainian territory and was planned to carry 63 bcm per year by 2017, passing under the Black sea and then through Bulgaria, Serbia, Hungary, and Slovenia (Kim, 2012). In 2014, when the pipeline was in its implementation period, the European Commission suspended the project and issued the following statement.

"New infrastructure investments promoted by dominant suppliers must adhere to all internal market and competition rules. This is why we said that the South Stream project should be suspended until full compliance with EU legislation is ensured and re-evaluated in light of the EU's energy security priorities" (EU Commission, URL, 2014).

In accordance with such a decision from the EU Commission, Bulgaria has also suspended the implementation of the 930km natural gas pipeline project (Vihma, 2015). Brussels put a lot of pressure on the countries that the proposed pipeline would have passed through. Even though Bulgaria, Serbia, Hungary, and Slovenia are highly dependent on Russian supplies, due to the fact that there have already been multiple gas transit disruptions between Russia and Ukraine, there are likely to be additional challenges for these countries in the future. Therefore, the implementation of the South Stream gas pipeline project in these countries would offer a significantly more secure and reliable pathway for Russian natural gas supplies. However, in a show of support to Ukraine from the European Union, especially after the annexation of Crimea, the EU Commission requested that these countries cease their cooperation with Moscow in regards to the implementation of the Southern Stream project until such time that Brussels officially confirms the project as approved. In response to the delay in approval of the South Stream project and subsequent suspension of the project, Moscow has responded by explaining that the South Stream gas pipeline project has been officially scrapped from its list of future planned projects (Vihma, 2015). However, Russia has criticized Bulgaria for its inability to act as a sovereign country, expressing that the government could have handled the situation in a much more proper manner. Russian president, Vladimir Putin, clearly portrays Russian sentiment in the following statement:

"If Bulgaria is unable to behave like a sovereign country, then they should at least ask the European Commission for compensation for the lost profits because only the direct income to the state budget from transit taxes would be of no less than €400 million per year. But at the end, it's Bulgaria's choice" (Zunino, URL, 2015).

President Putin's quick decision to completely remove the project from Russia's energy agenda took many observers by surprise. However, Moscow's new alternative proposed project to the South Stream took everyone by an even greater surprise when it was revealed to in fact be the Turkish Stream natural gas pipeline.

Construction of the Turkish Stream natural gas pipeline became the main agenda of Moscow after the failure of the implementation of the Southern Stream. This decision of Moscow has favored Ankara because Turkey's main goal is to become the transit route for the European Union energy supplies. The lifting of sanctions on the Islamic Republic of Iran, the potential development of huge gas reserves in Iraq, new discoveries in the Levant basin, and the construction of the TANAP gas pipeline project in collaboration with Azerbaijan are all providing viable prospects to interested players. These events have provided even greater number opportunities to Turkey's ambitions to implement its strategy in order to become a multi-regional energy hub. Therefore, Moscow's Turkish Stream proposal, which was formulated at the end of 2014, has facilitated a situation in which Turkey has become significantly more privileged in terms of becoming a vital country and trading partner for the European Union (Karagol and Kizilkaya, 2015). However, as mentioned in previous chapters, due to the ongoing conflict in Syria after the Arab Spring, as well as the shooting down of a Russian jet by a Turkish F-16, relations between the two countries have been impacted in a very negative way. After the jet crisis, Moscow immediately suspended talks on the Turkish Stream gas pipeline project and the same steps were taken from the Turkish side, both parties essentially abandoned the project overnight. However, after the initial cool down of events the Turkish President, Recep Tayyip Erdogan, expressed his "deep condolences" to the bereaved family members of pilots who had lost their lives in the tragic jet crisis. This statement subsequently stimulated the partial restoration of previous relations between the two countries to levels similar to what they had been before Turkey shot down the jet, which had violated its airspace, resulting in the breakdown of the bilateral relations. In accordance with the normalization period, Russia and Turkey have signed an intergovernmental agreement regarding the construction of the Turkish Stream gas pipeline project. This agreement was signed in Turkey during the 23rd World Energy Congress in 2016 and after the agreement Russian President Putin stated the following:

"You have now witnessed the signing of the intergovernmental agreement on the construction of the Turkish Stream. As part of this project and the broadening of our cooperation, we agreed on a mechanism by which to provide a discount on gas [for Turkey]" (Russia Today, URL, 2016).

This gas pipeline project has been designed to consist of two maritime pipelines and each pipeline could potentially deliver almost 16bcm per year to Turkish soil. This reconciliation between Moscow and Ankara as well as the rebuilding of a strategic alliance between the two countries clearly indicates that there are a number of additional energy projects that would serve the interest of both parties (Fatima, 2016). Furthermore, it is crucial to mention that in accordance with the agreement made with Russia during the 23rd World Energy Congress, Turkey will be provided with gas supplies at a discounted price. Since it is evident that the Turkish economy is highly dependent on energy resources, Moscow's discounted gas price only serves the interest of Turkey, which would only promote more economic development in the country. All this economic and geopolitical cooperation between the Turkish and Russian governments would only hurt the interests of the Western countries, particularly during this period of heightened tensions between Russia and the Western community. As Sebnem Merve says, "the Turkish Stream agreement is added to the list of developments that do not please the U.S. and as we know Washington is not a city that is just going to sit and watch" (Merve Sebnem, URL 2016). In the end, even after the strained period between Turkey and Russia, the two countries have clearly demonstrated that they will not only normalize their relations but furthermore, that Russia intends to diversify its gas transit route via Turkish soil and bypass Ukraine completely. This position not only provides an enormous opportunity to Russia to diversify its routes in reaching the EU gas market but it also provides Turkey with even more opportunity to become an energy hub for the European gas market. Both of these aspects do indeed render the EU countries vulnerable to Russia's 'energy weapon', and therefore the European Union should be extremely careful when considering the best direction to take in the building of its energy security policy. This is because Turkey is already becoming a prominent part of the Southern Gas Corridor through the construction of the TANAP natural gas pipeline, which will create a stable and secure access point to the Caspian Sea energy reserves. With Turkey implementing all of these new energy projects and the building of a strategic alliance with Russia, European energy security policy is being negatively affected. Moscow is taking serious measures to show EU countries that without Russia, the European Union cannot succeed in securing a reliable source of energy supplies. According to many analysts, if EU countries fail to build a common energy policy, Moscow will develop its current status in the EU energy market and significantly expand its political influence. On the other hand, if EU countries are successful in the diversification of their energy supplies and the implementation of the Energy Union priorities, then Moscow's energy policy will likely be weakened.

CENTRAL ASIA

Central Asia is a landlocked region situated in the heart of the Eurasian continent. It is bordered by the Caspian Sea to the west, China to the east, Russia to the north, and Iran and Afghanistan to the south. The Central Asian region has also been known as Turkestan, which means land of the Turkic peoples (Duarte, 2014). Kazakhstan, Turkmenistan, Uzbekistan, and Kyrgyzstan are considered to be Turkic countries, mainly due to the linguistic and cultural similarities. Over the millennia, many empires have conquered, ruled, and influenced this region. Civilizations such as the Persian Empire, the Mongolian Empire, the Huns, the Gokturks, and several other Turkic kingdoms and empires have juggled for control over this region for many centuries (Yunusbayev, Bayazit, ct al, 2015). In spite of its land-locked status and its isolating distance from other major civilization centers, the region was located on the historically strategic ancient Silk Road. The Silk Road that extended from China through the Middle East to the Mediterranean Sea and Europe, made the Central Asian region a strategically essential transit route for exotic goods. Since the Silk Road has been one of the key elements for the development of many empires' economic and territorial expansion throughout history, the transportation of so many goods has highlighted the strategic role of the central Asian region (Duarte, 2014).

Currently, the Central Asian region includes several states that are ex-soviet countries, such as Kazakhstan, Turkmenistan, Kyrgyzstan, Uzbekistan, and Tajikistan. Each of these countries is culturally and historically diverse and has their own specific national characteristics (Yunusbayev, Bayazit, et al, 2015). It is because of this reason that it is important to understand the major differences between each of these countries when analyzing the Central Asian region, even though most of the inhabitants of these countries are predominantly of Turkic and Islamic origin. For example, Kazakhstan, which is largest the land-locked country in the world and possesses enormous crude oil reserves, plays the driving role of the region from a trade and investment perspective. On the other hand, Turkmenistan boasts vast natural gas reserves, which make it home to the world's richest natural gas fields. Uzbekistan has a hugely advantageous strategic location because it shares borders with all of the Central Asian region's countries. It could be said that the country plays the role of human resources development. This is largely due to its huge population; currently, half of the Central Asian region's population resides in Uzbekistan. As for the last two countries, Kyrgyzstan and Tajikistan, their lack of energy resources and other geopolitical instruments has led to struggles in the implementation of the kind of regional diplomacy that the other central Asian countries have engaged in (Carrere and Grigoriou, 2011).

As a direct consequence of the fall of the Soviet Union in 1991, these countries have regained their independence and with their strategic geographic location and rich energy resources, primarily in Kazakhstan and Turkmenistan, they have become the center of attention in the global energy trade (Swanstrom, 2012). The region is in a position whereby it has access to the Caspian basin and it also shares borders with Russia, China, Iran as well as other significant regional powers. These factors have given rise to a broad range of political and diplomatic challenges in terms of their global strategy building. Therefore, Central Asian countries, from a geopolitical view, have struggled to develop and maintain independent and successful strategies since the beginning of their autonomy in the early 1990s. Nevertheless, its geographical and rich energy reserves have provided them with an important tool to rise up against those difficulties. Historically, central Asian countries have always been heavily influenced by the Tsarist Russian Empire, and later by the Soviet Union, and also by Iran (Khalid, Hashmi, and Ahmed, 2016). Since the fall of the Soviet Union, the Russian Federation has replaced the Soviet Union and up until the present time, Moscow has been using its authority to influence most of the central Asian countries in some form or another. Currently, Central Asian country's energy resources flow directly to the Russian Federation, travelling via Russian soil towards the European Union's energy market. However, over the last 10 years, Central Asian countries have adopted a strategy designed to diversify their energy markets and routes of transportation of energy reserves. Since China borders the Central Asian countries, it became a vital opportunity for building new energy infrastructure and accessing the growing Chinese energy market (Gidadhubli, 2015). Because China is currently in a position of development, its energy needs are growing quickly. As such, it is also very important for China to have access to Central Asian countries' energy resources. On the other hand, European countries consider Central Asian countries to be an important option in diversifying their own energy routes. Since the fall of the Soviet Union, EU countries have adopted a strategy of bringing central Asian countries closer on many policy-building areas (Plenta, 2011). These areas have included, energy security, economic transformation and development, and the construction of new alternative trade routes to access China, in favor of reducing Russia's transit role. Nonetheless, the main interest of the

European Union countries has been to create the energy infrastructure that would have access to the rich Central Asian energy fields. Especially when considering that Kazakhstan and Turkmenistan have some of the world's largest crude oil and natural gas reserves, together with a policy of building new modern energy infrastructure strategies and investments, Central Asian countries have successfully encouraged many countries to participate in these developments (Guliyev and Akhrarkhodjaeva, 2009). Therefore, the importance of central Asian countries over the last 10 years has increased and new global and regional players, such as China, the European Union, Turkey, India, and Iran have entered into the region in favor of receiving a slice of the cake. However, even after the fall of the Soviet Union, Moscow has still considered the region to be within its sphere of influence, in the same way, that it views the South Caucasus and Baltic states. This is particularly the case with Kazakhstan and Turkmenistan, which are Central Asian countries that border the Caspian Sea and have significant political and economic importance to the interests of Russia (Kostis, 2012). In particular, Kazakhstan currently holds existing economic and political ties with Moscow. As such, it is the only country that has experienced high levels of cooperation. This has been especially true since the creation of the Eurasian Economic Union together with Russia. Another country that has strong economic ties with Russia is Turkmenistan, an energy-rich country with huge natural gas reserves that currently exports its reserves to the Russian Federation. However, it is important to note that the Russian company, Gazprom, is in control of most of the important natural reserves in Central Asia. The Russian company has made agreements with almost all five of the above mentioned Central Asian countries (Arinc and Flik, 2010).

During the Soviet period, Moscow paid very little attention to the development of the Central Asian countries' energy infrastructure. This 'underdeveloped' status of energy infrastructure became more visible when the production of energy resources declined significantly in the initial years of the collapse of the Soviet Union (Ubiria, 2014). Therefore, most of the Central Asian countries invited international energy companies to create and develop modern energy infrastructure so as to have reliable and newly advanced production and export routes. Old energy pipelines, which were built during the Soviet Union period, served as an alarming message to these countries that progress is necessary. As such, invitations to Western energy companies have helped these countries to develop and expand their energy resources production and distribution. In recent years, discoveries of new crude oil and natural gas fields in Kazakhstan and Turkmenistan have brought more attention to the Central Asian region, especially to energy dependent countries such as China, India, countries within the European Union, and other global players that are developing a strategy to build and ensure long-term access to these vital reserves.

It is important to mention that according to many prominent geopolitical and geostrategic analysts, the Central Asian region has to be considered as one of the defining elements in building energy strategy on the Eurasian continent. Halford Mackinder, in his book, "The Geographical Pivot of History", presented an expanded geopolitical analysis and included the Central Asian region as the most important part of the Heart-land theory. The "Heart-land" region, stretching from the Volga River to the Himalayas, is considered to be the center of the world, and it is said that "who rules East Europe commands the Heartland: Who rules the Heartland commands the World-Island: Who rules the World-Island commands the World" (Blouet, pg. 322, 2004). This idea has been largely supported even until contemporary times, and current geopolitical affairs in the region demonstrate that the Central Asian region, which is located on the ancient Silk Road, is going to become a new type of

Silk Road, one that focuses on energy and other means of transportation routes. Central Asian countries that have regained their independence from the Soviet Union have started to play one of the main roles in regional cooperation. Being located in the heartland of the Eurasian continent, not only regional powers such China, India, Russia, and Turkey, but also the United States and the European Union see this territory as the main point in connecting North to South, and East to West (Blouet, 2004).

Deterioration in the relationship between Moscow and Brussels, mainly due to the war in Ukraine and the annexation of the Crimean region, has resulted in a slowing down of cooperation in many fields. The tension between the two sides has also negatively impacted energy relations and the gas issue that exists between the two sides has driven the European Union to pay more attention to the Caspian basin region. Turkmenistan, Kazakhstan, and Azerbaijan have become the main topic of the energy security discussions, and these countries are considered to be the key prospective partners in the energy diversification policy of the EU countries (Plenta, 2011). However, Moscow has been using its geopolitical tools of influence and control to protect its national interests. The European countries' strategy in accessing the Caspian energy resources and Russia's protective policy in preventing the European Union's entrance into the region bring even more challenges to South Caucasus and Central Asian countries. In many ways, these difficulties have impacted the strategies of these countries in terms of their avoidance of a potential situation in which their territories become a battlefield between two opposing forces. The main strategy of the current diversification policy of the European Union is based on the geopolitical importance of the Central Asian region and thus accepts Turkmenistan, Kazakhstan, and Azerbaijan as countries which are part of the critical transit and energy corridor (Guliyev and Akhrarkhodjaeva, 2009). This is because creating secure access to rich hydrocarbon resources in the Caspian basin via these countries would greatly assist in the securitization and stabilization of uninterrupted energy flow to the EU energy market. In recent years, the European Union has given a great deal of attention to Azerbaijan and Turkmenistan, in particular, due to their huge natural gas deposits. The proposed natural gas pipeline, known as the Trans-Caspian Gas pipeline, was once considered to be the main route for the EU countries to access Central Asian gas reserves (Kolb, 2012). In recent years, this issue has again become the main talking point of the European energy diversification discussions. When considering the fact that the TANAP and TAP projects are already under construction and that by 2018 the first phase of the construction will be completed, it makes sense that EU countries are pushing for the implementation of the Trans-Caspian pipeline as well. Currently, EU countries are promoting the proposed gas pipeline and have asked the EU Commission to resubmit the Trans-Caspian gas pipeline back on the energy agenda of the Union. The implementation of the Trans-Caspian pipeline would notably expand the east-west energy corridor, namely the Southern Gas Corridor, and would result in an energy corridor connection between Turkmenistan, Azerbaijan, Georgia, Turkey, and EU countries. However, this policy has been challenged by a few factors, and one of the main ones is the undefined legal status of the Caspian Sea (Cason, 2015). Therefore, in order to fully understand the future possibility of the implementation of an energy project in the Caspian basin, it is important to analyze the current geopolitical situation in the Caspian Sea. The unresolved status of the sea severely damages any potential chances for these countries to begin construction of the proposed energy pipelines. This is because, Moscow and Tehran have been using this issue as a grounding point to argue that such an energy pipeline could potentially harm the Caspian Sea's natural environment and ecosystems if there were to be some unforeseen incident in the pipelines (Cason, 2015).

THE CASPIAN SEA

The Caspian Sea is a landlocked body of water located in the middle of the Eurasian continent. It is also considered to be the largest inland saltwater lake in the world. The area of the Caspian Sea covers 386,000 square kilometers and borders Russia, Iran, Azerbaijan, Kazakhstan, and Turkmenistan (Bajrektarevic and Posega, 2014). The main sources of water that feed the Caspian Sea are the Volga and Ural Rivers. Throughout recorded history, the Caspian Sea has often been considered by many empires to be an extremely valuable and important body of water. This is because it not only has access to Central Asia, but also the Caucasus, Persia, and other regions that surround the sea. In the last two centuries, the Russian Empire and the Persian Empire were the only powers that ever shared the Caspian Sea. Even Marco Polo, who was a renowned Venetian traveler, came to visit the shores of the Caspian Sea in the 13th century (Ozyavas and Khan, 2012). During his expedition, he wrote the following:

"There is a fountain of oil which discharges so great a quantity as to furnish loading for many camels. The use made of it is not for the purpose of food, but as an unguent for the cure of itching in men and cattle, as well as other complaints; and it is good for burning. In neighboring country, it is used in their lamps, and people come from distant parts to procure it" (Exploring history, URL, 2016).

From this statement, we can see that even in the 13th century, Marco Polo saw that crude oil was being used by the local people in the fueling of their lamps, without realizing that in the distant future this fuel would become the

184

main element in the energy security of all the countries of the world. Thus, after 6 centuries the importance of the Caspian Sea became more visible when the world's first oil well was drilled near the city of Baku, located on the western shores of the Caspian Sea. Beginning in the late 19th century, the Nobel brothers entered the Caspian basin and started drilling for oil. It wasn't long before other oil companies followed them and together they industrialized the oil sector and laid the infrastructural foundations for energy extraction on a massive scale. This situation continued until the 1920s when the Soviet Union gained control of most of the Caspian region together with Iran (Ziyadzade, 2015).

The legal status of the Caspian Sea has become one of the most controversial topics since the fall of the Soviet Union. During the Soviet Union period, control of the Caspian Sea was distributed between Moscow and Tehran (Dar, 2013). However, when the South Caucasus and Central Asian countries regained their independence after the collapse of the Soviet Union, it resulted in the long lasting and undefined nature of the legal status of the Caspian. The only international document that exists which concerns the status of the Caspian is the Soviet-Iran Trade and Navigation Agreement that was signed in 1940 (Bajrektarevic and Posega, 2014). However, the five current littoral states of the Caspian Sea, namely Russia, Azerbaijan, Kazakhstan, Turkmenistan, and Iran, have found themselves in the middle of discussions and negotiations for a definitive agreement on the matter. The unresolved status of the Caspian Sea and the varied positions held by each littoral state regarding its demarcation process has not only obstructed the settlement of the legal status but it has also worsened the bilateral relations between some of these countries. Disagreements on the legal status of the Caspian Sea are often based on the notion of whether the body of water is a lake or a sea and applying the law based on one of these two alternatives has become the main topic of the negotiation process. Internationally accepted law of the sea and customary international law are the two decrees that are being taken into consideration in defining the status of the Caspian Sea. They respectively propose to either settle the demarcation with the coastline and equidistance measurements, as per the law of the sea, or with the 15 nautical miles from the shores of each country, as per the customary international law, if it is considered to be a lake (Bajrektarevic and Posega, 2014). All of the 5 littoral countries of the Caspian Sea have met almost every year in the hopes of achieving some form progress in resolving the unsettled situation regarding the Caspian Sea. The last Caspian Summit, which took place in Russian Federation in 2014, is one of the examples of this process. However, it is very important to mention that all the states in the Caspian Sea hold specific agendas and therefore different positions and these positions are highly connected to both economic and political interests. In a 2016 Working Group that took place in Turkmenistan, the littoral countries were still unable to reach any positive statements in terms of resolving the final status of the Caspian Sea (Bajrektarevic and Posega, 2016). Since these concerns are considered to be national interests, it becomes very visible that a circumstance in which all five of the countries are able to reach an agreement in defining the final legal status of the Caspian will be very difficult to achieve. Currently, Azerbaijan, Russia, and Kazakhstan share the same positions on the demarcation of the Caspian Sea under the law of the sea, and in 2002 the 3 countries had already defined their national sectors. Azerbaijan and Kazakhstan share Russia's view of "common waters, divided approach" because the majority of natural gas and crude oil reserve fields are generally located in the middle of the sea (Abilov and Isayev, 2015). However, Turkmenistan and Iran still haven't agreed on the status of the Caspian Sea. The main reason for this is that both countries have had massive disagreements with the Republic of Azerbaijan. Turkmenistan, Iran, and Azerbaijan have had disputes over their maritime borders and as a result, the planned implementations of major regional projects are being postponed. These proposed projects are primarily composed of energy pipelines that were to connect the east and west side of the Caspian Sea with energy infrastructure.

The Caspian Sea, which divides the European and Asian continents, is located in one of the most geopolitically critical regions in the world. Most of the global and regional powers' political, economic, and security interests coalesce in this region and this causes conflicts of many interests, especially in the implementation of mutually beneficial energy projects. When taking into consideration the long-lasting discussions and negotiations on the legal status of the Caspian sea, it can be seen that there are a significant number of negative impacts that occur due to the discovery of energy fields and the subsequent implementation of energy projects. This is mostly due to the blocking of production and the high likelihood of delays in the construction of natural gas and crude oil pipelines in the region. This situation is most visible when investigating the implementation of the Trans-Caspian natural gas pipeline project, which is intended to connect the South Caucasus with Central Asian countries, such as Azerbaijan and Turkmenistan. The implementation of the project would most importantly link Turkmenistan and Kazakhstan's energy resources to the European energy market. However, the European Union countries' dependency on the Russian energy exports as well as the important potential benefits of developing the Caspian basin and its energy reserves, puts the countries of Azerbaijan, Turkmenistan, and Kazakhstan in a most difficult situation (Emadi and Nezhad, 2011). Therefore, the legal status of the Caspian Sea would definitely provide significantly more support to these countries in the construction of energy pipeline projects intended for the transportation of their fossil fuels to the European energy markets. Proposed projects, such as the Trans-Caspian natural gas pipeline, are driven by the idea that the countries of the European Union must ensure that they decrease Russian domination over the European energy market and build a diversified network of alternatives for the ultimate security of their energy policy. However, this proposed pipeline project puts involved countries at risk of annoying the Russian Federation. In particular, Turkmenistan would receive increased pressure from Moscow and Iran due to ongoing disagreements and argue over the still unresolved status of the Caspian Sea (Shaffer, 2005). As a result, Turkmenistan is very cautiously walking a fine line as it attempts to avoid creating further confrontations between itself and Moscow.

On the other hand, Azerbaijan has been actively participating in the energy fields of the national sector of the Caspian Sea. The country has played a huge role in implementation, development, and production in the Southern Gas Corridor. As a consequence of this, Azerbaijan has served as a key player in the creation of an access corridor for EU countries to reach the Caspian hydrocarbon resources. Also, Azerbaijan is working very tightly with the Russian Federation and Iran and is continuing to cooperate within the Caspian Sea energy field. In 2016, Baku hosted the first Trilateral Summit, which created a new platform to foster healthy relations between the Russian Federation, the Islamic Republic of Iran, and Azerbaijan so that they can discuss further cooperation, especially on future projects within the Caspian Sea. During the Summit, the President of Russia, Vladimir Putin stated the following:

"Russia, Iran and Azerbaijan can discuss the implementation of new energy and transport projects in the Caspian Sea. We really have something to talk about in this format. There may be new projects in the Caspian Sea, and in a broader context, I mean transportation, energy, and the diversification of trade and economic relations" (Sputnik, URL, 2016).

This statement clearly demonstrates that Russia is willing and able to work together with the rest of the Caspian Sea states so as to create a network of energy cooperation that would benefit the bordering countries. Vladimir Putin evidently delivered a message suggesting that in the near future there are serious plans to expand Russia's priorities within the context of the renewed energy cooperation between Iran and Azerbaijan. Putin further stated, "Implementing oil and gas exploration and development projects, primarily in the Caspian region, are seen as priorities. We are ready to discuss mutually beneficial plans for the shared use of pipeline infrastructure to transport raw materials" (Sputnik, URL, 2016). There is a likely chance that Turkmenistan also will be invited to participate in the development of this cooperation. It is believed to be beneficial to have the modern and securitized infrastructure, especially with neighboring countries. However, this cooperation of Azerbaijan with the Russian Federation and the Islamic Republic of Iran does not mean that the country will decrease its energy relations with EU countries. As a matter of fact, Azerbaijan is currently involved in the construction of the TANAP gas pipeline project and is engaged in the sale of its natural gas and crude oil resources to the EU energy market via the BTC and BTE pipelines. Even with the undefined legal status of the Caspian Sea, Azerbaijan is nonetheless exploring its new potential energy fields whilst cooperating with Russia and Iran in the Caspian Sea and building its diversified energy infrastructure so as to create an energy corridor for other energy markets, particularly those in Europe. Within this policy of Azerbaijan, Turkmenistan is also considering the role and experience of Azerbaijan. Turkmenistan is showing significant interest in the diversification of the routes by which it exports its natural gas reserves, for example via the proposed Trans-Caspian pipeline that crosses the Caspian Sea.

CENTRAL ASIA IN EUROPEAN ENERGY GEOPOLITICS

After the collapse of the Soviet Union, Turkmenistan regained its independence and resumed control of its decision-making. This brought about an opportunity for Turkmenistan to consider its potential for exporting natural gas reserves in various directions (Gidadhubli, 2015). The country has a huge volume of natural gas reserves, currently holding the rank of sixth largest reserves in the world. Because of this and since its independence, Turkmenistan is seriously considering the possibility of entering new gas markets. However, the country has also considered the construction of modern crude oil and natural gas infrastructure as a means of entering the lucrative European energy market. Therefore, with its strategy of implementing a scheme to successfully development the energy sector, the country aims to strengthen its role in the global gas market. However, despite its huge natural gas reserves, the country is still in the early stages of its independence. As such, it is not yet a major energy player in the global gas market. This is also due to a lack of modern energy infrastructure. Without a diversified network of gas pipelines and the technological structures required to increase production, Turkmenistan's capability to export its natural gas reserves will remain severely limited (Onur, 2014). Over the last decade, the country has made the decision to develop its energy infrastructure by exporting gas reserves to China. The state-owned company, Turkmengaz, has control of the natural gas sector of the country and all the foreign energy companies that wish to participate and invest in the gas sector must become partners with the Turkmengaz Company. Since 2010, Turkmenistan has exported 120 bcm of natural gas to China (Arinc and Elik, 2010). The country also exports gas to Iran with a total capacity of 12bcm per year. However, Turkmenistan has considered the creation of infrastructure that has the capability of reaching the EU gas market. The proposed subsea Trans-Caspian Gas pipeline is the only alternative route for Turkmenistan to reach the European energy market. Turkmenistan has taken some steps towards the realization of this project and the largest gas fields that are located on the eastern side of the country are being developed in anticipation of this (Swanstrom, 2012). Furthermore, the country is building new energy infrastructure on the Eastern coast of the Sea, near the port city of Turkmenbashy. Turkmenistan considers this port city to be the main gateway to export its natural gas reserves to the European gas market. However, the current situation regarding regional energy geopolitics, which involves Russia, Iran, and now China, is creating obstacles for Turkmenistan to export its gas reserves via Azerbaijan's energy infrastructure in order to reach the EU energy market (Pomfret, 2012). Dependence on access to Russian soil for the transport of its natural gas reserves has made Turkmenistan very vulnerable to economic disruption. In 2016, when the President of Turkmenistan met with his German counterpart in Berlin, they discussed various energy export possibilities. As a result, the president of Turkmenistan, Kurbanguly Berdymukhamedov, stated "we in Turkmenistan are interested in delivering our energy resources to the West" (Roberts, URL, 2016). It was the first time that a Turkmen leader has announced that his country is ready to work together on legal and technical issues so as to implement the necessary infrastructure in the near future. This important step has reignited talks and negotiations about the implementation of the proposed Trans-Caspian Gas pipeline (Mustafayev, 2016).

Over the last couple of years, Azerbaijan is another country that has announced that it would provide all the necessary support for connecting the two coasts of the Caspian Sea via a gas pipeline. Since the coastal distance between the shores of Azerbaijan and Turkmenistan is not more than 300 km, it puts both sides in a situation in which they must seriously consider the implementation of the proposed gas pipeline (Kostos, 2012). There are currently a few disagreements between the two countries in terms of disputed oil and gas fields in the middle of the Caspian Sea. However, as the SOCAR's first vice president, Khashbakht Yusifzade, states "I think that we will resolve this issue in the near future" (Natural Gas World, URL, 2016). However, it is also important to mention that Azerbaijan's energy infrastructure has developed so much that Baku has created not only inland energy infrastructure but also offshore energy infrastructure, as Yusifzade further stated, "we have pipelines stretching to the middle of the Caspian Sea which are at a small distance from Turkmenistan" (Natural Gas World, URL, 2016). Given the high level of development of Azerbaijan's energy infrastructure, the implementation of an energy project could potentially be an important opportunity for Turkmenistan to consider in the near future. Essentially, Azerbaijan has offered two practical options to Turkmenistan, as Azerbaijan's minister of energy says "there are two pragmatic ways; first is the construction of a Trans-Caspian pipeline and the second option is linking the platforms in Caspian Sea through undersea pipeline" (Natural Gas World, URL, 2016). As can be interpreted, Azerbaijan has offered its two excellent opportunities to Turkmenistan in assisting in the creation of an energy corridor for Ashgabat. Also, the European Union has already indicated that Turkmenistan is one of the countries that would play an important role in the diversification of energy imports. As the European Commission Vice President, Maros Sefcovic, stated, "we agreed that we would work in the format of Turkmenistan, Turkey, Azerbaijan, and the EU and that we will invite Georgia, because it is an important transit nation from the point of view of the southern gas corridor" (Gurt, URL, 2015). According to this statement, the European Union has pushed the European Commission to work within the Energy Union of the EU countries to help in the implementation of the energy infrastructure needed to access Turkmenistan's gas reserves. This is largely due to the worsening relations with the Russian Federation relating to the annexation of Crimea from Ukraine. This clearly shows that the European Union has made important political decisions in an attempt to bring Central Asian countries closer to the EU gas market. In 2014, Turkmenistan and Turkey signed a gas supply agreement to transport energy via the TANAP pipeline project and the European Union considers this agreement to be very important in order to expand its collaboration with Central Asian countries. Therefore, as Sefcovic states, "now there is a political decision that Turkmenistan will become part of this project and will feed the European direction" (Gurt, URl, 2015). Turkmenistan, with its proven and newly discovered natural gas reserves, is becoming more attractive to EU customers. Various stakeholders, including both high-level officials as well as private energy companies, are considering Turkmen gas as the key element in expanding the diversification strategy of the European energy policy.

On the other hand, Kazakhstan is an energy-rich country located on the northeastern shores of the Caspian Sea. It remains one the key energy producer that is continuing to play an influential role in the global energy market. The country considers itself to be an energy power due to its critical geographical location, in which crude oil and natural gas reserves transit from Central Asia towards the Russian Federation and China. Currently, Kazakhstan is a member of the Eurasian Economic Union together with Russia, Belarus, Kazakhstan, Armenia, and Kyrgyzstan. Kazakhstan is also one of the few nations in the world in which a Russian minority amounts to around one-fourth of the total population. Since its independence in 1991, the country has maintained close economic and political ties with Russia (Nichol, 2012). It is one of the few post-soviet countries that have continued to engage in warm and constructive relations with Moscow. Although the country is in the same alliance as the Russian Federation, Kazakhstan has demonstrated its inclination towards a policy of integration with other regions of the world. Kazakhstan, like Turkmenistan, has considered having access to the new energy markets, including the European energy market. The country is the major economic and political power in Central Asia and has determined that the energy resources of the region are the main tools that can be utilized in order to achieve successful integration with the other regions of the world. When the Baku-Tbilisi-Ceyhan (BTE) crude oil pipeline became operational, Kazakhstan used this opportunity to export its crude oil to the world market. The BTE pipeline was the first pipeline that opened up the Caspian hydrocarbon resources to the rest of the world. It was also the first time that Kazakhstan had ever exported its crude oil bypassing the Russian Federation (Dessislava, 2011). In 2007, the European Union adopted the Strategy for Central Asian countries, and this helped to create a strong foundation for future collaboration in the energy sector. Recently in 2015, Kazakhstan and the European Union signed the 'Enhanced partnership and cooperation agreement', which called for both sides to engage in cooperation on a much deeper level in the energy field. However, it is very important to mention that once the country regained its independence, it invited most of the prominent international oil companies to assist the newly established country in exploring and producing new energy fields. Furthermore, these companies were invited to help the country to create a network of modern energy infrastructure. China to the east, has seriously considered the Kazakh energy resources and therefore, in 2004, a 2,798km long Kazakh-China Oil pipeline was constructed and it resulted in the linkage of the two countries with an energy pipeline for the first time (Khalid, Hashimi, and Ahmed, 2016).

Even though Kazakhstan had been broadening its energy markets, there was no proper pipeline that connected Kazakhstan with the EU energy market. The conflict in Ukraine and its impact created not only new policy strategies for EU countries, but it also brought new dilemmas to Astana, especially on the security level. In response to this, dialogue and plans for higher levels of cooperation between the European Union and Kazakhstan have become clearer and more positive, especially from an energy security perspective in recent years. Supplies of Caspian Sea hydrocarbon resources of Kazakhstan have become the primary topic of the discussions. The relatively new country with its huge natural gas reserves has also been invited to participate in the TANAP and TAP natural gas pipeline projects. Kazakhstan has already shown its enthusiastic interest in cooperating on trilateral agreements between Azerbaijan, Turkey, and Turkmenistan, whereby this would lead to Kazakhstan's decision to join the Trans-Caspian pipeline via Turkmenistan. Russia clearly takes any challenges to its monopoly in the EU energy market seriously, especially in the gas market. In particular, the Southern Gas Corridor project together with its TANAP and TAP projects, have already shown signs that Moscow is highly considering the challenge and will use any means necessary to prevent the construction of the Trans-Caspian gas pipeline. With its new gas pipeline project 'Turkish Stream', Moscow considers the Southern Gas Corridor to be a form of competition and therefore a threat to its own economic prosperity (Karagol and Kizilkaya, 2015).

Over the last few years, the European Union's energy strategy with Kazakhstan on gas supplies has become very complicated. This is largely due to Russia's objection and opposition to such cooperation. Furthermore, the entrance of Chinese interests into Central Asia and the implementation of newly proposed gas pipeline projects weaken the possibility of the European Union's energy diversification policy with the collaborative participation of Kazakhstan. The European Union needs to consider regional player's interests and cannot avoid the strategic and geopolitical vested interests of the countries in Central Asia. However, the Ukrainian crisis and the establishment of the Energy Union by the EU countries has resulted in intensified talks on the possibility of creating an energy corridor that has the capability of reaching both Turkmenistan and Kazakhstan's hydrocarbon resources, especially their natural gas reserves. And it is clearly visible that there are challenges for Kazakhstan, just as there are for Turkmenistan, in terms of implementing such an energy policy. As discussed above, there are important options that need to be thoroughly considered by both sides before progress can be made. One of the main options is the currently under construction Azerbaijani TANAP natural gas pipeline, which is the main part of the Southern Gas Corridor (Volkan, Yavuz, and Tokgöz, 2015). Starting from the western shores of the Caspian Sea and passing through Georgia and Turkey and finally reaching the currently being built TAP gas pipeline, it will subsequently allow access to the European gas market via Italy. Both Kazakhstan and Turkmenistan need to take important steps to fit into this proposed situation. Also, the European Union's commitment is very crucial in the decision making the process of encouraging eastern Caspian countries to join the TANAP and TAP pipelines. While the South Caucasus countries have become the energy partners of the EU countries, the European Union also needs to help Central Asian countries to become their energy partners.

CHAPTER FIVE – OTHER DEVELOPMENTS

INTRODUCTION

Energy security and diplomacy is such a complex and wide field that it brings together a multitude of geo-political and geo-economic interests from around the globe. The strategic implications of the European Union's diversification policy of its energy routes have resulted in many other political and economic developments. The complexity of the energy policy has created a rather intricate situation on the Eurasian continent. As such, the European Union's energy policy has had a major impact on most of the conflicts in the Eastern European and South Caucasus regions. In some way, within this framework, the European Union's energy expansion towards the Caspian basin gives a feeling that is similar to NATO's expansion towards the Eastern regions of Europe (Cirdei, 2014). In this sense, the strategic implications of NATO enlargement and the potential role played therein by the US in post-Cold war Europe highly relates to the energy security strategy which is followed by Europe, especially in the face of a gradual disassociation of the European Union with the Russian Federation. In particular, both conflicts over Georgia and Ukraine are closely related to Russian perceptions of NATO enlargement and the European Union's energy expansion strategy (Spassov, 2014). Looking back at the last 20 years of history, the clash of interests in Eurasia, especially in Eastern Europe between the Russian Federation and the West have increased to a higher level. The wars in Georgia in 2008 and in Ukraine in 2014 were actually the result of NATO's post-Cold war ambitions to expand their sphere of influence to include eastern countries in Europe that were previously under the dominion of Russia, pushing deep into post-Soviet space (Demir, 2015). This strategy of the Euro-Atlantic community has not only irritated Moscow, but it has also driven Russia to consider its energy strategy and to continue to place Eastern European countries in a position in which they are dependent on Russia as a source of economically essential energy. A successful energy security policy of any country is vital to ensuring political and economic stability in a country. Therefore, Russia's energy strategy is an important tool that it can use to show its intolerance towards the NATO's expansion towards the ex-Soviet countries (Grison, 2013). The high reliance of the Eastern EU states on Russian energy supplies, especially on natural gas, adds to the risks associated with the economic security of those states. A number of conflicts have occurred over the energy resources in the past and countries in the European Union are working tirelessly to secure their own energy imports. From the Eastern European countries' point of view, reaching this objective has been difficult and thus, the necessity for decreasing the reliance on Russian natural gas supplies is obvious (Kolb, 2011). However, as it was mentioned above, due to the complexity of the energy security policy, and its influence over the politics of many countries it does bring about several difficulties in strategy building (Yildiz, 2012).

When taking into consideration all of the intricacies of global energy policy building, it becomes clear that it is a very important feature of modern geopolitics that is having an effect on many developments around the globe. A thorough understanding of contemporary energy relations will be necessary in order to understand the future of the successful energy security diplomacy of the countries of the European Union. The role that is played by the major conventional overseas power, the United States, and on the other hand, the major emerging overseas power, China, show a potential clash of interests in the future, especially from a conflicting energy perspective (Jacob, 2015). These two global players have been engaged in disagreements over the geopolitical situation in the Caspian basin, the Middle East, and even in parts of Africa. China's entrance into the Central Asian region after the fall of the Soviet Union and the implementation of new energy infrastructure with Kazakhstan and Turkmenistan to secure its energy imports have already put the Euro-Atlantic community under threat (Qazi, 2015). The same strategy has been followed by the Russian Federation in Central Asia as a means of maintaining its dominant role and to prevent the European Union's access to rich energy reserves within the region. Unlike China, Russia's energy infrastructure in central Asia has existed since the Soviet period. Also, Russia's geographic position and the already existing Soviet pipeline infrastructure prevent Central Asian countries from directly reaching the European energy market. However, China doesn't have any geographic obstacles to overcome in order to access the Central Asian countries and with its heavy investment in energy infrastructure, it could potentially become the dominant energy market for Kazakhstan and Turkmenistan to sell their energy reserves to in the close future (Khalid, Hashmi and Ahmed, 2016). It is important to mention the role of Iran in the Central Asian region as well in order to understand the complexity of energy interests in the region. The Central Asian region is completely landlocked; surrounded by the Russian Federation to the north, China to the east, and Iran to the south. This situation allows no other option for the Euro-Atlantic countries to access the Central Asian region but from the western shores of the Caspian Sea, which is known as the South Caucasus (Grison, 2013).

Despite the successful energy cooperation between The European Union and the South Caucasus, particularly with regards to the existing energy corridor involving the help of Turkey, Georgia, and Azerbaijan, the European Union has not made any strong commitments to enter the Central Asian countries and create energy infrastructure as a way to secure its energy policy. This is due to European Union's divergent interests when it comes to the implementation of such a policy. Within the European Union, the major industrial economies and energy consumers and importers, such as Germany, France, and Italy, do not reach agreement on a set of common policies (Irime, 2014). This is the case because all of the countries that make up the European Union have had a long history of tending to have divergent priorities and allies. For example, Germany, which is currently the main continental power in Western European, is traditionally oriented towards the Eastern regions of Europe (Osica, 2010). Consequently, when it comes to the country's foreign policy interests, Eastern European countries, including the Russian Federation, play the most important role in terms of its priorities. France and Italy are traditionally oriented towards the Mediterranean and North African region (Dale, 1999). Before BREXIT the United Kingdom, as a part of the European Union, had traditional strategic ties with the Middle East. In addition to this, the United Kingdom has long been an important maritime power and for this reasons, it is historically oriented towards the Atlantic region and specifically to the United States (Negut and Neacsu, 2012). The examples given here only scrape the surface of the issue of finding common accord amongst EU member states. All of these divergent interests within the European Union and difficulties regarding the creation of a common policy on energy security diversification has resulted in a weaker implementation of energy infrastructure directed towards the east, specifically to the Central Asian region (Ugur, 2016). The postponed proposed energy pipeline, known as the Trans-Caspian natural gas pipeline, is an important example that demonstrates how the European Union's commitments are not strong from an energy perspective. The position of the European Union becomes even weaker with the emergence of the regional powers, such as Turkey, Iran, Israel, and Saudi Arabia. In particular, the emergence of Turkey as the key regional power on European Union's path to the Middle East and the Caspian basin creates huge concerns for the countries of the European Union. Different views of Turkey and the Euro-Atlantic countries on regional issues, and Turkey's involvement in the Middle East Conflict (civil war and ISIS in Syria, Iraq, Libya, Yemen) puts the European countries in a position in which they have no choice but to negotiate with Turkey in order to have successful access to the energy-rich Caspian basin and Middle East regions (Bilgin, 2015). Also, Turkey's lost hopes for European Union membership have enormously damaged the trust between the two sides. Specifically, on 15th of July in 2016, when there was the failed coup attempt in Turkey, none of EU countries supported Turkish government in its successful prevention of the coup (Ferguson, 2017). Furthermore, the failed migration agreement between the two sides has finally broken the cooperation between two sides (Najimdeen, 2016). As a result, in late 2016 the EU Parliament made the decision to freeze talks on Turkey's future membership in the European Union. Even though the decision wasn't ratified and it was only a recommendatory decision of the EU parliament, it had further negative impacts on relations (Bhutta, 2016). When taking into consideration the fact that Turkey is the gateway for the European Union to reach the Levant and Caspian basins, the attitude of EU countries is unclear. If the current situation continues on the same track, then the European Union will lose the opportunity to further its goals regarding the implementation of energy security strategy for its diversification. If the European Union shows the same level of reaction as it did during the Ukrainian conflict, which left Ukraine alone in the face of Russia, then regional powers, such as Turkey, Israel, and Iran will change the direction of their presently Western-oriented integration in favor of a more reliable partner (Bebler, 2017).

The nuclear deal between P5+1 countries and the Islamic Republic of Iran is an important opportunity for the European Union's policy to decrease

Russia's dominance in its energy market (Popova and Rasoulinezhad, 2016). However, due to the relatively weak level of energy infrastructure currently established in Iran as a result of the years of economic and political sanctions, there have been obstacles preventing EU countries from fully accessing Iranian natural gas fields in the short-term period. Nonetheless, a very important development occurred in late 2016 in terms of energy developments between Iran and the Euro-Atlantic community (Iran Infrastructure Report, 2016). The nuclear deal was agreed upon with the previous Obama administration. However, this agreement may not have the same foundation as it did when it was signed due to the recent US presidential election in late 2016 and the subsequent victory of Donald Trump. In light of his many controversial statements on US foreign policy, many allied countries have expressed their concern, including Iran itself. As such, the new foreign policy of the United States with the newly elected President Donald Trump has shifted many plans for developing strong relations with the Islamic Republic of Iran (Erdbrink, and Krauss, 2016). Since energy resources are the main product that Iran possesses as a means to redevelop its economy and get back on track, a new foreign policy of the United States appears as though it will render many already accepted programs in a state of postponement. However, EU countries are still willing to continue their work with Iran within the framework of the energy cooperation. However, it is more than possible that in the future Washington DC will again block the full capacity of the energy cooperation between Iran and potential trading partners (Erdbrink, and Krauss, 2016).

As it has been mentioned before, the implementation of energy projects is equal to the implementation of any kind of foreign policy and diplomacy, which is necessary in order to reach the new energy destinations. Within the European Union and Russia's perspective, their energy cooperation is visibly shadowed by too many political disagreements and divergent agendas. This situation is driving other energy-rich countries to establish strong and long-term energy partnerships with any country that is willing to purchase their energy reserves. Throughout the research, it has become abundantly evident that the Caspian basin and Levant basin countries are trying hard not to involve themselves too heavily in any of the international politics relating to the energy security policy implementation (Lewis, 2015). The main aim of the energy-rich countries in the Caspian basin and Levant basin is to establish safe and stable access to energy markets. The European Union is a great example of a reliable energy consumer to which countries of this region could sell their energy reserves to, and for the last couple of years, these countries have established Western-oriented energy infrastructure development. Central Asian, South Caucasus, and Middle Eastern countries have proposed that their mainly natural gas reserves should be directed towards the European Union's energy market (Esen, 2016). Their goal is not to replace the dominant role that Russia plays in the European energy market, but rather to contribute to European energy security in exchange for the opportunity to receive advanced Western technologies and cooperate in educational, scientific, and other fields so as to develop their economies and standards of living. In particular, countries in the Middle East have suffered from the Arab spring and the following civil wars that have damaged most of the sectors of these countries (Kadercan, 2016). In response to this, countries like Iraq, Iran, and Syria are willing to establish long lasting energy cooperation with Western nations, which have the means to provide them the necessary factors to re-develop their economies.

GAZPROM AND SOCAR – GAS DEAL

The State Oil Company of Azerbaijan Republic (SOCAR) is the leading natural gas and crude oil company of the Republic of Azerbaijan. SOCAR is currently participating in all the energy projects of the Southern Gas Corridor. Since the independence of Azerbaijan, the role-played by SOCAR in existing and proposed infrastructure has been very crucial and therefore, in order to define the future of Azerbaijan's commitments, it is important to understand and analyze the investment strategy roadmap of SOCAR. SOCAR is responsible for the production of crude oil and natural gas in the Republic of Azerbaijan and its main goal is to ensure that all the energy pipelines that are operational in the country achieve their objectives. SOCAR is ranked as one of the largest crude oil and natural gas corporations in the global energy market. The company has made large investments in the European energy market. Also, SOCAR's direct participation in building new energy infrastructure to the European energy market has turned SOCAR into one of the major energy companies in Europe (Kolb, 2011).

Despite the fact that EU countries are striving to diversify their energy routes, the implementation of this policy has not shown any significant improvement. This became very evident with the failed implementation of the proposed Nabucco natural gas pipeline. As it was mentioned earlier, Azerbaijan has never politicized its energy resources because of regional and global politics and Azerbaijan has always followed the policy of creating balance and accord with regard to the key regional and global players. Russia located on the northern borders, Turkey on the western borders, Iran on the southern borders, and Central Asian countries on the eastern borders have naturally put Azerbaijan in a situation in which it must create and facilitate a harmonious political relationship with all of the involved countries. Since its independence until the current period, Azerbaijan has followed its national interests and created regional projects that have involved most of the countries in the South Caucasus region – specifically Georgia and Turkey (Ibrahimov, 2015). However, despite the fact that Iran was under strong western sanctions, Azerbaijan did not take part in any of these sanctions. The same strategy has been followed by Russia. After the collapse of the Soviet Union, most of the ex-soviet countries created aggressive position against Russia, whereas Azerbaijan re-developed its relations with the new post-Soviet Russian Federation (Topal. 2014). Unlike other newly established former Eastern Bloc nations, the Azerbaijani government did not close any Russian high schools or universities and created new economic cooperation strategies with Russia, as well as other ex-soviet countries. By facilitating an environment of friendship and mutual support on the political stage, Azerbaijan has proven itself to be a proactive and reliable partner regionally and on a global scale (Hill and Kirisci, 2015).

After the fall of the Soviet Union, the Euro-Atlantic community demonstrated important commitments by entering the South Caucasus, exclusively to the Baku energy fields, and building important energy infrastructure directed towards the EU energy market. Successful implementation of energy policy during the 1990s resulted in the beginning of the construction of the BTC and SCP energy pipelines. However, when it comes to further development of this energy cooperation, EU countries displayed very little commitment. This situation became clearly visible when the highly anticipated Nabucco pipeline was cancelled and the Trans-Caspian pipeline lost its support from the European Union. Therefore, it can be said that weak decision-making, divergent interests, and a lack of common EU policy within the EU countries have prompted countries like Azerbaijan to discover new routes and energy policies for the welfare of its nation. This factor led to the development of a deal between Gazprom and SOCAR and this was a clear example of the result of the European Union's weak stand (Paxton and Soldatkin, 2010). The Russian company committed to increasing its purchases of natural gas from Azerbaijan to 2 bcm in early 2011 (Blank, 2011). This deal not only increased the volume of the natural gas traded between the two countries, but it will also increase the future volume of gas that is traded between the two countries to much higher than 2 bcm of natural gas. In the beginning, the subsequent result of this deal was that it extinguished EU optimism that the Republic of Azerbaijan could potentially develop as an important contribution to the source of rivals to Russian energy supplies to the European gas market.

As a matter of fact, Republic of Azerbaijan and Russian Federation share a long historical relationship and this cooperation not only covers the oil and gas related collaborations (Musayeva, 2009). Within this framework, the agreement was not a surprise to numerous policy makers but it could not be conclusively understood by European countries, many of which have already named the Republic of Azerbaijan as the one of the main countries in Caspian basin for building alternative energy routes to its gas market (Pinar, 2009). Azerbaijan does not hold the same levels of natural gas reserves as Russia, and certainly not the amount necessary in order to become an important competitor to Russia in the European energy market (Hill and Kirisci, 2015). However, Azerbaijan's contributions even in small percentages do play an important role in some of the eastern European countries and some of them are 90% dependent on Russian supplies. Therefore, Azerbaijani natural gas contribution in general numbers could be represented as low as 1%, however, countries in the eastern European Union do need diversified resources of imports. Therefore, the Azerbaijani deal with the Russian energy giant, Gazprom was a huge surprise for Eastern EU countries (Azerbaijan Oil &

Gas Report, 2015). For many policy makers, the deal made between Azerbaijan and Russia may only seem like a move that was steered by the history shared between the two countries, but this claim disregards the power that Azerbaijan could use when negotiating the prices for its natural gas exports to the countries of the European Union (Rusnak, 2011). Moreover, the Republic of Azerbaijan has reminded the Euro-Atlantic nations that it has some degree of independence in its energy policy building and that Azerbaijan is more than just an energy supplying country to the European Union's energy market.

Furthermore, when analyzing the decision of the two countries, it becomes clear that that there are several economic justifications. Economically, the decision that led Azerbaijan to agree to transport a minimum of 2 bcm of natural gas to Russian Federation has created lots of opportunities to the country. First of all, the existing energy infrastructure between the two countries, together with shared territorial boundaries, suggested that Azerbaijan could gain ideal economic benefit by supplying natural gas resources to only the Russian Federation with little investments (Blank, 2011). Instead, of investing in proposed energy infrastructures that is led by the European Union, Azerbaijan, having very little investment in existing energy infrastructure with Russia, could gain more economic benefits. Therefore, the deal with Russia has been logical for the country to create a long-term natural gas deal with Moscow to ensure higher income from its natural gas exports (Kazanstev, 2010). From the European perspective, the decision that was taken by the Republic of Azerbaijan was not the best of commercial choice in terms of the future concerns of the deal. Many policy makers claim that Baku, by agreeing to sell its natural gas resources to Gazprom even in small volumes, may slowly affect its future position in the European gas market (Emadi and Nezhad, 2011). This claim has been backed up by the existing situation in Turkmenistan and Kazakhstan in terms of selling most of their gas reserves at very low prices to Russia as the single purchaser of their gas and this was also the case during the post-Soviet period when they had no other option but to sell their natural gas resources to other markets due to a lack of diversified energy infrastructure. Therefore, many policy makers have warned Azerbaijan not to end up in the same situation as its Central Asian neighbor countries (Blank, 2011). Though, in the case of Azerbaijan, Moscow is not the sole buyer of Azerbaijani gas reserves. Since its independence, Baku has created vital energy infrastructure to transport its crude oil and natural gas reserves to additional energy markets as well and this argument can be easily demonstrated by examining the existing and operational BTC and SCP pipelines.

Also, it is clearly evident that Moscow uses its energy supplies to benefit its political influence in other countries (Kolb, 2011). Actually, in 2006 and in 2009 Moscow did cut its natural gas supplies to the European Union countries to promote and put forward its political interests (Perovic, 2009). European countries have certainly been looking to find a way forward in determining the most suitable approach to expanding their natural gas supplies so as to decrease the high reliance on Russian gas supplies.

Overall, when analyzing the decision of the Republic of Azerbaijan in 2011, it becomes evident that the gas deal with Russia carries many diplomatic and geopolitical implications. The agreement eventually gave Azerbaijan the necessary tools and power to promote its energy agenda in the European energy security policy. The gas deal between Azerbaijan and Russia has driven the European consumer representatives to take major and rapid steps towards realizing the proposed energy projects and also to pay a better price for natural gas supplies via proposed pipelines. Therefore, the gas deal in

2011 has improved the position of Azerbaijan and it has moved EU consumers' attention to the Caspian basin since it has served as an alarm for EU countries to unite their agendas and take conclusive steps in developing a common energy security policy within the European Union before it is too late (Bishku, 2012).

ARMENIA-AZERBAIJAN NAGORNO-KARABAKH CONFLICT

The Armenian-Azerbaijani Nagorno-Karabakh conflict started in the period of the collapse of the Soviet Union and this resulted in Armenian armed forces occupation of 20% of the internationally recognized territories of Azerbaijan (UN Security Council, 1993). This conflict and its aftermath left more than 1 million Azerbaijanis under IDPs and refugee status (Najafizadeh, 2015). It has now been more than 2 decades and Armenia still retains its occupation of the said 20% of the internationally recognized territories of Azerbaijan and continues to violate the territorial integrity of the Republic of Azerbaijan. Due to this conflict, Azerbaijan has created an energy infrastructure that bypasses the Armenian Republic and as a result of this policy, Armenia has been left out of any major regional projects for more than 20 years (Nichol, 2014). Therefore, all of the existing energy projects, as well as the proposed ones, pass through Georgia instead of Armenia. All of the existing and proposed pipelines start from Azerbaijan and pass through Georgia towards Turkey to ultimately reach the EU energy market. This policy of Azerbaijan has left Armenia not only out of regional and global energy projects but it has also excluded Armenia from important economic and developmental projects. Examples of projects that Armenia has missed out on include the currently being constructed transportation infrastructure project (Baku-Tbilisi-Kars (BTK) railway project, which is also known as the Iron Silk road, joint production factories, and a number of other important projects. In particular, the BTK project has created an increasing level of concern in Armenia that the country will become more isolated and will lose the opportunity to become involved in other interregional projects (Shiriyev and Davies, 2013). These worries are understandable because the energy route corridors have already been created via the same route as the transportation corridor, the further development of the Azerbaijani-Georgia energy corridor has further pushed for the transportation development. As the prime minister of Azerbaijan, Artur Rasizade states, "For the present, Baku-Tbilisi-Kars railway pipeline is being implemented and the project will be launched this year. Above-mentioned projects are strategic and serve the increase of welfare in Azerbaijan and Georgia. These are practically international projects" (APA Agency, 2016).

Due to the Nagorno-Karabakh conflict, Azerbaijan has been following the isolation policy of Armenia, which excludes it from any interregional projects (UN Security Council, 1993). This policy of Azerbaijan has created a huge concern among Euro-Atlantic countries. This concern was highlighted due to the fact that the increased cooperation of Azerbaijan with Euro-Atlantic countries, together with Georgia, increases the possibility of isolating and pushing Armenia towards Tehran and Moscow (Dogru, 2015). This concern over the last several years has pushed EU countries to show little support for the Trans-Caspian natural gas pipeline, and it is clear that EU countries could push Azerbaijan or Turkey to open their borders and invite Armenia to all the interregional projects. The weak policy-making of the European Union and the underestimation of Azerbaijani and Turkish cooperation have resulted in failed attempts of negotiations involving the orientation of Armenia into interregional projects. The Euro-Atlantic community policy makers do not fully appreciate that without the return of the internationally recognized territories of Azerbaijan to their traditional custodians, Armenia will become even further isolated and fall behind in terms of global advancement, and as a result, it will be difficult for Armenia to continue its sovereignty and it will leave Azerbaijan with no other option but to use its military power to re-establish the territorial integrity of the country. Four UN Security Council resolutions (Resolution 822 - 30 April 1993, Resolution 853 - 29 July 1993, Resolution 874 - 14 October 1993, Resolution 884 - 12 November 1993) outline the official international positions (UN Security Council, 1993). However, the situation appears to be frozen and it looks as though this will continue, as Armenia falls deeper into isolation (UN Security Council, 1993). The periodic escalations over the occupied territories of Azerbaijan bring a great deal of concern and raise threats to the security of the BTC and BTE pipelines as well as in terms of the general energy infrastructure in the South Caucasus region. The unpredictable aggression and position of Armenia, and the ongoing occupation of Azerbaijani territories not only creates instability in the region, but it also forces other global powers to try to put down any escalation in the contact line to prevent further threats to Western-oriented energy pipelines. Armenia could join the interregional energy and economic projects only with the withdrawal of its troops from the occupied Azerbaijani territories. In general, security in the South Caucasus region starts from Azerbaijan due to the strategic energy infrastructure and energy resources. Security that the country provides to NATO's European allies brings about an important level of status and respect for Azerbaijan within the Caspian basin. Any interrupted energy supplies from Azerbaijan due to any war in South Caucasus would without a doubt damage the European energy diversification policy and threaten the energy security of Europe.

The Republic of Azerbaijan understands its importance in playing an important role in the energy diversification policy of European countries. This role is very important to Azerbaijan because the energy cooperation promotes and stimulates the continuing development of its national economy. Also, cooperation with European countries promotes the important status of the country in the Caspian basin region (Pinar, 2009). In light of this, the country is developing its own strategy to play the most critical role in the energy diversification policy of the European Union. The foreign policy of Azerbaijan aims to help European countries in some way to secure their energy security. In the long-term, Azerbaijan, with its independent and diversified exports energy routes, aims to securely deliver its resources to the European energy market. In this manner, European countries will receive a number of alternative sources in order to counteract any disruption from one route in case there are any political or environmental disasters, which are more than likely in the foreseeable future (Kolb, 2011). Due to its sensitive geopolitical location, Azerbaijan is a country that considers all the security guarantees over its energy infrastructures. NATO has been involved in providing the necessary resources and consultation needed to help Azerbaijan to protect its energy infrastructures, such as transferring important defensive devices for the energy pipelines. But in the future, once the TANAP and TAP projects together with the Trans-Caspian pipelines become operational, then NATO could further help Azerbaijan to develop an air-defense system for the pipelines and train military forces to better protect the pipelines. This training and the assistance of NATO would be extremely crucial for Azerbaijan, especially within the creation of the Southern Gas Corridor (Neag and Halmaghi 2016).

GEORGIA – RUSSIA WAR IN 2008

The European countries' strategy to develop reliable and secured diversified energy supplies has been delayed due to many political and economic conflicts and the war in Georgia in 2008 is one example of this (Aras and

Akpinar, 2011). The war between Russia and Georgia was primarily a war over the territory that involved separatist groups, which claimed independence from the sovereign Georgian territory. However, the war that took place in Georgia provided Russia with an important tool to implement its interests and prevent any further Euro-Atlantic entrance into the region. Therefore, during the period of war, Russian military jets attempted to shoot and bomb energy infrastructure that was being used to transport resources to the European energy market. Since Georgia is considered to be one of the main energy routes for Azerbaijan and European countries, any bombing and destruction of energy infrastructure during the war would have resulted in significant delays (Papava and Tokmazishvili, 2010).

During the period of war, Russia succeeded in interrupting the energy transportation routes and through its military activities, Moscow effectively forced Tbilisi and other involved countries to reduce the energy transportation via Georgia to very minimal volumes. During and after the period of war, the same situation regarding energy transportation continued. Therefore, South Caucasus states, together with Euro-Atlantic countries, developed a strategy to ensure that the energy resources via pipelines within the South Caucasus region are completely expanded in higher volumes (Ozkan, 2010). The energy corridor that was built between Azerbaijan and Georgia created the main panic during the war. This is because the energy corridor is the main passage that exists from the Caspian basin and energy infrastructure could have been harshly destroyed throughout the war in 2008 (Sestanovic, 2008). When the Russian Federation initiated military activity in Georgia, Moscow also dealt a substantial blow to the European hopes of diversifying their energy resources (Papava and Tokmazishvili, 2010).

During the war in 2008, military aircrafts accidentally or intentionally tried to bomb the crude oil and natural gas pipeline infrastructure. The main strategy of Moscow was to ensure that the European countries should understand the implications of their strategy to decrease Russia's role in the European energy market. For example, Russia jets targeted some parts of the BTC crude oil pipeline to send a message to European consumers. This is one of the main pipelines and pumps more than a million barrels of crude oil every single day (Sadri and Burns, 2010). Since the BTC pipeline involved the Turkish Republic, the bombing would also affect the relations between the two states as well. The attempted bombing of the BTC pipeline could have automatically nullified all the efforts and plans in building the proposed energy pipelines. However, on the other hand, even the attempts of the Russian jets were enough for European countries to be sure that alternative energy routes, even with small volumes, are critical to their national security (Burbach, 2011).

Within the 2008 conflict, Russian jets not only targeted the energy pipelines, but they also attempted to destroy one of the main pieces of critical infrastructure that would have harmed the Georgian state significantly. Therefore, when jets hit a critical bridge on the Georgian railway route it also affected the transportation of the energy resources from the Caspian basin to European market. Georgian railway routes are also responsible for the transport of crude oil to the European market (Tsiaras, 2010). The bombing of the bridge stopped the transportation of crude oil and resulted in significant disruptions (Nichol, 2014). With the destruction of a section of the railway line, Russia succeeded in disrupting crude oil transportation to the European market. (Aras and Akpinar, 2011). Thus, in a nutshell, the war in 2008 was an important step and a signal predicting further military escalation by Russia within post-soviet countries in the future. The results of the prediction became visible with the war in Ukraine and annexation of the Crimean Peninsula. The war in Georgia was a reaction from Moscow to prevent any further Euro-Atlantic integration to the South Caucasus and Central Asian regions. However, it was not until after the war in 2008 that European countries developed the European Neighborhood Policy and Eastern Partnership Programs to further enter towards the East. It is important to mention that these geopolitical moves are transforming Eastern European countries into battlefields for these global powers.

UKRAINE – RUSSIA CRIMEAN CONFLICT IN 2014

When the conflict took place in Ukraine, the first thing those western countries worried about was the energy security of the EU countries. Since these countries have always considered that Moscow plays the energy card as a political instrument, their worries have become highly evident. This is because the countries of the European Union have faced the same difficulties during the 2006 and 2009 gas disputes between Ukraine and Russia. These two events left most of the EU countries without gas supplies during the cold winter months and as a result, this created a huge security threat towards their economies. Since energy resources are considered to be the lifeblood of a country's economy, the EU countries made the decision to decrease their dependency on Russian supplies. Since the last gas dispute in 2009, the countries of the European Union made the decision to diversify their energy routes, however, due to a weak response from various governments and no common policy within the European union countries, this has resulted in a little decrease of the Russian dependency. As such, the conflict in Ukraine has become the most problematic issue within the framework of the gas supplies. When considering that most of the EU countries that are situated in the east, close to Ukrainian border, such as Latvia, the Czech Republic,

Slovakia, etc., are completely dependent on Russian gas supplies, the conflict in Ukraine had a huge effect on their energy supplies. Even though Russia did not cut any gas flow to the European Union during the conflict in Ukraine, this has, however, increased the security measures that have been taken by the EU countries (Oguz, 2015). As a result of the conflict in Ukraine and due to economic sanctions against Russia, a decision was made in 2014 to create the Energy Union of the EU countries. As stated by the European Commission "The Council welcomed the goal of the European Council to build an Energy Union aiming at affordable, secure and sustainable energy, and supports the work underway to achieve a fully functioning and interconnected internal EU energy market, as laid out in the conclusions of the European Council of 23 October" (Federal Information & News Dispatch, URL, 2014). To reiterate, as a consequence of the conflict in Ukraine circumstances have pushed EU countries to finally create a common energy policy. Although the European Union has placed sanctions on Russia, it has not put any sanction on energy imports. Therefore, the response of the EU countries towards Russia over the annexation of the Crimean peninsula was only to implement relatively small economic sanctions, which did not have a significant effect on the Russian Federation. During the period of the conflict in 2014, the European Union and the United States held a joint press release and in their announcements, both parties made the following statement:

"The Council welcomed the trilateral gas accord of 30 October 2014 mediated over the course of the last eight months by the European Union, and acknowledged the support of the United States and other parties in this achievement. The accord is an important contribution to ensuring Ukraine's security of gas supply this winter, provides relief to the citizens of Ukraine, and ensures the reliable transit of gas to Europe. Beyond its immediate impact on the supply of gas, it demonstrates that it is possible to de-escalate the conflict, and provides a template on which further action could be built. Without prejudice to the outcome of the cases lodged with the Stockholm International Court of Arbitrage, the Council reaffirmed the importance of reaching a long-term gas agreement between Russia and Ukraine" (Federal Information & News Dispatch, URL, 2014).

As it is visible from the statements, the reaction of the Western countries to the Ukrainian conflict was highly related to their own energy security interests and was generally viewed as a reflection of their own agenda. The Euro-Atlantic countries' position in the Ukrainian conflict showed very clearly that a lack of common foreign policy, including in the energy field, brings about a significant amount of economic and political troubles for all the involved parties (Oguz, 2015). This was very evident with the BREXIT decision when the United Kingdom left the European Union and took a different path in order to fulfill its own economic and political needs. There is a possibility that the lack of a common position held by EU countries will inevitably cause more countries to leave the union and follow their own path in the future, and the main motivation for this expectation is the lack of energy security decision-making amongst European governments. In some ways, the conflict in Ukraine has woken up the EU countries and shown them that now is the time to finally create a common energy policy and develop new energy routes of infrastructure (Gümüscedil and Yasin, 2015). Rich energy countries in the Caspian basin, Levant basin, and the Middle East might be the solution for EU countries but again with such a weak response to economic and political developments, the European Union might continue its highly risky dependency on Russian gas supplies.

TURKISH – RUSSIAN COALITIONS

On 24th of November 2015 when a Turkish F-16 fighter jet shot down a Russian military aircraft near the Turkish-Syrian border, it almost led to the destruction of years of successful cooperation between Moscow and Ankara (Sutyagin, 2016). Economic and political relations between the two countries fell so badly that all of the surrounding regions and countries have subsequently suffered from this tension. Sanctions that were implemented by Russia against Turkey became a major obstacle in the development of the entire surrounding region, such as in the Caspian and the Black Sea basins. Turkey and Russia have been cooperating with each other since 1992 with the creation of Black Sea Economic Cooperation and all the surrounding countries had been receiving the advantageous benefits of cooperation under the protocols of this agreement (Tanrisever, 2012). Russia, with its energy, especially with natural gas reserves, plays an important role in the energy security of the Turkish Republic. However, Turkey has always taken care not to become overly dependent on Russian exports (Karagol, 2015). Nonetheless, after the jet crisis, the country faced huge challenges. There was a lingering threat that Russia would put sanctions on its energy exports towards Turkey. This situation has prompted Turkey to continue deeper collaboration with the energy-rich Caspian basin countries and fasten the implementation of TANAP and the Trans-Caspian natural gas pipeline projects. In a nutshell, the jet crisis has very quickly pushed Ankara to expand towards the eastern part of the country. In particular, as a result of its political tensions with the European Union over issues of mass migration and EU membership, Turkey has directed all of its attention towards the South Caucasus and Central Asian countries energy reserves. It is important to mention that these countries are Turkic nations by ethnicity and therefore this has significantly motivated the Turkish government to move its orbit towards the east. Additionally, Iran became another alternative for Turkey however, due to small volumes and price disagreements Turkey has still been very much dependent on Russia.

Things changed in the middle of 2016 when Turkey and Russia decided to leave behind the Jet crisis and start a new chapter in all the sectors of their long cooperation. Particularly since the failed coup attack on 15th of July in Turkey, Russia has become the main supporter of the Turkish government. Unlike its NATO allies, Turkey has received significant support from Moscow and this has resulted in a coalition between Turkey and Russia. The full normalization process between these two powers, from economic to political spheres, caught the Euro-Atlantic countries by surprise, and this coalition became especially evident with regard to energy cooperation. Gazprom selected Turkey as the country to bring back the implementation of the Turkish Stream project and allow Turkey to become a major transit country for its natural gas exports to the European energy market (Karagol, 2015). Since the Ukrainian conflict became the main obstacle for Gazprom to further increase the volume of its natural gas transportation, after the normalization process with Turkey, the country came to be in the center of attention in the creation of an alternative energy route to Ukraine. Therefore, the energy coalition between Turkey and Russia would not only weaken the role of Ukraine but also increase the further importance of the Turkish Republic. Turkey has faced many challenges from the side of the European Union in terms of its membership in the union, yet after the implementation of the major energy pipeline projects Turkey will use this opportunity to dictate its own interests to the European Union. In the end, if energy pipelines, such as the TANAP, Trans-Caspian, and Turkish Stream pipelines become operational, then it is obvious that Turkey, along with its NATO allies, will play significant roles in the energy games of the future. Another important project being implemented between Russia and Turkey is the 20 billion US dollar Akkuyu nuclear power plant (Telli, 2016). This nuclear power plant would be the first of its kind to be constructed on Turkish territory. Furthermore, at the beginning of 2017, both countries, together with Iran, agreed to continue the Syrian cease-fire.

In general, the Turkish-Russian coalition has significantly worried Turkey's NATO allies. Despite the fact that Russian and Turkish relations were worsened due to the jet crisis, after the coup attempt in Turkey, Russia was the first country to support the Turkish government and offer its help (Durdag, 2016). This was followed by the visit of the two presidents to each other's capitals and in the end, a decision was made to restore the previous relations but with even higher levels of economic and political cooperation. This cooperation includes mainly the implementation of the Turkish Stream natural gas pipeline and the selling of natural gas to the Turkish market with lower prices. These events clearly show that NATO's failed foreign policy, as well as the European Union and the United States' isolation policy, has encouraged Turkey to create a coalition with the Russian Federation and other regional powers in the eastern world (Içener, 2016). Turkey's change in inclination and its clear position shows that despite the political difficulties, Turkey will continue its cooperation with EU countries, especially in the energy security framework however, the Turkish foreign policy will never again be Western-oriented, despite the fact that it is still one of the NATO member countries. Since 1963, the European Union has been keeping Turkey waiting at the door for EU membership, and despite the deep period of negotiations, no success has been made. Therefore, Turkey has been asking EU countries to make the final decision in saying yes or no to its EU membership process. It is very important to mention that the European Union's security is highly dependent on Turkey. Particularly with respect to the migrant crisis and the energy diversification policy, Turkey's role in the European Union's future security will be very important. As the prime minister of Turkey Binali Yildirim states "European security starts from Turkey. If Turkey is not safe, then Europe cannot be safe" (Yeni Safak, 2017). It is for this reason that the European Union cannot say no to Turkey's membership and divert its NATO ally, and main strategic Islamic country, away from its foreign policy. However, the key question is this: once the European Union makes up its mind and decides to accept Turkey as an EU member, will Turkey be still available?

CHAPTER SIX – EVALUATION AND CONCLUSION

GENERAL EVALUATION

As it has been analyzed throughout my research, the study has attempted to investigate the geopolitical and geo-economic factors within the framework of contemporary European energy security.

The research in this study has endeavored to understand the current European energy security situation and examine Azerbaijan's possible contribution. Within this study, research has underlined the following vital evidence: 1) Azerbaijan could contribute to the European reliance on Russian gas; 2) Azerbaijan, Georgia, and Turkey's BTC and BTE pipelines have proven that the Southern Gas Corridor involves trustworthy partner countries that are ready to contribute to some of the EU countries' energy supplies; 3) With the construction of the TANAP and TAP pipelines, Azerbaijan has committed to transporting its natural gas; and 4) As a transit corridor for gas resources from Central Asian countries, Azerbaijan is seen as the most important in reaching the European energy market. The abovementioned promises have been studied and the results have been analyzed.

The results of the research have linked to the research objectives and this has contributed to the aim of the research. Starting from the historical background, the energy history of Azerbaijan has been highlighted and it was very important to have a general look at the analysis of my study. The energy history of Azerbaijan presented an overall view of the position of the country, which comes from its historical practice. The production and sale of crude oil to global markets have already been adopted as an important part of the Republic of Azerbaijan's agenda. Even during the Soviet Union period, despite the fact that Azerbaijan could not sell its crude oil to the European market, the country has always redeveloped and generated many engineers and oil professionals in its energy industry in order to innovate and introduce new technologies. However, due to weak innovative attempts of the Soviet Union, the Republic of Azerbaijan not only lost its access to the European energy market, but it has also lacked behind the modern global technological advancements in the energy production industry. Since its independence from the USSR, Azerbaijan quickly reduced all these negative impacts and chose a path of its own. Therefore, the new energy strategy of the country started with the fall of the USSR in 1991 and, with the signing of the "Contract of the Century" in 1994, Azerbaijan became one of the main European partners in the frame of the energy policy.

At the beginning of its independence, the country faced significant levels of chaos as a result of the economic crisis, political instability, and even occupation of its territories by Armenia. During this chaotic period, the only options left for the country were to use its rich energy reserves to stabilize its political and economic sectors, to prepare a balanced foreign policy, and to facilitate its access to the Western energy markets. Azerbaijan is one of the few post-Soviet republics that have been successful in the creation of a foreign policy that builds its energy infrastructure towards the European energy market. Azerbaijan joined the Production Sharing Agreements (PSA) for the exploitation of hydrocarbons resources in its national sector of the Caspian basin (Pinar, 2009). In addition to the investments in its energy infrastructure, Azerbaijan has called for and promoted Western companies to invest in Georgian energy infrastructure in order to quickly transport Caspian hydrocarbon resources to the European market. Furthermore, Azerbaijan itself invested in Georgia so as to build an oil terminal in the city of Kulevi in order to receive greater entrance to the EU oil and gas market. The exploitations of hydrocarbon resources in the Caspian basin and the resulting discovery of the Shah Deniz natural gas field has helped Azerbaijan to develop its role as a natural gas producer. The Shah Deniz natural gas field drew more western investors seeking to build direct access to the Caspian Sea via Georgia and Azerbaijan. All of these energy developments, which occurred right after the fall of the Soviet Union, concerned the Russian Federation, especially in the framework of its role in the European gas market. Despite the fact that Azerbaijan initially received many political and economic pressures, the country's successful regional balance with all the players has significantly helped Azerbaijan to supply the European energy market without any conflicts.

The construction of the Baku-Tbilisi-Ceyhan (BTC) crude oil and Baku-Tbilisi-Erzurum (BTE) natural gas energy pipelines have added an important factor to the infrastructure network and has laid down strategic foundations for the furthering of the diversification policy of energy security of the European Union. This paper argues that the realization of these pipelines between Azerbaijan, Georgia, and Turkey has essentially created the backbone of alternative energy routes. With these operational energy pipelines, Azerbaijan has proven that it is a reliable country in terms of its ability to contribute to and supply European countries with energy reserves. As these were the first two energy pipelines that bypassed Russian soil, their continuity up until the present time have proven that the diversification of European energy security through the South Caucasus region could be expanded and developed to an even greater extent. This policy has corresponded clearly to the conclusion that Azerbaijan, with its existing pipelines, does contribute to Europe's energy security and provides a reliable partnership.

An essential part of the study was to analyze the proposed energy pipelines because these future pipelines will have huge capacities of transportation and as such promise to play an important role in Azerbaijan's contribution to the European energy security. This thesis has been expanded to examine each of the proposed energy pipelines. The study has so far indicated that Azerbaijan and European countries have selected the TANAP and TAP natural gas pipelines as the main energy projects for the implementation of successful energy infrastructure. The decision of both sides to select these pipelines has demonstrated that strong commitments and clear desires will bring about the successful realization of the proposed projects in the near future. It is clearly visible that the determination of Azerbaijan has been highly considered by the European countries, and throughout the construction of the TANAP and TAP proposed pipelines, Azerbaijan will make a greater contribution to the energy security of Europe. Also, it is very important to mention that these projects, which were agreed upon between Azerbaijan and the European Union, are the most valuable pipelines in terms of the diversification policy of European energy security. Throughout the research, it has become evident that proposed projects like Nabucco have been cancelled due to the fact that the European Union has shown very little interest in its success and weak commitments towards its realization. Therefore, it is necessary to ensure strong commitments of Azerbaijan to Turkey and even stronger commitments to build the TANAP natural gas pipeline project. The economic and political support for this pipeline evidently implies that the construction works will be completed and operational by 2018 (Sevim, 2013).

Given the fact that all of the planned projects (such as BTC and BTE) have been constructed, it is obvious that the TANAP and TAP proposed energy infrastructure would be realized and finalized ahead of their planned schedule. Situated in a strategic location in Eurasia and having a proven 2.6

trillion cubic meters of natural gas reserves, Azerbaijan has been successful in attracting European consumers and the country has officially stated that it is ready to supply the European market with its natural gas reserves in higher volumes through the currently contracted pipelines once they are operational (Khan, 2016). In addition to this, the European Union has expressed its readiness to give all the political, economic, and legal support necessary to implement and secure Europe's access to the gas reserves of Azerbaijan. Since obtaining its independence, the country has signed several memoranda of understanding with the European Union in the framework of energy cooperation. Azerbaijan and the European Union signed a joint declaration to develop the Southern Gas Corridor and to realize the proposed projects within this energy corridor. In February of 2017, the president of the Republic of Azerbaijan paid an official visit to the European Union capital, Brussels. During his visit, president Aliyev made a start on the negotiations to discuss the new Strategic Partnership agreement with the European Union. He stated during his meeting with the president of the European Council, Donald Tusk, that "I'm pleased that we will start the negotiations on the new agreement with the EU tomorrow" (Today News Agency, URL, 2017). He continued by indicating the unchanged position of Azerbaijan in cooperating with the European Union on the energy security framework. As he stated "The Southern Gas Corridor project is a project of energy security and energy diversification. And when I say diversification, I mean not only routes, but also sources. Europe is our major investor and main trading partner. We supply oil to some European countries and we hope that we will soon provide gas as well" (President.az, 2017). As it is seen from the statements of the president Ilham Aliyev, Azerbaijan is very well committed to the bringing the role of Azerbaijan to the forefront of negotiations and development from the European energy security perspective. Therefore, Azerbaijan is working hard with the European Union to complete the implementation of the Southern Gas Corridor. The official representatives of the European Union have indicated the same position. In 2017 president of the European Council, Donald Tusk stated the following:

"Azerbaijan is an important partner for the European Union, whose independence, sovereignty and territorial integrity we support. We want to build on our reliable and strategic partnership in the energy field. Azerbaijan is important for Europe's energy security and diversification of supplies. We have a shared commitment to finalize the Southern Gas Corridor; in fact, it is a key priority for both sides" (EU Press Release, URL, 2017).

It is clearly indicated by the statements of the officials of both sides that Azerbaijan and the European Union are working hard to finalize the works on the proposed energy infrastructure stipulated under the proposal of the Southern Gas Corridor. Thus, one can conclude that the gas strategy of Azerbaijan under the Southern Gas Corridor is being successfully implemented. Azerbaijan's transportation of natural gas and the country's position in the Eurasian region have always been a good indicator that the country is eager to sell its resources to Europe in as much volume of natural gas as needed. Throughout the research, it has become obvious that Azerbaijan has no possibility of competing with the volume of the Russian exports in the European gas market but it can definitely contribute to the implementation of the proposed TANAP and TAP pipelines.

Azerbaijan's geographic location and its existing transportation infrastructure make it a major transit country in the Southern Gas Corridor. This status of the country provides an important opportunity for the transportation of energy reserves from Central Asia to mainly European markets. Based on the research, the main pipelines from the South Caucasus region, namely the Baku-Tbilisi-Ceyhan crude oil pipeline and the Baku-Tbilisi-Erzurum (SCP) natural gas pipeline, are considered to be important elements of the backbone of European energy security because they serve to provide alternative routes and because they increase the levels of cooperation with energy-producing countries from the Caspian basin region. This cooperation has mainly been concentrated on the supply of the natural gas to European markets from the Azerbaijani section of the Caspian Sea. But this experience has opened up the chapters for the Central Asian countries to transport their own energy reserves via Azerbaijan. The possibility of supplying Central Asian gas reserves via the proposed Trans-Caspian pipeline has become one of the factors that could contribute to the long-term stability of the European gas market. The proposed Trans-Caspian project for the future supply of natural gas is under extensive review. However, the present study has made it thoroughly clear that Russia's position of gas supremacy over the European energy market has caused the EU countries a great deal of concern and has led them to search for alternative routes, thus placing Azerbaijan into one of the centers of Europe's energy policy. In addition to this, Azerbaijan's access to the Caspian Sea and its role as a gateway between Europe and Central Asia has made it a considerably more strategic partner for the European Union.

The abundant gas reserves in central Asia, particularly in Turkmenistan, have drawn the attention of Europe. Their interest has prompted them to expand Azerbaijan's role as a transit corridor for the transport of natural gas from Turkmenistan to the European market. As noted earlier in this study, the Trans-Caspian pipeline, which connects the two shores of the Caspian Sea between Turkmenistan and Azerbaijan, performs a principal role in the supply of additional amounts of natural gas to the EU energy market. The analysis and evaluation of all of the geopolitical and geo-economic aspects of the energy diplomacy of the European Union reveal that Azerbaijan, largely due to its energy reserves in the Caspian basin and its role as a transit hub for Central Asian energy reserves, can contribute significantly to the diversification of European energy security. Even though this contribution would not generate a very high level of competition for the Russian gas supplies, it would nonetheless give European consumers the opportunity to balance the gas prices in the energy market with other energy players. This would consequently provide European countries with a greater level of leverage during negotiations with its energy suppliers. As this research has demonstrated, many scholars agree that under the Southern Gas Corridor, cooperation among Azerbaijan, Georgia, Turkey, and Central Asian countries will increase and all of the countries that are participating in this strategic energy corridor will profit from the project.

REGIONAL PERSPECTIVE

As has been discussed throughout the present research, with the existing and proposed infrastructure, Azerbaijan's role in achieving the diversification of European energy security has been clearly determined. This being the case, however, Azerbaijan's ongoing cooperation with the regional countries and the building of new strategic relations has brought about many challenges to the country's foreign policy. Furthermore, Azerbaijan's relations with Moscow have played an important role in its foreign policy. It is very obvious that Russia never has and never will accept the entrance of the non-regional countries, especially the European Union and the United Sates, into the South Caucasus and Caspian basin regions. Azerbaijan, being the largest and the richest country in South Caucasus, has been facing many challenges in striving to achieve a balance between the various regional and non-regional powers, and the energy reserves of the country are playing a key role in maintaining such a policy. The role that Azerbaijan is currently playing in the region has great importance to the implementation of a number of regional projects. Azerbaijan's political and economic alliance with Turkey has provided an important and advantageous tool to the country's control over regional balance. Azerbaijan's alliance with Georgia and Turkey has not only isolated Armenia from the strategic and important regional projects, but it has also discharged any influences that the other regional countries may have on its foreign policy. Azerbaijan has chosen to cooperate with Georgia and Turkey in the building of an energy infrastructure network that would enable access to the European energy markets. However, this has disturbed Russian interests in the South Caucasus region because all of the pipelines that bypass Russia decrease its level of influence in the region. This frustration was clearly indicated in 2008 when Russia and Georgia were involved in an armed conflict. During the ensuing chaos, Russia bombed some of Georgia's energy infrastructure. This action caused great concern to countries of the South Caucasus, particularly Azerbaijan and Georgia, so much so that both countries have rapidly accelerated their integration towards the Western world in the period since. Within this framework, Azerbaijan and Georgia have tightened their relations to become even closer together but unlike Georgia, Azerbaijan has maintained a balanced regional policy with all the regional and non-regional players. However, it appears that Turkey's involvement in this cooperation has created an even more pro-European atmosphere in the region during the period of 2008. Of course, Turkey, as a member of the North Atlantic Treaty Organization (NATO) and a candidate country for the European Union, has contributed significantly to the South Caucasus countries' integration towards the European Union. However, the relations between Turkey and the European Union have worsened in recent times due to a weak support of the Turkish government during the period of the failed coup attempt in 2016 as well as the failed migration agreement. Both of these factors have increased the levels of tension between the two sides. Despite the tension between Russia and the Euro-Atlantic community over the annexation of Crimea, after the jet crisis, Turkey and Russia changed their policies towards each other and Turkey allied itself with Russia to promote cooperation in all areas. The Turkish-Russian coalition has been involved in the development of many fields. In particular, the energy transportation framework has begun to worry the governments of the European Union. Turkey and Russia have already set their targets in terms of the implementation of the proposed Turkish Stream natural gas pipeline. However, despite the fact that the current EU and Turkish relations are experiencing their worst period, energy cooperation has still continued nonetheless and both sides are working hard to complete the TANAP and TAP projects ahead of their planned schedule. The same direction of energy pipeline construction policy is followed by the Russian Federation.

As the cooperation between Azerbaijan, Georgia, and Turkey intensifies, the energy corridor will strengthen under the Southern Gas Corridor commitment. This EU-backed corridor has highly concentrated on all the mentioned countries and has supported the proposed TANAP and TAP projects through this corridor to diversify its energy supplies. General agreements and earlier experiences from the previous pipelines have made it easier to bring the Southern Gas Corridor countries together as a team in order to construct the proposed projects. In addition, Azerbaijan, Georgia and Turkey have united their economic ambitions and political interests less than one roof to effectively implement their strategic goals. What is useful in this partnership is that the common policy of Azerbaijan and Georgia makes it easier to achieve Europe's entrance into the South Caucasus region.

These examinations and analysis show the following, 1) that geo-politics in the region is highly concentrated on the energy pipelines; 2) that without the common policy of the Southern Gas Corridor countries, proposed pipelines, such as TANAP and TAP could not be implemented; 3) that Azerbaijan, as a producer and as a transit country, plays a significant role in supplying Europe with alternative energy reserves; and 4) that by promoting the political balance between regional and non-regional actors, the energy security for the European Union could be realized with the participation of the regional countries.

CONCLUSION

Throughout this study, there has been a concentration on the role of Azerbaijan in the diplomacy and geopolitics of the European energy security. The collection of all the data and the subsequent examination of regional and global approaches of different countries, as well as an analysis of many other developments in the different regions, comprised the study of Azerbaijan's contribution in supplying alternative routes towards European energy markets. This study revealed that within the South Caucasus and Caspian regions, under the leadership of Azerbaijan, Europe's diversified energy policy could be effectively secured and implemented.

This research has also examined the existing pipeline infrastructure (BTC and BTE) in order to determine Azerbaijan's role in such an energy policy and it has analyzed the ways in which previous pipelines have served as the backbone for the further development of energy infrastructure with Azerbaijani, Georgian, and Turkish participation. In addition, the proposed TANAP and TAP natural gas pipelines have been examined so as to understand how Azerbaijan could contribute further to the European Union's energy security. With the strong commitments of Azerbaijan's leadership in the region under the guidance of president Ilham Aliyev, it is easily possible to determine that the TANAP and TAP proposed pipeline projects will be realized, and it is apparent that this proposed infrastructure will be constructed in the near future as a way to diversify such energy supplies towards the European energy market. Moreover, Azerbaijan's important role as a transit hub for Turkmen gas to be transported via the Trans-Caspian pipeline to the European energy market has been confirmed. However, the unsettled status of the Caspian Sea area greatly reduces the chance of accessing central Asian gas reserves in very near future. Furthermore, Iran and Russia's position on blocking the Trans-Caspian pipeline projects has caused further delays in the realization of this infrastructure. Nevertheless, the war in Georgia in 2008 and Ukraine in 2014, together with other key developments, indicate that the European Union's strong commitment and Turkey's involvement in negotiations with Turkmenistan have significantly increased the probability that the Trans-Caspian pipeline will be implemented. Azerbaijan has officially announced that the country is very much open to the idea of playing a role in the implementation of the Trans-Caspian natural gas pipeline and the country welcomes any initiative for Turkmenistan and Kazakhstan to join the Southern Gas Corridor to assist in the transportation of their energy reserves.

In contemporary times, there have been a number of political and economic clashes taking place around the world. These include, but are not limited to, the ongoing civil wars in Iraq and Syria, tensions between Russia and the Euro-Atlantic countries, NATO's enlargement policy towards the eastern regions of Europe, unstable relations of the Euro-Atlantic countries with the Islamic Republic of Iran, and the United Kingdom's 'BREXIT' from the European Union. This instability will directly or indirectly cause many circumstances that will have an effect on the Southern Gas Corridor. If the implementations of TANAP and TAP's construction works are not regulated together with geo-politics and other developments, it could cause extensive delays in the development of such projects, thus affecting European energy security. Therefore, Azerbaijan's very active talks regarding the acceleration of the construction works of the new pipelines, namely the Trans-Anatolian and Trans-Adriatic projects, has led officials to announce that the construction works will have greater support and will be completed ahead of their planned schedule. Also, Azerbaijan and Turkey's decisive role in realizing the TANAP project have raised hopes for the diversification of

European energy supplies in the near future. It is expected that the TANAP project will serve as a role model for other proposed projects and that it will provide the impetus that is necessary for the realization of other projects that Europe has been hoping for. As previously stated, these developments would potentially affect the politics of Eurasian energy, and they would increase Azerbaijan's role in Europe's energy security.

As this research has demonstrated, energy politics will continue to play an important role in the diversification policy of European energy security, which involves the establishment of alternative routes. The development of such alternative routes alongside Russian borders greatly increases the levels of political pressure in the region. As Azerbaijan is situated between Russia and Iran, an increase in the targets against it will bring much more challenges to its participation in such an energy policy. For this reason, the study has determined that with cooperation between Azerbaijan, Georgia, and Turkey, such an energy policy will be realized and these countries will help to develop a healthy balance between regional and non-regional players. Consequently, by delivering a number of important arguments from the perspectives of the regional players of the South Caucasus and the Caspian Sea basin, this paper proposes that the European Union's diversified energy policy from the direction of the Caspian basin will be successfully implemented with the participation of The Republic of Azerbaijani.

BIBLIOGRAPHY

Academic Articles and Books

1) Aalto Pami And Dicle, K, Temel. "European Energy Security: Natural Gas and the Integration Process". JCMS 2014 Volume 52. Number 4. pp. 758–774

2) Abilov, Shamkhal, and Ismayil Isayev. "Azerbaijan-Russian Relations: Azerbaijan's pursuit of successful balanced foreign policy/Azerbaycan-Rusya Iliskileri: Azerbaycanin basarili denge politikasi arayisi" *Orta Asya ve Kafkasya Arastirmalari*, vol. 9, no. 19, 2015, pp. 113-143

3) Aktar, Cengiz. "The Positive Agenda and Beyond: A New Beginning for the EU-Turkey Relations?" *Insight Turkey*, vol. 14, no. 3, 2012, pp. 35-43,

4) Alipour, Ali. "Turkey's Stance Towards the Main Developments in the South Caucasus." *Insight Turkey*, vol. 17, no. 1, 2015, pp. 191-211

5) Aras, B., and Akpinar, P. The Relations Between Turkey and the Caucasus. *Perceptions, 16*(3), 2011. pp. 53-68.

6) Arinc, I., and Elik, S. "Turkmenistan and Azerbaijan in European Gas Supply Security". *Insight Turkey, 12*(3), 2010. pp. 169-190.

7) Arinc, Ibrahim,S., and Levent Özgül. "Exportation of EastMed Gas Resources: Is it Possible without Turkey?" *Insight Turkey*, vol. 17, no. 2, 2015, pp. 117-140

8) Ayman, S. G. "Turkey And Iran: Between Friendly Competition And Fierce Rivalry." *Arab Studies Quarterly*, vol. 36, no. 1, 2014, pp. 6-26,

9) Baev, P. K; Øverland, I. The south stream versus Nabucco pipeline race: Geopolitical and Economic (ir)rationales and Political Stakes in Mega-projects. *International Affairs, 86*(5), 2010 pp. 1075-1090.

10) Bahgat, Gawdat. "Global Energy Outlook: Opportunities and Challenges." *Perceptions*, vol. 19, no. 3, 2014, pp. 5-14

11) Bahgat, Gawdat. "The Iranian Nuclear Crisis: An Assessment." *Parameters*, vol. 43, no. 2, 2013, pp. 67-76

12) Bahgat, Gawdat. North Africa and Europe: Energy Partnership. *Opec Review Journal.* 3 December, 30.2: 2009, pp105-123.

13) Bajrektarevic, Anis H., and Petra Posega. "The Caspian Basin: Geopolitical Dilemmas And Geoeconomic Opportunities." *Geopolitics, History and International Relations*, vol. 8, no. 1, 2016, pp. 237-264

14) Bajrektarevic, Anis H., and Petra Posega. "The Caspian Basin: Territorial and Status- Related Disputes, Energy Transit Corridors, and their Implications for EU Energy Security." *Seton Hall Journal of Diplomacy and International Relations*, vol. 16, no. 1, 2014, pp. 85-107

15) Banciu, Roxana I. "NORD STREAM 2 and its Soft Power - an Unfolding Playground for European Union." *Romanian Journal of European Affairs*, vol. 16, no. 2, 2016, pp. 83-91

16) Banciu, Roxana I. "South Stream Project and the Ukrainian Factor." *Romanian Journal of European Affairs*, vol. 15, no. 1, 2015, pp. 55-69

17) Barysch, Katinka. "Should the Nabucco Pipeline Project Be Shelved?" Centre for European Reform - Policy Brief, 2010, p. 1.

18) Bebler, Anton. "On the Geopolitical Aspects of the Conflict Over Crimea." *IUP Journal of International Relations*, vol. 11, no. 1, 2017, pp. 7-26

19) Belyayev, Alexey V. *Changes on the European Gas Market: Implications for Gazprom*, University of Washington, Ann Arbor, 2013,

20) Belyi, Andrei, Sophie Nappert, and Vitaliy Pogoretskyy. "Modernising the Energy Charter Process? the Energy Charter Conference Road Map and the Russian Draft Convention on Energy Security." *Journal of Energy & Natural Resources Law*, vol. 29, no. 3, 2011, pp. 383-399

21) Berger, Michael. "Motives for the Foundation of the ECSC." *The Poznan University of Economics Review*, vol. 13, no. 3, 2013, pp. 55-90

22) Bhat, Mukhtar A. "Iran-China Relations: A Challenge for U.S. Hegemony 1." *Quarterly Journal of Chinese Studies*, vol. 3, no. 2, 2014, pp. 113-125

23) Bhutta, Tahir. "The European Neighbourhood Policy And The Prospects For Turkey's Inclusion In The Eu." *Journal of European Studies*, vol. 32, no. 2, 2016

24) Bilgin, M. "Energy Security and Global Security". *Hampton Roads International Security Quarterly*. 2010, 5153

25) Bilgin, Mert. "Turkey's Energy Strategy: Synchronizing Geopolitics and Foreign Policy with Energy Security." *Insight Turkey*, vol. 17, no. 2, 2015, pp. 67-81

26) Bishku, M.B. "Azerbaijan Since Independence". *Middle Eastern Journal* 66(2), 2012, pp. 369-370

27) Blank, S. (2011). Russian energy and Russian security. *The Whitehead Journal of Diplomacy and International Relations, 12*(1), pp. 173-188.

28) Blouet, Brian W. "The Imperial Vision of Halford Mackinder." *The Geographical Journal*, vol. 170, 2004, pp. 322-329

29) Bradshaw, Michael J. "Global Energy Dilemmas: A Geographical Perspective." *The Geographical Journal*, vol. 176, 2010, pp. 275-290

30) British Petroleum. "BP in Azerbaijan Sustainability Report". British Petroleum Report. 2009

31) Burbach, D. T. A little war that shook the world: Georgia, Russia, and the future of the west. *Naval War College Review, 64*(1), 2011 pp. 155-157.

32) Calanter, Paul. "Policies For The Development Of The Energy Sector At The Level Of The European Union And Romania." *Calitatea*, vol. 17, 2016, pp. 275-278

33) Carrere, Cé, and Christopher Grigoriou. *Landlockedness, Infrastructure and Trade: New Estimates for Central Asian Countries.* Federal Reserve Bank of St Louis, St. Louis, 2011

34) Carroll, T. The Cutting Edge of Accumulation: Neoliberal Risk Mitigation, the Baku-Tbilisi-Ceyhan Pipeline and its Impact. *Antipode, 44*(2), 2012 pp. 281-302.

35) Cason Bryce. A. "The Trans-Caspian pipeline: implications for the five littoral states". *J World Energy Law Bus* 2015, pp. 474-484

36) Christoffersen, Gaye. "The Role of China in Global Energy Governance." *China Perspectives*, no. 2, 2016, pp. 15-24

37) Cîrdei, Ionut A. "National Security And Collective Security From The Perspective Of Ensuring Energy Security." *Land Forces Academy Review*, vol. 19, no. 2, 2014, pp. 145-151

38) Codoban, Alin. "The European Union's Quest For Energy Policy: A Geo-Economic Approach." *Romanian Journal of European Affairs*, vol. 11, no. 3, 2011, pp. 38-59.

39) Comsa, Mircea Leonard. "Energy Policy And Geopolitical Considerations In The South-East Of Europe." *Journal Of Criminal Investigations* 8.1 (2015): 14-30.

40) Cornell, Svante E. "The Caucasus in Limbo." *Current History*, vol. 110, no. 738, 2011, pp. 283-289

41) Costel, S. "Future Developments on Oil and Gas Transport in the Black Sea Region". *Universitatii Maritime Constanta. Analele, 15*, pp. 2011, 107-110.

42) Dagdemir, Elif U. "Trade-Related Aspects Of The European Neighbourhood Policy And The Prospective Role Of Turkey In Energy Trade." *Economic and Business Review for Central and South - Eastern Europe*, vol. 10, no. 2, 2008, pp. 153-171.

43) Dagoumas, Athanasios, and Floros Flouros. "Energy Policy Formulation in Israel Following its Recent Gas Discoveries." *International Journal of Energy Economics and Policy*, vol. 7, no. 1, 2017

44) Dale, Reginald. "The Search for a Common Foreign Policy." *Europe*, no. 388, 1999, pp. 25-29

45) Darnirchi, EltefatVazifeh, Mahabbat M. Ashir, and AliasgarAliyov. "Success In Investment And Investing In Azerbaijan Republic." *International Journal of Management Research and Reviews*, vol. 3, no. 8, 2013, pp. 3289-3299.

46) Dannreuther, Roland. "Energy Security and Shifting Modes of Governance." *International Politics*, vol. 52, no. 4, 2015, pp. 466-483

47) Dar, F. Caspian Sea: A Case Study of Economic Conflict. *Current Politics and Economics of Russia, Eastern and Central Europe*, 2013, vol. 28, no. 2. pp. 115-130

48) Dargay, Joyce M., and Dermot Gately. "World Oil Demand's Shift Toward Faster Growing and Less Price-Responsive Products and Regions." *Energy Policy*, vol. 38, no. 10, 2010, pp. 6261

49) Davenport, Kelsey. "Iran Nuclear Deal Implemented." *Arms Control Today*, vol. 46, no. 2, 2016, pp. 48-49

50) Davenport, Kelsey. "Sanctions Relief Timing Key to Iran Deal." *Arms Control Today*, vol. 45, no. 2, 2015, pp. 20-21

51) Demir, Sertif. "Is end of a dream reassessing the NATO enlargement policy toward the Black sea and Caucasus regions *." *Karadeniz Arastirmalari*, no. 46, 2015, pp. 1-22

52) Dilbazi, Eltay. "Energy Security and Alternative Sources in the Caspian Sea Region." *International Issues & Slovak Foreign Policy Affairs*, vol. 19, no. 1, 2010, pp. 79-94

53) Dogru, Ahmet. "Nationalism and Democratization Process in Armenia: Impacts of the Nagorno-Karabakh Issue/Ermenistan'Da Milliyetcilik Ve Demokratiklesme Süreci: Daglik Karabag Meselesinin Etkisi." *Gazi Akademik Bakis Dergisi*, vol. 8, no. 16, 2015, pp. 207-236

54) Doukas, Haris, et al. "EU-GCC Cooperation for Natural Gas: Prospects and Challenges." *International Journal of Energy Sector Management*, vol. 7, no. 2, 2013, pp. 194-222

55) Draghicescu, M. Environment Policy in the European Union. case study: Romania. *Economics, Management and Financial Markets, 6*(1), 2011. pp. 620-628.

56) Dreyer, Iana. "International Energy Security Challenges for Europe in the Coming Years." *International Issues & Slovak Foreign Policy Affairs*, vol. 22, no. 3, 2013, pp. 3-19,123

57) Duarte, Paulo. "CENTRAL ASIA: THE BENDS OF HISTORY AND GEOGRAPHY." *Revista de Relaciones Internacionales, Estrategia y Seguridad*, vol. 9, no. 1, 2014, pp. 21-35

58) Dumitru, Raluca-Ana-Maria, and Marin Dumitru. *Energy Security In The Context Of European Integration And Sustainable Development*, vol. 1, "Carol I" National Defence University, Bucharest, 2014.

59) Durdag, Celil, et al. "The Effect of Political Crisis between Countries on International Trade and International Logistics: A Qualitative Study on Turkey-Russia Relations." *Journal of Economic and Social Thought*, vol. 3, no. 4, 2016, pp. 497-508

60) Dusciac, Dorin, Nicu Popescu, and Victor Parlicov. *Eu - Russia and the Energy Dimension of the Eastern PARTNERSHIP*, vol. 8, Alexandru Ioan Cuza University of Iasi, Centre for European Studies, Iasi, 2016.

61) Efe, H. Turkey's role as an energy corridor and its impact on stability in the south Caucasus. *Orta Asya Ve Kafkasya ArastIrmalarI/Journal of Central Asian & Caucasian Studies, 6*(12), 2011 pp. 118-147.

62) Egan, Matt. "After 40-Year Ban, U.S. Starts Exporting Crude Oil." *CNN Wire Service*, Jan 28, 2016

63) Emadi, S.E; Nezhad, H. Energy Market for Caspian Sea Oil and Its Supply. International Black Sea University Scientific Journal (5.2), 2011. pp. 21-34

64) *Emerging Europe Oil and Gas Insight - February 2013*, Business Monitor International, London, 2013.

65) Environmental Policy and Law Journal. "European "Energy Union" Becomes a Reality", 04, 2015, vol. 45, no. 2. pp. 85-87

66) Erdbrink, Thomas, and Clifford Krauss. "Iran Races to Clinch Oil Deals before Donald Trump Takes Office. "*ProQuest Central*, Dec 08 2016,

67) Erdemir, H. The Policies Around the BTC Pipeline. *Alternatives: Turkish Journal of International Relations, 8*(4), 2009 pp. 20-44.

68) Erkan, Anil Ç. "Enerji Ithalatinda Tedarikçilerin Çesitlendirilmesi: Rus Gazina Alternatif Azerbaycan Gazi." *Karadeniz Arastirmalari*, no. 50, 2016, pp. 17-44,

69) Esen, Ömer. "Security of the Energy Supply in Turkey: Prospects, Challenges and Opportunities." *International Journal of Energy Economics and Policy*, vol. 6, no. 2, 2016

70) Fackrell, B.E. "Current Developments in Regional Energy Security and Turkey". Insight Turkey, 2013, vol. 15, no. 1. pp. 63-72

71) Fatima, Agha S. "PRESENT-DAY RUSSIA: CHALLENGE FOR EUROPEAN UNITY?" *Journal of European Studies*, vol. 32, no. 2, 2016

72) Feller, Gordon. "Turkey's New Government Looking again to the Caucasus and Central Asia." *The Washington Report on Middle East Affairs*, vol. XVI, no. 4, 1997, pp. 26,

73) Ferguson, Yale H. "Competing Identities and Turkey's Future." *European Review*, vol. 25, no. 1, 2017, pp. 81-95

74) Fernandez, R. Nabucco and the Russian Gas Strategy vis-à-vis Europe. Post - Communist Economies, 23(1), 2011 p. 69.

75) Fiedorczuk, Monika, and Jerzy Grabowiecki. "Economic and Financial Crises and Changes in Corporate Governance in Russia (Part 2)." *Ekonomia i Prawo*, vol. 15, no. 3, 2016, pp. 307-316,

76) Finon, D. "The EU Foreign Gas Policy of Transit Corridors: Autopsy of the stillborn Nabucco project". *OPEC Energy Review, 35*(1), 2011 pp. 47-69.

77) Floridan, Goran. "Improvements In The Development Of A Common European Energy Policy In The Years 2007-2011." *Journal of Comparative Politics*, vol. 6, no. 1, 2013, pp. 43-60

78) Frances, G.E. (2011). Market or Geopolitics? The Europeanization of EU's Energy Corridors. *International Journal of Energy Sector Management,* 5(1), pp. 39-59

79) Georgescu, Constantin. "Energy Terrorism Security of Energy in Romania and European Union NATO's Role in Security of Energy Endogenous and Exogenous Influencing Factors." *Knowledge Horizons. Economics*, vol. 7, no. 2, 2015, pp. 172-175

80) Gheorghe, Corina. *The EU Relations with the Middle East and North Africa*, vol. 1, "Carol I" National Defence University, Bucharest, 2013

81) Gidadhubli, R. G. "Caspian Genesis of Energy Politics." *The Journal of Central Asian Studies*, vol. 22, no. 1, 2015, pp. 73-I

82) Gjelten, Tom. "THE DASH FOR GAS: The Golden Age of an Energy Game-Changer." *World Affairs*, vol. 174, no. 5, 2012, pp. 43-52

83) Götz, R. "The Nabucco Gas Pipeline: Problems and Alternatives". Osteuropa, 2009 54(1-2), pp. 1-8.

84) Grewlich, Klaus W. "International Regulatory Governance of the Caspian Pipeline Policy Game." *Journal of Energy & Natural Resources Law*, vol. 29, no. 1, 2011, pp. 87-116

85) Grinberg, Alex. "Iran and Russia: similarities and implications for decision making." *Middle East Review of International Affairs (Online)*, vol. 19, no. 2, 2015, pp. 26-32

86) Grison, Nathan R. "NATO's Energy Security Policy Put to the Caspian Test." *Connections: The Quarterly Journal*, vol. 12, no. 2, 2013, pp. 83-94

87) Groszkowski, Jakub. "European Policies of the Visegrad Countries." *International Issues & Slovak Foreign Policy Affairs*, vol. 22, no. 1, 2013, pp. 71-90,132

88) Guliyev, F., & Akhrarkhodjaeva, N. The Trans-Caspian Energy Route: Cronyism, Competition and Cooperation in Kazakh Oil Export. *Energy Policy, 37*(8), 2009, pp. 3171-3182.

89) Gümüscedil, and Yasin K. . "How Secure is the EU Energy Policy After the Ukraine Crisis?" *International Journal of Energy Economics and Policy*, vol. 5, no. 4, 2015

90) Guney, N.A. and Korkmaz, V. The Energy Interdependence Model between Russia and Europe: An Evaluation of Expectations for Change. *Perceptions*, Autumn, 2014, vol. 19, no. 3. pp. 35-59

91) Gupta, Anshuman, and Surbhi Arora. "Control the Oil, Rule the World: The Energy Games Nations Play." *IUP Journal of International Relations*, vol. 9, no. 1, 2015, pp. 52-65

92) Hey, Christian. "Low-Carbon and Energy Strategies for the EU: The European Commission's Roadmaps: A Sound Agenda for Green Economy?" *Gaia*, vol. 21, no. 1, 2012, pp. 43-47

93) Hill, Fiona, and Kemal Kirisci. *U.S., EU, and Turkish Engagement in the South Caucasus*, Brookings Institution Press, Washington, 2015.

94) Holgate, Michael, and Jay Wagner. "European Unconventionals Sector must Forge its Own Path." *Petroleum Economist*, 2013

95) Houshisadat, Mohammad. "Persian Gulf Gas and LNG in the EU's Goals for Security of Gas Supply by 2030." *The Polish Quarterly of International Affairs*, vol. 24, no. 1, 2015, pp. 7-II

96) Iacob, Valentin. "Exploring European Union Security Alternatives - Is Europe Ready To Move On?" *Strategic Impact*, no. 54, 2015, pp. 7-21

97) Ibrahimov, Rovshan. "Turkish-Azerbaijani Energy Relations: Significant Leverage in the Implementation of the Foreign Policy Interests of both Countries." *Insight Turkey*, vol. 17, no. 2, 2015, pp. 83-100

98) İçener, Erhan. "Turkey - EU Relations After the Failed July 15 Coup Attempt/15 Temmuz Basarisiz Darbe Girisiminin Ardindan Türkiye - AB Iliskileri." *Bilig*, vol. 79, 2016, pp. 69-87

99) Indeo, Fabio. *Azerbaijan: A Strategic Actor in the Regional Energy Chessboard*, Federal Reserve Bank of St Louis, St. Louis, 2013.

100) Irimie, Rada C. "European Union: A Global Actor in Challenging Times." *Studia Universitatis Babes-Bolyai. Studia Europaea*, vol. 59, no. 4, 2014, pp. 101-133

101) Jain, A. "Baku-Tbilisi-Ceyhan Oil Pipeline Vital Link for East and West". *Pipeline & Gas Journal, 232*(8), 2005. pp. 60-64

102) Jarosiewicz, A. (2012). Southern Corridor Managed by Azerbaijan and Turkey. Center for Eastern Studies/Osrodek Studiow Wschodnich, July 18, p.76.

103) Javed, Faisal, and Ayaz Ahmed. "The Iran Nuclear Deal." *Defence Journal*, vol. 19, no. 8, 2016, pp. 17-25

104) Jensehaugen, Helge. "The Northern Cypriot Dream - Turkish Immigration 1974-1980." *The Cyprus Review*, vol. 26, no. 2, 2014, pp. 57-83,10

105) Johnson, Michael L. "From the Big Bang to Baku: A Primer on the Beginnings of the Petroleum End Times." *Southwest Review*, vol. 95, no. 3, 2010, pp. 426-443

106) *Joint Statement of the U.S.-EU Energy Council*, Federal Information & News Dispatch, Inc, Lanham, 2014.

107) Kadercan, Burak. "What the ISIS Crisis Means for the Future of the Middle East 1." *Insight Turkey*, vol. 18, no. 2, 2016, pp. 63-81

108) Kaplan, Muhittin, Abdullah Yuvaci, and Shatlyk Amanov. "One Nation, Many Voices? External Cohesion of the Turkic Council States in the United Nations General Assembly, 1993-2011." *Bilig*, vol. 74, 2015, pp. 125-149

109) Karagol, Erdal T., and Mehmet Kizilkaya. "The Turkish Stream Project in the EU-Russia-Turkey Triangle." *Insight Turkey*, vol. 17, no. 2, 2015, pp. 57-65

110) Kardas, S. (2011). Geo-strategic Position as Leverage in EU Accession: The case of Turkish-EU negotiations on the Nabucco pipeline. *Southeast European and Black Sea Studies, 11*(1), pp. 35-52.

111) Karimov Fatih. "Iranian Gas Delivery to EU Via Azerbaijan Easier than Direct Export." *Trend Capital. English*, Aug 18 2015,

112) Kazantsev, A. "The Crisis of Gazprom as the Crisis of Russia's "Energy Super-State" Policy Towards Europe and The Former Soviet Union". Caucasian Review of International Affairs (4.3) 2010, pp. 271-284

113) Khalid, Iram, Rehana S. Hashmi, and Zainab Ahmed. "China-Central Asia Relations: A Socio-Economic and Security Analysis of Bilateral Ties." *Journal of Political Studies*, vol. 23, no. 1, 2016, pp. 49-62

114) Khan, Shazia M. "Heydar Aliyev's Political and Socio-Economic Achievements and Azerbaijan-Pakistan Bilateral Relations." *Defence Journal*, vol. 20, no. 5, 2016, pp. 36-45

115) Khatinoglu, Dalga. "BP Hopes to See Iran's Gas in Southern Gas Corridor." *TCA Regional News*, Oct 18 2016,

116) Kim, Younkyoo, and Stephen Blank. "Russo-Turkish Divergence (Part Ii): The Energy Dimension." *Middle East Review of International Affairs (Online)*, Vol. 16, No. 3, 2012, Pp. 18-30

117) Kirisci, Kemal. "Turkey and its Post-Soviet Neighborhood." *Current History*, vol. 112, no. 756, 2013, pp. 271-276

118) Kirshner, Sheldon. "The Flotilla and Israel's Blockade of Gaza." *Canadian Jewish News*, Jun 16, 2011, pp. 11,

119) Kirvelyte, Laura. "The Dilemma of Azerbaijan's Security Strategy: Energy Policy Or Territorial Integrity?" *Lithuanian Annual Strategic Review*, vol. 10, no. 1, 2012, pp. 199-n/a

120) Kocaslan, Gelengul. "International Energy Security Indicators and Turkey's Energy Security Risk Score." *International Journal of Energy Economics and Policy*, vol. 4, no. 4, 2014, pp. 735-743

121) Kolb, R. "Geopolitics Threats To World Energy Markets". *The Journal of Social, Political, and Economical Studies,* 36.(2), 2011 pp. 154-196

122) Kolb, Robert W. "The Natural Gas Revolution and Central Asia." *The Journal of Social, Political, and Economic Studies*, vol. 37, no. 2, 2012, pp. 141-180

123) Koolaee, Elaheh, and Mahnaz Goodarzi. "Turkey-Armenia Rapprochement and its Impact on Iran-Armenia Relations." *Hemispheres*, vol. 30, no. 2, 2015, pp. 57-73,

124) Kosolapova, Elena. "Iranian Gas Industry to Require Massive Investments to Meet European Demands." *TCA Regional News*, Jan 27 2016,

125) Kunu, Serkan, and Sertaç Hopoglu. "Turkey and Iran: An analysis based on mutual trade and defense spending." *Kafkas University. Faculty of Economics and Administrative Sciences. Journal*, vol. 7, no. 12, 2016, pp. 109-124,

126) Lashaki, A.B., Goudarzi, M.R. and Amraei, D. The Roots of Tension in South Caucasus: The Case of Iran- Azerbaijan Relationship. *Journal of Politics and Law*, 12, 2013, vol. 6, no. 4. pp. 141-149

127) Leal-Arcas, Rafael. "How Governing International Trade in Energy can Enhance EU Energy Security 1." *Renewable Energy Law and Policy: RELP*, vol. 6, no. 3, 2015, pp. 202-219

128) Lewis, Ian. "Regional Report: Eastern Mediterranean." *World Oil*, 2015

129) Lu, Jing M., and Wen L. Gao. "Shale Gas Development Environmental Impacts and Consideration." *Applied Mechanics and Materials*, vol. 521, 2014, pp. 831-836

130) Luciani, Giacomo. "EU-RUSSIA GAS BLUES." *Journal of International Affairs*, vol. 69, no. 1, 2015, pp. 19-IX

131) Mankoff, Jeffrey. "Russia's Asia Pivot: Confrontation Or Cooperation?" *Asia Policy*, no. 19, 2015, pp. 65-87

132) Maracz, Laszlo. "The Strategic Relevance Of AGRI In Europe's Southern Gas Corridor." *Karadeniz Arastirmalari*, no. 28, 2011, pp. 19-28

133) Marketos, T. Eastern Caspian Sea Energy Geopolitics: A litmus test for the U.S. - Russia - China Struggle for the Geostrategic Control of Eurasia. *Caucasian Review of International Affairs, 3*(1), 2009, pp 2-19.

134) Matthews, Owen, and Bill Powell. "As in the Cold War, Russia is Vulnerable on Energy." *Newsweek*, vol. 162, no. 15, Apr 18, 2014

135) McLaughlin, Daniel, and Vanessa Mock. "New Cold War Breaks Out After Russia Turns Off Gas Supplies." *The Independent*, Jan 07, 2009, pp. 2,

136) Mehdi Sepahvand -. "Recent Azerbaijan-Iran MoUs 'Momentous' - Azerbaijani Ambassador." *Trend News.English*, Feb 29 2016,

137) Mikail, Elnur H. "SECURITY DIMENSION OF CAUCASIAN POLITICS OF THE USA26." *TURAN : Stratejik Arastirmalar Merkezi*, vol. 2, no. 5, 2010, pp. 55-62

138) Moradi, M. Caspian Pipeline Politics and Iran-EU Relations. *UNISCI Discussion Papers,* 2006, (10), pp. 173-184.

139) Musayeva, A. A. "Managerial organization in the CIS region: The case of Azerbaijan oil market". *European Research Studies, 12*(2), 2009. pp. 149-156.

140) Mustafayev, Nurlan. "The Southern Gas Corridor: legal and regulatory developments in major gas transit pipeline projects". *J World Energy Law Bus* 2016 pp. 370-387

141) Najafizadeh, Mehrangiz. "Poetry, Azeri Idp/Refugee Women, And The Nagorno-Karabakh War." *Journal of Third World Studies*, vol. 32, no. 1, 2015, pp. 13-43

142) Najimdeen, Bakare. "Middle East Refugees' Crisis Europeans' Three Dimensional Approaches." *Policy Perspectives*, vol. 13, no. 2, 2016

143) Namazova, A. A., and T. Q. Taghizada. "Bioethics in Azerbaijan." *Asian Bioethics Review*, vol. 7, no. 5, 2015

144) Neag, Mihai, and Elisabeta-Emilia Halmaghi. *Energy Security. Black Sea - Caspian Sea Corridor*, Romanian National Defense University, Regional Department of Defense Resources Management Studies, Brasov, 2016

145) Negut, Silviu, PhD., and Marius-Cristian Neacsu PhD. "The European Union Between "The United States Of Europe" And "European Union Inc."." *Strategic Impact*, no. 43, 2012, pp. 45-50

146) Nichol, J. "Armenia, Azerbaijan, And Georgia: Political Developments And Implications For U.S. Interests". *Current Politics and Economics of Russia, Eastern and Central Europe*, 2014, vol. 29, no. 2. pp. 193-279

147) Nichol, Jim. "Armenia, Azerbaijan, And Georgia: Political Developments And Implications For U.S. Interests*." *Current Politics and Economics of Russia, Eastern and Central Europe*, vol. 29, no. 2, 2014, pp. 193-279

148) Nichol, Jim. "CENTRAL ASIA: REGIONAL DEVELOPMENTS AND IMPLICATIONS FOR U.S. INTERESTS *." *Current Politics and Economics of South, Southeastern, and Central Asia*, vol. 21, no. 3, 2012, pp. 261-349

149) Nichol, Jim. "Russia-Georgia Conflict In August 2008: Context And Implications For U.S. Interests." *Russia, China and Eurasia*, vol. 28, no. 1, 2012, pp. 1-49

150) Oguz, Safak. "NATO'S MISTAKES THAT PAVED THE WAY FOR RUSSIA-UKRAINE CRISIS." *Karadeniz Arastirmalari*, no. 45, 2015, pp. 1-12

151) Ojeaga, Paul, and Odejimi Deborah. "Demand for Energy and Energy Generation: Does Regional Energy Policy Play a Role?" *Computational Methods in Social Sciences*, vol. 2, no. 1, 2014, pp. 5-20

152) Onur Cobanli. "Central Asian gas in Eurasian power game". Energy Policy, Volume 68, May 2014, Pages 348-370

153) Osica, Olaf. "Taming Chaos: The Future of EU External Relations in Light of the Treaty of Lisbon." *The Polish Quarterly of International Affairs*, vol. 19, no. 2, 2010, pp. 79-95

154) Ostrander, Ian, and William R. Lowry. "Oil Crises and Policy Continuity: A History of Failure to Change." *Journal of Policy History: JPH*, vol. 24, no. 3, 2012, pp. 384-404

155) Ozdemir, Volkan. "Balkan Piyasalarini Hedef Alan Dogal Gaz Boru Hatti Projeleri Arasinda Rekabet: NABUCCO-Güney Akim Ve Trans-Adriyatik Boru Hatti (TAP) Projeleri Örnegi/Competition between Natural Gas Pipeline Projects that Target Balkan Markets: In the Case of NABUCCO-South Stream and Trans-Adriatic Pipeline (TAP) Projects." *Sosyoekonomi*, no. 2, 2014, pp. 253-272,426

156) Ozkan, G. (2011). The Nabucco Project within the Context of Energy Supply Security and International Politics. *China-USA Business Review, 10*(8), pp. 689-699.

157) Ozkan, Gokhan. "Georgia's NATO Membership Within Context of The Black Sea Dimension Of "The New Great Game"." *Karadeniz Arastirmalari*, no. 27, 2010, pp. 1-22

158) Ozyavas, Aziz, and Shahab D. Khan. "The Driving Forces Behind the Caspian Sea Mean Water Level Oscillations." *Environmental Earth Sciences*, vol. 65, no. 6, 2012, pp. 1821-1830

159) Paliwal, Monika. "Natural Gas Is It The Alternate Fuel?" *Energy Future*, vol. 5, no. 2, Jan 2017, pp. 46-51.

160) Papatulica, Mariana. "EU Foreign Energy Policy - the Vulnerable Part of Energy Union Strategy." *Global Economic Observer*, vol. 4, no. 2, 2016, pp. 1-9

161) Patterson, Robert G. "*Russian-EU Energy Interdependence and Security in Europe*". University of Washington, Ann Arbor, 2013

162) Peachey, R. Petroleum investment contracts after the Baku-Tbilisi-Ceyhan (BTC) pipeline. *Northwestern Journal of International Law & Business, 31*(3), 2011 pp. 739-769.

163) Perovic, J. "*Russian energy power and foreign relations: implications for conflict and cooperation*". Routledge, Taylor & Francis Group, 2009.

164) Pinar, I. "Azerbaijan's Foreign Policy and Challenges For Energy Security". *The Middle Eastern Journal*. 2009, pp. 227-239

165) Plenta, Peter. "The European Union and Central Asia." *International Issues & Slovak Foreign Policy Affairs*, vol. 20, no. 3, 2011, pp. 82-85

166) Poladian, Simona M., and Andreea-Emanuela Dragoi. "Sweden And Turkey: Two Models Of Welfare State In Europe." *Global Economic Observer*, vol. 1, no. 2, 2013, pp. 72-79

167) Pomfret, Richard. "The Economic Future of Central Asia." *The Brown Journal of World Affairs*, vol. 19, no. 1, 2012, pp. 59-68

168) Popova, Liudmila, and Ehsan Rasoulinezhad. "Have Sanctions Modified Iran's Trade Policy? an Evidence of Asianization and De-Europeanization through the Gravity Model." *Economies*, vol. 4, no. 4, 2016, pp. 24-n/a

169) Poyraz, Emel. "Evaluation of the Partnership and Cooperation Agreement between the European Union & Russia from the Public Diplomacy of Russian Perspective." *Uluslararasi Hukuk ve Politika*, vol. 7, no. 27, 2011, pp. 141-158,186,

170) Prisecaru, Petre, and Al D. H. Ali. "Natural Gas Boom in the Middle East." *Global Economic Observer*, vol. 2, no. 1, 2014, pp. 11-21

171) Qazi, Muhammad S. "Central Asia: Crossroads for Global Economic Stratagem." *Journal of Political Studies*, vol. 22, no. 1, 2015, pp. 289-301

172) Raczka, W. A Sea or a Lake? the Caspian's Long Odyssey. *Central Asian Survey, 19*(2), 2000. pp. 189-221.

173) Radu, Carmen, and Liviu Radu. "PUBLIC POLITICS IN THE ENERGY FIELD." *Challenges of the Knowledge Society*, 2015, pp. 879-885

174) *Rafael L.R, Juan.R & Constantino. Journal of World Energy Law Business (2015) 8 (4):* 291-336.

175) Rafique, Najam, and Babar Shah. "Political and Economic Impact of Nuclear-Related Sanctions on Iran and its Foreign Policy Options." *Strategic Studies*, vol. XXXII-XXXIII, no. 4-1, 2013

176) Rafique, Najam, and Babar Shah. "Political and Economic Impact of Nuclear-Related Sanctions on Iran and its Foreign Policy Options." *Strategic Studies*, vol. XXXII-XXXIII, no. 4-1, 2013

177) Richard Y. "Energy Security: Europe's new foreign policy challenge". London, Routledge. 2009

178) Richardson, Ronny, et al. "Economic Development Perspectives of Eurasia: Exploration and Concise Synopsis." *International Management Review*, vol. 12, no. 1, 2016, pp. 5-10,70

179) Rocco, A. The Energy Charter Treaty's Failure? the Different Perceptions of Energy Security: Within the European Union and Beyond its Borders. *Eurolimes*, Spring, 2013, vol. 15. pp. 101-116

180) Rosenberg, Elizabeth, et al. *The New Great Game*, Center for a New American Security, Washington, 2016.

181) Rufiz Hafizoglu -. *Azerbaijan, Turkey, Russia to Create Trilateral Co-Op Format - Erdogan (UPDATE).* Baku: , Aug 09, 2016

182) Rufiz Hafizoglu. "Iraq's Gas to Europe through TANAP." *Trend Capital. English*, May 14 2015,

183) Ruggiero, Francesco, et al. "Energy Cooperation - The Strength Of The Eu's Economic Development." *Amfiteatru Economic*, Vol. 17, No. 40, 2015, Pp. 1080-1094

184) Ruseckas, Laurent. "Turkey and Eurasia: Opportunities and Risks in the Caspian Pipeline Derby." *Journal of International Affairs*, vol. 54, no. 1, 2000, pp. 217-236)

185) Rusnak, U. "Turkey as the Key Element to the EU's Southern Gas Corridor". *International Issues and Slovak Foreign Policy Affairs* (20.1), 2011 pp. 70-82

186) Rustamov, R., & Stergiopoulos, F. (2011). European Energy Security, Gas Supply and Demand: Suppliers from Caspian region countries. *Economics, Management and Financial Markets*, 6(1), pp. 776-789.

187) Rustamov, Rufat, and Fotis Stergiopoulos. "European Energy Security, Gas Supply And Demand: Suppliers From Caspian Region Countries." *Economics, Management And Financial Markets*, Vol. 6, No. 1, 2011, Pp. 776-789

188) Sadri, Houman A., and Nathan L. Burns. "THE GEORGIA CRISIS: A NEW COLD WAR ON THE HORIZON?" *Caucasian Review of International Affairs*, vol. 4, no. 2, 2010, pp. 126-144

189) Sales, Ben. "Israel-Turkey Relations on the Mend?" *Washington Jewish Week*, Feb 18, 2016, pp. 1-19,

190) Sancak, Kadir. "Soft Power as an Effect Instruments in Foreign Policy's Soft Power Analysis and the Assessment of its Soft Power Capacity on Azerbaijan." *Turkish Economic Review*, vol. 3, no. 1, 2016, pp. 225-234

191) Schubert, Samuel R., Johannes Pollak, and Elina Brutschin. "Two Futures: EU-Russia Relations in the Context of Ukraine." *European Journal of Futures Research*, vol. 2, no. 1, 2014, pp. 1-7,

192) Sefcovic, Maros. *The Energy Union, Status and Way Forward: Remarks from Maros Sefcovic, European Commission Vice-President for the Energy Union*, Brookings Institution Press, Washington, 2016.

193) Sestanovich, S. What has Moscow Done? *Foreign Affairs, 87*(6), 2008. pp. 12-28.

194) Sevim, T.V. "Importance of TANAP in Competition between Russia and Central Asia". *International Journal of Energy Economics and Policy*, 2013, vol. 3, no. 4. pp. 352-n/a

195) Shaffer, B. From Pipedream to Pipeline: A Caspian Success Story. *Current History, 104*(684), 2005 pp. 343-346.

196) Shaffer, Brenda. "Europe's Natural Gas Security Of Supply: Policy Tools For Single-Supplied States." *Energy Law Journal*, vol. 36, no. 2, 2015, pp. 179-201

197) Shaffer, Brenda. "Securing Europe's Natural Gas Supply." *Hampton Roads International Security Quarterly*, 2014, pp. 71

198) Sharipov, Ilkhom, and Sergey Lisnyak. The Current State And Prospects Of Economic Development In The EU's EaP Countries, vol. 8, Alexandru Ioan Cuza University of Iasi, Centre for European Studies, Iasi, 2016.

199) Shieber, Jonathan. "Emerging Energy Meets Emerging Markets." *The Private Equity Analyst*, 2012

200) Shiriyev, Zaur, and Celia Davies. "The Turkey-Armenia-Azerbaijan Triangle: The Unexpected Outcomes of the Zurich Protocols." *Perceptions*, vol. 18, no. 1, 2013, pp. 185-206

201) Shokri Kalehsar, Omid. "Iran-Azerbaijan Energy Relations in the Post-Sanctions Era." *Middle East Policy*, vol. 23, no. 1, 2016, pp. 136-143

202) Siddig, Khalid, and Harald Grethe. *No More Gas from Egypt? the Israeli Gas Sector between Offshore Discoveries and Import Uncertainty.* Federal Reserve Bank of St Louis, St. Louis, 2013,

203) Sierra, O.P. "A Corridor Through Throns: EU energy security and the Southern Energy Corridor". European Security (19.4), 2010 pp. 643

204) Sierra, Oscar P. "A Corridor through Thorns: EU Energy Security and the Southern Energy Corridor." *European Security*, vol. 19, no. 4, 2010, pp. 643

205) Smil, Vaclav. "Energy Transitions, Renewables and Rational Energy use: A Reality Check." *Organisation for Economic Cooperation and Development. The OECD Observer*, no. 304, 2015, pp. 36-37

206) Sotolongo, Kristie. "EU ENERGY POLICY: No One-Size-Fits-all Solution." *Fuel*, 09, 2014, pp. 54-57

207) Souleimanov, Emil, and Josef Kraus. "Turkey: An Important East-West Energy Hub." *Middle East Policy*, vol. 19, no. 2, 2012, pp. 157-168

208) Spassov, Philip. "NATO, Russia and European Security: Lessons Learned from Conflicts in Kosovo and Libya." *Connections: The Quarterly Journal*, vol. 13, no. 3, 2014, pp. 21-40

209) Stefan, Georgescu, et al. "The Importance of Relations Between Georgia And Romania for the Progress of Energy Projects." *Universitatii Maritime Constanta. Analele*, vol. 13, no. 18, 2012, pp. 283-288

210) Stefanova, Boyka M. "European Strategies for Energy Security in the Natural Gas Market." Journal of Strategic Security, vol. 5, no. 3, 2012, pp. 51-68

211) Sutyagin, Igor. "Dealing with NATO's Security Challenges -Where the East Merges with the South." *The Polish Quarterly of International Affairs*, vol. 25, no. 1, 2016, pp. 115-V

212) Swanstrom, Niklas. "Central Asia and Russian Relations: Breaking Out of the Russian Orbit?" *The Brown Journal of World Affairs*, vol. 19, no. 1, 2012, pp. 101-113

213) Szurlej, Adam, and Piotr Janusz. "Natural Gas Economy in the United States and European Markets." *Gospodarka Surowcami Mineralnymi*, vol. 29, no. 4, 2013, pp. 77-94

214) Talus, Kim. "Application of EU energy and certain national laws of Baltic sea countries to the Nord Stream 2 pipeline project". *J World Energy Law Bus* 2017; pp. 30-42.

215) Tanrisever, Oktay F. "The Black Sea Economic Cooperation Organization And Its Strengths And Weaknesses In Promoting The Globalization Of The Black Sea Region: 1992-2012/Karadeniz Ekonomik Isbirligi Teskilati Ve Karadeniz Bölgesinin Küresellesmesini Desteklemekteki Güçlü Ve Zayif Yönleri: 1992-2012." *Orta Asya ve Kafkasya Arastirmalari*, vol. 7, no. 13, 2012, pp. 57-72

216) Tanrisever, Oktay F. "Türkiye-Rusya Krizinin Dinamikleri Ve Ikili Iliskilere Etkileri." *Bilge Strateji*, vol. 8, no. 14, 2016, pp. 7-17,

217) Tantau, Adrian D., and Mohammadreza Khorshidi. "New Business Models for State Companies in the Oil Industry." *Management & Marketing*, vol. 11, no. 3, 2016, pp. 484-497

218) Teixeira, Cé, et al. "Convergence to the European Energy Policy in European Countries: Case Studies and Comparison." *Socialines Technologijos*, vol. 4, no. 1, 2014

219) Telli, Azime. "Türkiye'Nin Nükleer Enerji Açiliminin Içerik Analizi: Çsitlendirme Mi, Teslimiyet Mi?/Content Analysis of Turkey's Nuclear Energy Initiative: Diversification Or Submission?" *Bilge Strateji*, vol. 8, no. 14, 2016, pp. 47-75

220) Tichy, L. and Kratochvil, P. "The EU-Russia Energy Relations Under the Prism of the Political Discourse". *Perspectives*, 2014, vol. 22, no, 1. pp. 5-32,113-114

221) Topal, Ömer F. "Power Games In The Caucasus: Azerbaijan's Foreign And Energy Policy Towards The West, Russia And The Middle East." *Orta Asya ve Kafkasya Arastirmalari*, vol. 9, no. 17, 2014, pp. 193-195

222) Trenin, Dmitri. *Russia and Iran: Historic Mistrust and Contemporary Partnership*. Carnegie Endowment for International Peace, Washington, 2016

223) Tsiaras, A. Pipeline Wars. Yale Economic Review, 6.(2), 2010, pp. 21-25

224) Tunc, Zeynel. "Energy: Full of Energy." *International Financial Law Review*, 2012, 2

225) Ubiria, G. "Central Asia and the Rise of Normative Powers: Contextualizing the Security Governance of the European Union, China, and India". *Asian Studies Review*, 09, 2014, vol. 38, no. 3. pp. 511-512

226) Ugur, Ömer. "The Europeanization of National Foreign Policies: The Examples of Germany and France within the Framework of Ukraine Crisis." *Turkish Economic Review*, vol. 3, no. 3, 2016, pp. 527-536

227) Umbach, F. "Energy: Why ''TANAP'' is changing the Eurasian Pipeline Competition". Geopolitical Information Service (GIS). 2012, 27 March.

228) Urutchiev, V. Energy Dependence: The EU's Greatest Energy Security Challenge? *European View*, 12, 2014, vol. 13, no. 2. pp. 287-294

229) Vihma, Antto, and Umut Turksen. "THE GEOECONOMICS OF THE SOUTH STREAM PIPELINE PROJECT." *Journal of International Affairs*, vol. 69, no. 1, 2015, pp. 34-X

230) Volkan Özdemir, H. Buğra Yavuz, Emine Tokgöz, 2015. The Trans-Anatolian Pipeline (TANAP) as a unique project in the Eurasian gas network: A comparative analysis. *Utilities Policy Journal, 2015 (1-7)*

231) Voskopoulos, George. "The Arab Spring Phenomenon and European Security: Change and Continuity Under the Spectrum of Securitized Idealism." *IUP Journal of International Relations*, vol. 9, no. 3, 2015, pp. 23-34

232) Winrow, Gareth M. "The Southern Gas Corridor and Turkey's Role as an Energy Transit State and Energy Hub." *Insight Turkey*, vol. 15, no. 1, 2013, pp. 145-163

233) Yanik, Lerna, Dr. "Keep(Ing) Calm and Carry(Ing) on Business? Turkey-Russia Relations, as seen from Turkey 1." *Turkish Review*, vol. 5, no. 5, 2015, pp. 366-375,

234) Yasar, Ayse G. "Turkey: Challenges to the Liberalisation of Natural Gas Markets: The Turkish Case." *European Networks Law and Regulation Quarterly (ENLR)*, vol. 4, no. 2, 2016, pp. 163-168,

235) Yesevi, Cagla G., and Burcu Y. Tiftikcigil. "Turkey-Azerbaijan Energy Relations: A Political and Economic Analysis." *International Journal of Energy Economics and Policy*, vol. 5, no. 1, 2015, pp. 27-44

236) Yildirim, Zerife, and Ayse A. Yasa. "The Relation between the Budget Deficit and Energy Demand in the Selected European Countries and Turkey: Panel Cointegration Analysis." *International Journal of Trade, Economics and Finance*, vol. 5, no. 6, 2014, pp. 482-489

237) Yildiz, Ugur B. "The Union for the Mediterranean: Why did it Fail and how should it be Effective?" *Uluslararasi Hukuk ve Politika*, vol. 8, no. 32, 2012, pp. 117-148

238) Yunusbayev, Bayazit, et al. "The Genetic Legacy of the Expansion of Turkic-Speaking Nomads Across Eurasia." *PLoS Genetics*, vol. 11, no. 4, 2015

239) Ziyadzade, Ziyad. "Drilling for Black Gold: The Demarcation of Hydrocarbon Resources in the Caspian Sea." *Chicago Journal of International Law*, vol. 16, no. 1, 2015, pp. 312-339

News Articles and Online Publications

240) ABC News. "Natig Aliyev: DESFA deal failure and Italian referendum not to affect TAP gas pipeline". ABC News. 2016. URL: http://abc.az/eng/news/100596.html

241) Agayeva, S. "Foreign Ministry: Azerbaijan's Foreign Policy has always been Multi-Vector and Balanced." *McClatchy - Tribune Business News*, Feb 29 2012,

242) Anadolu Agency. "Turkish FM: Turkey a central country rather than a bridge". 2012.

243) APA Agency. "BTK to be launched this year – Prime Minister". APA Agency. 2016. URL: http://m.apa.az/en/infrastructure/btk-to-be-launched-this-year-prime-minister

244) Asharq Alawsat "Erdogan is Sorry and Moscow: 'He Apologized'... the Result is Quick Normalization of Ties." Jun 28, 2016,

245) Asia News Monitor. "European Union: Towards Energy Union: The Commission Presents Sustainable Energy Security Package." Feb 22, 2016

246) Azernews. "Iran Voices Readiness to Sell gas to Europe for Political Purposes"., 2015. URL: http://www.azernews.az/region/89506.html

247) Azpromo. "Turkish trade minister sees trade with Azerbaijan rising five-fold by 2023" Azpromo, 2015. URL:http://www.azpromo.az/uploads/bne_invest_in_azerbaijan_may_20 15.pdf

248) AzVision. "The fifth meeting of Turkey-Azerbaijan High Level Strategic Cooperation Council will be held in Ankara instead of Baku." Azvision, 2016. URL: http://en.azvision.az/Turkey-Azerbaijan_High_Level_Strategic_-32760-xeber.html

249) BankWatch "Southern Gas Corridor/ Euro-Caspian Mega Pipeline" BankWatch, May 12, 2016. URL: http://bankwatch.org/our-work/projects/southern-gas-corridor-euro-caspian-mega-pipeline?page=1

250) Badalova, A. "Richard Morningstar: Nabucco is Good, but Not Only Project." Trend News. English, Dec 09 2010,

251) Badalova, Aygun. "TAP to be Major Asset in European Energy Security Tool Box - Sefcovic." TCA Regional News, May 17, 2016

252) BBC Monitoring Middle East. "Iran Resumes Natural Gas Swap with Azerbaijan.", Jul 11 2013,

253) Caspian Energy, (2016). "Southern Gas Corridor is a project of Global Energy Security – Ilham Aliyev" available on: URLhttp://caspianenergy.net/en/oil-and-gas/36300-2016-10-25-08-48-07#

254) CC Law Office. "TAP, Albania Will Play a Key Role for Supplying Balkan States". CC Law Office. 2015. URL: http://www.cclaw.al/tap-albania-will-play-a-key-role-for-supplying-balkan-states/

255) CFR – Council on Foreign Policy. "A Literal Cold War: The EU-Russian Struggle Over Energy Security". CFR – Council on Foreign Policy, 2016. URL: http://blogs.cfr.org/zenko/2016/10/06/a-literal-cold-war-the-eu-russian-struggle-over-energy-security/

256) Common Space EU. "Tensions in Russian-Turkish relations have serious negative impact on region". CommonSpace EU, 2015.URL: http://commonspace.eu/index.php?m=23&news_id=3420

257) Daily Mail. "Rosneft-led consortium plans to complete Essar acquisition next month –sources" Daily Mail, 2017.URL: http://www.dailymail.co.uk/wires/reuters/article-4242094/Rosneft-led-consortium-plans-complete-Essar-acquisition-month-sources.html

258) Dessislava Dimitrova. *Barroso is looking for Caspian for Europe.* Euinside News. 2011 URL: http://www.euinside.eu/en/news/barroso-is-looking-for-caspian-gas-for-europe

259) Environmental Policy and Law. "European "Energy Union" Becomes a Reality." *Environmental Policy and Law*, vol. 45, no. 2, 2015, pp. 85-87

260) EU Commission Press Release. "Towards Energy Union: The Commission presents sustainable energy security package". EU Commission Press Release, 2016.URL: http://europa.eu/rapid/press-release_IP-16-307_en.htm

261) EU Commission. "European Energy Security Strategy: key priorities and actions". EU Commission, 2014.URL: http://europa.eu/rapid/press-release_SPEECH-14-505_en.htm

262) EU Press Release. "Statement of President of the European Council – Donald Tusk". EU Press Release.URL: http://www.consilium.europa.eu/en/press/press-releases/2017/02/06-tusk-remarks-president-azerbaijan-aliyev/

263) Eur-Lex. "Communication From The Commission To The European Parliament, The Council, The European Economic And Social Committee And The Committee Of The Regions Energy Roadmap 2050". Eur-Lex, 2011.URL: http://eur-lex.europa.eu/legal-content/EN/TXT/?uri=CELEX%3A52011DC0885

264) Euractive. "Pipeline focus at Istanbul World Energy Congress". Euractive, 2016.URL: http://www.euractiv.com/section/energy/news/pipeline-focus-at-istanbul-world-energy-congress/

265) European Security Strategy. "A Secure Europe in Better World – Council of the European Union", 2003

266) Exploring history. "How did the Baku Oil Industry Grew Under Tsarist Russia?". 2016. URL: http://exploringhist.blogspot.ch/2016/01/how-did-baku-oil-industry-grew-under.html

267) Express, News n. "Rosneft to Buy Essar Oil, Vadinar Port for $12.9 Bn." *Indian Express*, Oct 16, 2016

268) Fedorenko, Vladimir. "Turkey as Viewed from Central Asia" Rethink Institute, 2016.URL: http://www.rethinkinstitute.org/wp-content/uploads/2016/04/Fedorenko-Turkey-As-Viewed-From-Central-Asia.pdf

269) Financial Times. "Work begins on Trans Adriatic gas Pipeline". Financial Times, 2016.URL: https://www.ft.com/content/da3ceeae-1c29-11e6-b286-cddde55ca122

270) Financial Tribune. "Tehran's Gas Strategy, Global Trends Discussed". Financial Tribune. 2016.URL: https://financialtribune.com/articles/energy/33755/tehran-s-gas-strategy-global-trends-discussed

271) Gastech News. "Analysis: Iran eyes European Gas Market". Gastech News, 2016.URL: http://www.gastechnews.com/processing-technology/analysis-iran-eyes-european-gas-market/

272) Global Insight. "Azerbaijan, Georgia, Romania Sign Trilateral LNG Terminal Deal". Global Insight. 14 April 2010

273) Gurt, Marat "Exclusive: European Union sees supplies of natural gas from Turkmenistan by 2019". Reuters, 2015. URL: http://www.reuters.com/article/us-turkmenistan-gas-europe-exclusive-idUSKBN0NN0FM20150502

274) Hurriyet Daily News. "TANAP's construction accelerates, costs decrease: Project Chief " *Hurriyet Daily News. English*, Dec 12, 2016.URL: http://www.hurriyetdailynews.com/tanaps-construction-accelerates-costs-decrease-project-chief.aspx?pageID=517&nID=107181&NewsCatID=345

275) IENE – Institute of Energy for South East Europe Journal. "Iran Can Join TANAP to export its Gas to Europe: Azerbaijan" Institute of Energy For South East Europe Journal - IENE. 2016.URL: http://www.iene.eu/iran-can-join-tanap-to-export-gas-to-europe-azerbaijan-p2017.html

276) Independent. "Ukraine crisis: Putin will cut gas to Europe unless Russia is paid by the end of the week". Independent, 2015.URL: http://www.independent.co.uk/news/world/europe/ukraine-crisis-putin-will-cut-gas-to-europe-unless-russia-is-paid-by-the-end-of-the-week-10071475.html

277) Interfax: Ukraine Business Daily (B) "World; Nord Stream 2 Must Comply With Eu Environmental Standards, Laws - Ec Vp." Apr 07, 2016

278) Interfax: Ukraine Business Daily. "World; Azerbaijan Examines Option Of Shipping Iranian Gas To TANAP." *Interfax : Ukraine Business Daily*, Aug 29, 2016,

279) Issayeva Meyramgul., Lidiya Parchomchik. "Current Situation over the AGRI Project (Azerbaijan-Georgia-Romania Interconnection). Eurasian Research Institute. 2015
URL: http://eurasian-research.org/en/research/comments/energy/current-situation-over-agri-project-azerbaijan-georgia-romania

280) Journal of European Studies. "European Commission High Representative Of The European Union For Foreign Affairs And Security Policy." vol. 31, no. 2, 2015

281) Kaya. K, (2012). Trans-Anatolian Pipeline: Geopolitical achievement, but no panacea for Turkey's Energy Independence. *International Middle East Peach Research Center*. IMPR advisor. URL:http://www.impr.org.tr/en/trans-anatolian-pipeline-a-geopolitical-achievement-but-no-panacea-for-turkeys-energy-independence/

282) Khlebnikov, Alexey. "Increased Iranian oil production is no threat to Russia". Russia Direct, 2016. URL: http://www.russia-direct.org/analysis/increased-iranian-oil-production-no-threat-russia

283) Kostis, G. (2012). EU bets on Gas From Azerbaijan, Turkmenistan for Trans-Caspian Pipe. New Europe Agency. URL:

http://www.neurope.eu/article/eu-bets-gas-azerbaijan-turkmenistan-trans-caspian-pipe

284) Marie-Claire Aoun et al. (eds.), "Strengths and weaknesses of the European Union gas security of supply", in INSIGHT_E Hot Energy Topics, May 2014, URL:http://insightenergy.org/ckeditor_assets/attachments/28/het1_-_final.pdf

285) Merve Sebnem, Oruc. "Turkish Stream: Dynamics in the region changing once again". Daily Sabah Columns, 2016. URL: https://www.dailysabah.com/columns/merve-sebnem-oruc/2016/10/15/turkish-stream-dynamics-in-the-region-changing-once-again

286) Natural Gas Asia. "Turkey Remains Very Important for Europe's Energy Security, Says EU". Natural Gas Asia, 2016. URL: http://www.naturalgasasia.com/turkey-remains-key-for-europes-energy-security-says-eu-17585

287) Oil and Energy Trends. Caspian: Plenty of Pipelines, but where is the gas? *32*(7), 2007 pp. 7-8.

288) Oxford Analytica. (2010) *BULGARIA/AZERBAIJAN: Black Sea CNG has wider potential*. Oxford, United Kingdom.URL: http://www.oxan.com/display.aspx?ItemID=DB162572

289) Papava, Vladimer & Michael Tokmazishvili. *Russian Energy Politics and The EU: How to Change the Paradigm.* Caucasian Review of International Affairs. Vol. 4(2) – Spring 2010 URL: http://www.cria-online.org/11_2.html

290) Pasturia, Nino. "Georgia Pumped Up About Project with Azerbaijan, Romania." Eurasianet Journal. 4 May 2010.URL: http://www.eurasianet.org/node/60980

291) Political Transcript Wire. "Special Envoy For Eurasian Energy Richard Morningstar Holds A Briefing On U.S.-Eu Energy Council, As Released By The State Department." Nov 05 2009,

292) President Az. "Statement of President Ilham Aliyev". Official web page of the President of the Republic of Azerbaijan.URL: http://en.president.az/articles/22706

293) RBTH - Russia and India Report. "Russia to increase petroleum exports to India". RBTH - Russia and India Report, 2016. URL:http://in.rbth.com/economics/business/2016/10/12/russia-to-increase-petroleum-exports-to-india_638053

294) Report News Agency. "4 bln USD will be attracted to TANAP Project " *Report News Agency. English*, Dec 16 2016.URL: https://report.az/en/energy/4-bln-usd-will-be-attracted-to-tanap/

295) Richard Youngs. Europe's External Policy: Between Geopolitics and the Market. No. 278, November 2007.URL: http://aei.pitt.edu/7579/

296) Roberts, John. "Turkmenistan Lobbies Germany on Gas". Natural Gas World. 2016. URL: http://www.naturalgasworld.com/turkmenistan-lobbies-germany-on-gas-31342

297) Robin Paxton, Vladimir Soldatkin. *Gazprom aims to double Azeri Gas purchases in 2011.* Reuters, Jan 2010.URL:http://uk.reuters.com/article/2010/01/21/gazprom-azerbaijan-idUKLDE60K19620100121

298) RT – Russia Today. "Turkish Stream gas pipeline: Moscow & Ankara sign agreement in Istanbul". RT – Russia Today, 2016.URL: https://www.rt.com/business/362279-gazprom-turkish-stream-pipeline/

299) Socor, Vladımır. "Azerbaijan, Georgia, Romania Launch LNG Project in the Black Sea". Moldova Press, 16 April 2010.URL: http://economie.moldova.org/news/azerbaijan-georgia-romania-launch-lng-project-in-the-black-sea-208221-eng.html

300) Socor, Vladimir. (2012). *Azerbaijan did what European could not.* Region Plus Azerbaijan journal. URL: http://www.regionplus.az/en/articles/view/1671

301) Sek, A. (2012). Economic Commission For Europe. Regional Advisor – Sustainable Energy Division.

302) Sputnik. "Russia Ready to Discuss Joint Caspian Pipeline Use With Iran, Azerbaijan – Putin" Sputnik, 2016. URL: https://sputniknews.com/business/201608081044065312-putin-pipeline-talks/

303) TCA Regional News. "Israel and Turkey Reach Deal to Restore Relations." Jun 27, 2016,
   Time. "Europe Still Can't Break Its Addiction to Russian Energy". Time, 2014. URL: http://time.com/2828086/europe-oil-gas-russia-g7/

304) Today News Agency. "President Aliyev: Azerbaijan-EU cooperation is very fruitful, sincere". Today News Agency. 2017. URL: http://www.today.az/news/politics/158385.html

305) Trend Capital. *English* "Ilham Aliyev: Azerbaijan-Iran Relations must further Develop.", Oct 18 2016,

306) Trend News. "Ilham Aliyev: Shah Deniz 2 of Great Importance for Azerbaijan (UPDATE 5), Sep 01 2016

307) Trend News. "Iraq, Azerbaijan can co-op in oil and gas sector for benefit of both sides – Iraqi Minister " *Trend News. English*, Jun 2, 2015. URL: http://www.hurriyetdailynews.com/tanaps-construction-accelerates-costs-decrease-project-chief.aspx?pageID=517&nID=107181&NewsCatID=345

308) UN Security Council. "Security Council Resolutions 822, 853, 874, 884 on Azerbaijan-Armenia". 1993.URL:http://www.un.org/en/sc/documents/resolutions/1993.shtml

309) Ünay, Sadik, and Serif Dilek. "July 15: Political Economy of a Foiled Coup." *Insight Turkey*, vol. 18, no. 3, 2016, pp. 205-231,URL: http://aa.com.tr/en/turkey/turkish-fm-turkey-a-central-country-rather-than-a-bridge/333854

310) Vardaryildiz, Sinem. (2012). *USAK Analysis: TANAP Project is taking shape*. The Journal of Turkish Weekly.URL: http://www.turkishweekly.net/news/141872/-usak-analysis-tanap-project-is-taking-shape.html

311) World Bank Group, & Gerner, F. 2009. *The Future of the Natural Gas Market in Southeast Europe*. New York: World Bank Publication. URL:http://issuu.com/world.bank.publications/docs/9780821378649

312) Yeni Safak. "Erdogan Welcomes Turkmen President at Presidential Palace". Yeni Safak. 2015.URL: http://www.yenisafak.com/en/news/erdogan-welcomes-turkmen-president-at-presidential-palace-2090817

313) Zunino, di Dreta. "Russia drops South Stream pipeline to EU and courts Turkey" The Fielder, 2015.URL: http://thefielder.net/en/21/01/2015/russia-drops-south-stream-pipeline-to-eu-and-courts-turkey/

*Data Reports and Programs

314) European Union 2030 Policy Framework for Climate and Energy - A Detailed Analysis, Global Data Ltd, London, 2014.

315) Eurostat. Energy Imports and Exports EU World. 2016, p15.

316) Greece Oil & Gas Report - Q1 2016. London: Business Monitor International. First, 2016

317) Iran Infrastructure Report - Q2 2016, Business Monitor International, London, 2016.

318) Iran Power Report - Q3 2016, Business Monitor International, London, 2016.

319) Norway Oil & Gas Report - Q3 2016. Business Monitor International, London, 2016

320) State Oil Company of the Azerbaijan Republic - *Oil & Gas - Deals and Alliances Profile*, Global Data Ltd, London, 2017.

321) TAP - Trans Adriatic Pipeline - Greece - Construction Project Profile. Progressive Media Group, London, 2016.

322) Trans Adriatic Pipeline (TAP) - Italy, Greece, Albania. *MENA Report*, Jul 25, 2015

323) Azerbaijan Oil & Gas Report - Q1 2015, Business Monitor International, London, 2015.

324) Energy Information Administration. *Azerbaijan Energy Data, Statistics and Analysis – Oil, Gas, Electricity, Coal.* November 2010

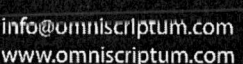

Printed by
Schaltungsdienst Lange o.H.G., Berlin

—